Hugh Macmillan

The True Vine

Or the Analogies of our Lord's Allegory

Hugh Macmillan

The True Vine
Or the Analogies of our Lord's Allegory

ISBN/EAN: 9783337016517

Printed in Europe, USA, Canada, Australia, Japan

Cover: Foto ©Lupo / pixelio.de

More available books at **www.hansebooks.com**

THE TRUE VINE;

OR

THE ANALOGIES OF OUR LORD'S ALLEGORY.

BY THE

REV. HUGH MACMILLAN, LL.D., F.R.S.E.,

AUTHOR OF "BIBLE TEACHINGS IN NATURE," "HOLIDAYS ON HIGH LANDS,"
"THE MINISTRY OF NATURE," ETC. ETC.

THIRD EDITION.

London:

MACMILLAN AND CO.

1875.

Printed at the University Press,

BY MACLEHOSE AND MACDOUGALL,

GLASGOW.

" La Nature est une image de la Grace."—*Pascal.*

I T is a well-known fact, that the sunbeam is invisible until it impinges upon earthy particles. In like manner, the light of Divine Truth would be invisible to us were it not reflected by images derived from the common things around us. As the optician fashions out of the materials of nature, instruments which will help him to penetrate the hidden arcana of nature, so the student of Scripture may construct from the objects of the material world—from the studies of the scientific man—analogies which will enable him to understand, in some measure, the deep things of the spirit in man, and the deep things of God. Each science is an additional lens, as it were, to bring the spiritually distant near, and to enlarge the spiritually minute.

Comparative Physiology finds in the vegetable kingdom, on account of the simplicity of its structure, the key to the explanation of the higher animal structures—those profound analogies of organization which so strikingly attest the unity of creation. And may we not believe that there is also a Comparative Theology which finds in plants the analogies of the still higher mysteries of the spiritual world? There is surely a deeper reason than a mere utilitarian one, for the dual form—the animal and vegetable—in which organic life displays itself. God has closely connected the spiritual life of man with this strange plant-life, which runs parallel with his own. At the very beginning, the tree of the knowledge of good and evil in the garden of Eden represented to him all the unexplored mysteries of the moral and intellectual universe, and contracted within the narrowest compass the whole vast, delusive range of temptation. The tree of life was a faithful type, or pictured image of the blessed immortality consequent upon doing the will of God. And when man fell, his altered state was still as closely connected with plant-life.

God enjoined the cultivation of the thorny ground, that in it man might see reflected, as in a mirror, the Divine culture of himself, and, through it, be able to rise to the spiritual toil in the higher seed-field of the kingdom of heaven.

Through the "Gate Beautiful" of the vegetable kingdom we gain admission into the Spiritual Temple. For the unfolding of spiritual truth, the world of plants, in some respects, is better adapted than any other department of nature. Abundant proofs of this will be seen in the following pages. For the representation of the union of believers with Christ, for example, the vegetable, by the very peculiarity of its structure, is better fitted than the animal. St. Paul compares this union to that subsisting between husband and wife; but husband and wife are two separate individuals, and have a mutually independent life. He also compares it to the union subsisting between the head and the body; but the head and the members are only parts and organs of one and the same individual. But when our Lord says, "I am the Vine, ye are the branches," the union thus indicated is not only the closest possible—as close as that of the head with the body—but, as will be described fully in Chapter Third, it is also the union of separate independent individuals — like that of husband and wife in the intimacy of the marriage relation. The human-unions have indeed the advantage of conscious rational life—which the plant-union altogether lacks—and thus have a higher value; but, within the limits of its own capacity, the plant reveals to us more clearly the precise nature of the union.

An additional peculiarity of the plant may also be noticed, which admirably qualifies it for symbolising this mystical union. Animals grow by the substitution of new cells for the old, which are eliminated from their structure; plants grow by the addition of new cells to the old, which are hermetically sealed up in their structure. The existence of the animal depends upon the incessant and total change of the very substance of its fabric; whereas the bulk of the tree remains fixed and unalterable till the lease of the entire organism has run out—there being no provision in the plant for the renewing of tissues once completed. Vegetable growth goes on slowly, by repetition of the same parts; and what is added to the plant is never lost. In this contrast between the animal and the plant, we see how much more beautifully the plant symbolises the mode in which the Spiritual Vine grows, not by the substitution of living believers for dead, but by the addition of living believers to dead; we see the inseparable union of living and dead believers in Christ—and are impressively taught that nothing is lost in Him.

No more vivid and expressive type of immortality can be found in material nature than a tree. A tree is the most enduring of all things. The rock and the mountain are the helpless prey of every wind that blows and raindrop that falls. The golden finger of the sunbeam cannot touch them, however lightly, without helping to crumble away some portion of them. They have no power of resistance—no principle of renewal; and therefore, in the course of time they must inevitably succumb to all the forces of nature leagued against them, and disappear. But the tree has a principle of life and self-growth, which all nature helps to maintain and increase. The sunbeam touches it only to add to its stature and beauty, and the rain-drop falls upon it only to fill its veins with more and fuller life. And it is so constructed,—as we have seen,—that every addition of material which each summer makes to it, is retained, and goes to increase its size and strength. It is capable of going on indefinitely—producing a constant repetition of similar parts. It never presents indications of having passed the limit of its natural growth. It never assumes the appearance of natural old age. What remains living of the oldest tree,—though most of its trunk is a mere bleached, crumbling skeleton,—still forms every year new wood and bark,—still extends its roots and branches. Its leaves are as large and perfectly-formed, and the circulation of its sap as vigorous as in the days of its youth. For hundreds—ay, for thousands of years it lives on fresh and blooming, while all else is changing around. Season after season,—generation after generation, it renews its foliage, while individuals, and families, and whole races, that have dwelt under its shadow, and have eaten of its fruit, have passed away. There are trees still flourishing in our own country that bridge across the middle ages, and have lived through the whole history of England. I have seen a yew-tree that put forth its infant shoots when Solomon was studying the cedars of Lebanon and the hyssop on the wall—that had reached its prime when the Druids were offering their mysterious sacrifices under its shadow; and is still, after the lapse of more than three thousand years, —though reduced to a mere fragment,—putting forth every summer, leaves, and flowers, and fruit, as perfect as in its palmiest days. But for purely accidental causes, any or every tree—so far as its organization is concerned—might endure as long as the world itself, and go on growing and enlarging to any conceivable size. There is nothing in its own structure to limit the bulk of its form and the length of its days. In its own nature it is perennial. Is not the *Tree of Life* then a most significant symbol? Is not the prophecy of Isaiah invested with a higher value when looked at in this light?—"As the days of a tree so are the days of My people." Are not the words of our Lord full of new meaning when we thus consider the trees how they grow?—"I am the Vine, ye are the branches."

The analogies contained in the following pages are not exclusively drawn from the grape-vine. The great majority are derived from this source, in order to make the treatment of the subject as homogeneous as possible; but the whole range of the vegetable kingdom is laid under contribution for appropriate illustrations. The work is meant to be, not merely an exposition of the fifteenth chapter of St. John's Gospel, but also a general parable of spiritual truth from the world of plants. It describes some of the more prominent and apparent points in which the varied realm of vegetable life comes into contact with the higher spiritual realm, that includes it within its vast periphery; and shows how rich a field of promise lies before the analogical mind in this direction. I wish to draw special attention to this general comprehensive design of the book, lest it should be regarded by those who seek to view everything in its just limits, colouring and proportions, as open to the objection that the work goes beyond the material—that the illustrations are more than the thing illustrated. Some interesting and valuable suggestions have been received from Mr. Soltau, Professor Harvey, Archbishop Trench, Dr. Thomas Balfour, and Mr. Leo Grindon— all of whom have written, with deep insight, upon the subject of the typical meaning of nature, and the connection of the world of sense with the world of faith.

This new edition has been carefully revised. Many passages which appeared in the former have been omitted altogether, and others considerably altered; while a large amount of new matter has been added in the shape of explanatory foot notes and fresh illustrations in the text, which it is hoped will increase the value of the volume. I am conscious that it has still many imperfections which I cannot remedy. The mellow, rounded, graceful shadow projected against a wall by the living, flexible human figure, is not more different from the stiff, hard, grotesque shadow cast by a statue, than is the ideal as it exists in my own mind from the reality which I have been able to execute. Such as it is, however, I put forth anew this monograph upon a favourite subject, hoping that, like Newton's apple, it may help to suggest wider and grander thoughts to others than belong to itself.

H. M.

August, 1872.

CONTENTS.

THE TRUE VINE.

CHAPTER I.

THE TRUE VINE.

"I am the true Vine."—JOHN xv. 1.

PROFOUND and far-reaching meanings are often hid in words. Like boulders left on the strand, confirming a geologist's theory, they lie as it were on the shore of the present, and reveal to us strange glimpses of a former state of things. Among the most interesting of such terms is the word *parable*. It means literally a placing of one thing beside another, not for the purpose of comparison but of completion. And so interpreted, what a significant testimony does it bear to the blind and ignorant condition of fallen man! Previous to the expulsion from Eden, nature was a mirror in which heaven was seen as clearly reflected as the blue sky in the depths of a placid lake. There were not two separate worlds, but one. The earthly shadow was always associated in the mind of Adam with its heavenly substance. He needed no parable or symbol to teach

A

him the truths of the unseen and the eternal, for everything around him was symbolic of spiritual truth. Creation was one great revelation of God. This is abundantly evident from the fact that natural objects alone, as embodying spiritual truths, are mentioned in the beginning of Genesis; such as the garden, the tree of life, the tree of knowledge, the command "Be fruitful and multiply, and replenish the earth." But his iniquity separated between his soul and God, and then, as a necessary consequence, between the natural and the spiritual worlds. The eating of the forbidden fruit made him see double—resolved the one harmonious scheme of creation into two separate independent worlds, sweeping indeed round a common centre, and having a certain local contiguity, but never uniting with, or blending into one another. It brought the scales of unbelief over the purity of his vision, dropped a thick veil between him and the glory and meaning of the inner shrine of nature. The key of knowledge was taken away from him who aspired to be as God. He lost the power of deciphering the hieroglyphics inscribed on sky and stream and hill. Spiritually as well as literally, he hid himself from God, and God hid Himself from him among the trees of the garden. Walking among objects fitted by their very nature to suggest spiritual realities to his mind, he saw nothing but the common appearances of nature, and had no thoughts beyond their earthly uses. The articulate message of God seemed to be mere thunder, and the personal vision of His glory a mere lightning flash.

Such was the blindness, because of spiritual defection, which had fallen upon man, God's high-priest, in the very temple where formerly everything was as full of meaning to him as was the furniture of the tabernacle to Aaron. To cure this blindness, the second Adam came into the world. As the Living Ladder, in His descent and ascent—not in a dream but in open reality—He united earth to heaven. As the Mediator—the Son of God and the Son of man—He reconciled man to God. As the Creator and the First-Born of every creature, He joined together once more the seen and the unseen, which man's sin had divorced. He showed that nature was His Father's house—a grand temple with divinely-pictured windows. Standing without, man saw nothing but the merest outline of dusky shapes, and had no idea of the combined scheme and purport of the picture. But the True Light brought him through spiritual insight into the interior, and there every ray revealed a harmony of unspeakable splendours. Constantly, in His discourses, Jesus revealed the hidden glory of all creation. Not more frequently did He appeal to the written revelation of the Old Testament which He himself had given, in the formula "It is written," than He appealed to the older unwritten revelation in the works which He himself had made, in the formula "The kingdom of heaven is like unto a sower; like unto a grain of mustard seed; like unto leaven," &c. Seated by Jacob's well, He spoke of the living water; in the wilderness, after the miraculous feeding of the multitude, He drew attention to Himself as the true bread; in the homes of men, whenever He cured disease, He revealed Himself as the spiritual physician. The literal and the figurative ran side by side in all His words and acts; the natural and the spiritual were associated, as in statements like these,—" Except a man be born of *water* and of the *Spirit;*" "He shall baptise you with the *Holy Ghost* and with *fire.*" His miracles showed that the common forces of nature, constantly at work around us, and divested of all their inherent wonderfulness by their very uniformity and familiarity, were all direct powers of the Heavenly Kingdom. In His parables He lifted the veil from the face of nature, formerly despised or ignored; disclosed, in. living reality, to our eyes its wonderful spiritual beauty and significance, and connected the common sights and incidents of daily life with the laws and objects of that spiritual kingdom which He has opened up to all believers. "He expounded all things to His disciples;" or, as the original word for expounded *(epelue)*, means literally, He set free from its folds or wrappings, the meaning hid in the parables of nature, of which his own were faithful transcripts. His cross on Calvary was the very focus of symbolism, in which every spiritual truth connected with the finished work of redemption was shadowed forth in some material, visible form. He wore our human nature as the sign of His intimate union and communion with us in suffering; He was nailed to the cross as the picture of His spiritual sacrifice; the crown of thorns was the natural indication that by Him the original curse was overcome and removed;

the eclipse of the sun and the mid-day darkness were the outward representation of the dark cloud of spiritual desertion under which for a time His glory was eclipsed. In short, just as the Hebrew inscription on the cross was explained to the Greek and the Roman by the Greek and Latin equivalent by its side; just as the meaning of all Egyptian hieroglyphics was made known by the Greek translation placed side by side with the common and sacred Egyptian characters of the Rosetta Stone; so the meaning of all the objects and processes of nature is explained to us in the human and Divine language of the Bible, and in the human and Divine sayings and actions of Him who is the Living Word. Christ is the Alpha and Omega of creation; and as these letters include all the intermediate letters of the alphabet, and are necessary to make up every word of human language, by which we express our thoughts, so without Christ, the Word of God, was not anything made that was made; without Him there could have been no expression at first of the thoughts and qualities of God; and without His appearance on earth there could have been no explanation of the significance of creation to fallen man.

Throughout the earlier part of our Lord's ministry He discoursed exclusively in parables. We are told that without a parable spake He not unto the multitude. He sought to win the most careless and ignorant to the apprehension of the truth ; and therefore employed the most simple and familiar illustrations, borrowed from the scenes around them, and the common events of their daily life. His audience was composed almost entirely of the rustic multitudes of Galilee—the "warlike race," as Josephus describes them, who clung to the literal faith of their fathers in simplicity and zeal, and who wished to take Christ by force and make Him a king. And therefore pictures and external illustrations were the only suitable vehicles for their instruction. He made the world of nature and of human life to those child-like simple-hearted people, who were in closest contact with the culture of the soil—a *kinder-garten* in which they were taught by objects. And it was only the very little ones—those who had no spiritual susceptibility—who regarded the objects themselves. Hence the gospels, which describe the Galilean life of Jesus, abound in the parabolic element. This is their distinguishing characteristic. In them the ladder of Divine truth which reaches to heaven is set up on the earth. But towards the close of His ministry Jesus confined Himself almost exclusively to Judæa; and there He found a different class of people—more meditative than active, more prone to inquire than prompt to obey, trained to exercise their minds by reflection upon the mysterious problems of religion and of their own wonderful history. To suit these thoughtful minds, the form of Christ's teaching was altered. He adopted a more refined and abstract mode of instruction. To the closer circle of disciples, educated by intimate companionship with Himself, and growing in faith and in spiritual apprehension, He used a personal style of thought and language. He conveyed to their minds the highest verities of the Christian faith in the form of dialogues, special discourses, and spiritual revelations; and hence the gospel of St. John, which records at fullest length this part of Christ's ministry, which moves almost wholly within the circle of Judæa—St. John himself being probably a native of Jerusalem, dwelling there in his own house, except when he went annually to the Sea of Galilee during the fishing season,—is distinguished for the absence of the parabolic element. But there are links in this gospel which connect the later form of Christ's teaching with the earlier. At the close of the eleventh chapter of St. Matthew, we hear words so like those of St. John, that they seem a quotation from his gospel. " All things are delivered unto me of my Father; and no man knoweth the Son, but the Father; neither knoweth any man the Father, save the Son, and he to whomsoever the Son will reveal Him." "Come unto Me, all ye that labour and are heavy laden, and I will give you rest." So, on the other hand, in the tenth and fifteenth chapters of St. John, and in the 24th verse of the twelfth chapter, "Verily, verily, I say unto you, Except a corn of wheat fall into the ground and die, it abideth alone: but if it die, it bringeth forth much fruit. He that loveth his life shall lose it; and he that hateth his life in this world shall keep it unto life eternal;" and in the 21st verse of the sixteenth chapter, " A woman when she is in travail hath sorrow, because her hour is come; but as soon as she is delivered of the child, she remembereth no more the anguish, for joy that a man is born into the world.   And ye now therefore have sorrow; but I will see you again, and your heart shall rejoice, and your joy no man taketh from you."   In all these sayings of St. John we are brought back to the simple illustrations of St. Matthew, St. Mark and St. Luke, and hear parables, as it were transformed and suited to the new circumstances.

The narrative of the Vine is not, properly speaking, a parable; for a parable veiled the truth in a material illustration, and required to be afterwards unveiled or explained by an interpretation from without, like writing with sympathetic ink which needs the application of heat to bring out its characters.   It is rather an allegory, for it contains *within itself* its own explanation ; the lower object is put directly for the higher.   It is not necessary that Christ should interpret the vine to us, because the thing signified is interpenetrated with the thing signifying; the qualities of the one being attributed to the other, and the two thus blended into one form of speech.   In the allegory of the Vine we have our Lord's first and last teaching harmoniously combined ; the parabolic and the personal element beautifully blended; the ends of the Gospel united in a perfect circle of revelation.   We see in it the complete fulfilment of the promise given to the disciples as recorded by St. Matthew, and but partially fulfilled at the time,—" Unto you it is given to know the mystery of the kingdom of God ; but unto them that are without, all these things are done in parables.   For whosoever hath, to him shall be given and he shall have more abundance, but whosoever hath not, from him shall be taken away even that he hath."

The method of Christ's teaching seems to have depended largely on chances and occasions. Seeds of truth were blown from Him who is the Truth by every breeze of circumstance, like thistledown by the wind. The character of His words, and the mould in which they were cast, were suited to the moment. This seems to have been specially the case with the allegory of the Vine. It was doubtless suggested by some outward incident of the moment; not by the sight of a vineyard, as some suppose, for the imagery of St. John—the gospel not of action but of meditation—is derived not from the fields of nature but from the homes of men ; and Christ on this occasion was not in the open air, but in the upper chamber at Jerusalem. Some object in the room caught His eye while He was speaking to the disciples. Perhaps a portion of a trellised vine outside, peeping in through the latticed window, rustling in the evening breeze, or showing through its veined, transparent leaves the golden light of the setting sun; or, more probably still, the wine-cup before Him on the supper-table,—in which the Jewish Passover was transformed into the Christian Sacrament,—may have started the train of association which led naturally and easily from the juice of the grape, the symbol of His shed blood, to the vine that produced it, as the symbol of His own broken body. But while the form of Christ's teaching on this occasion was determined by the accident of the moment, it fell in, by a beautiful and Divine harmony, with the general analogy of Scripture teaching. The vine is one of the most familiar images in the Old Testament. We see it as an illustration of spiritual ideas as frequently within the sacred enclosure of Divine truth as we see it growing as a natural object in the fields of nature. The inspired writers cultivated it as assiduously for its higher uses, as the vine-dresser cultivates it for the sake of its natural uses. No less than five of our Lord's parables refer to it. The idea of the kingdom of God as a vine or a vineyard* runs throughout the whole Bible; and when our Lord appropriated it as an earthly symbol of Himself, He but fulfilled the highest meaning of the prophetic blessing pronounced by the dying Jacob upon the head of his son Judah; "The sceptre shall not depart from Judah, nor a lawgiver from between his feet, until Shiloh come; and unto him shall the gathering of the people be. Binding his foal unto the vine, and his ass's colt unto the choice vine; he washed his garments in wine, and his clothes in the blood of grapes; his eyes shall be red with wine, and his teeth white with milk." The Land of Promise was a land of vineyards; and Judæa especially, with its temperate climate,

---

* The prairie, or open moorland, although sown by the wind with the seed of trees, is bare of woods, because animals devour the young plants as soon as they appear above ground, and there is no shelter from the wind. But when a space is walled round, the seeds spring up in it freely, and in its favouring climate speedily become tall trees. So is it in the Church : it is a garden enclosed, a vineyard walled round from the open and exposed common of the world, in whose genial shelter plants of righteousness, the planting of the Lord, may grow up and flourish in God's holy place.

and elevated rocky slopes, was admirably adapted for the culture of the vine. A vineyard on a terrace or brow of a hill is the first object that strikes the eye of the traveller when he approaches Judæa from the desert; and the first of our Lord's parables which is suggested to his mind by the new scenery is that of the "Vineyard." Indeed, Hebron, according to Jewish tradition, is supposed to be the spot where the vine was created, and from whence, as a centre of distribution, it spread out to other lands. It was from the Judæan valley of Eshcol that the spies brought the enormous cluster of grapes, regarded by the Israelites as a remarkable specimen of the fertility of the land. A vineyard on a hill, fenced and cleared of stones, was the natural emblem of the kingdom of Judah; and this heraldic symbol was engraved on the coins of the Maccabees, on the ornaments of the temple, and on the tombstones of the Jews.

It is not without significance that the vine should be thus peculiar to Judæa. One of the most perfect of plants, it belongs to one of the most perfect of countries as regards its physical structure. Contrast the grapes of Eshcol with the richly variegated scenery of that valley, and its elaborate geological conformation, with the hard dry woody fruits of the dreary parched plains of Australia; a low type of fruit with a low type of country. There is a close typical relation between the character of a country and the character of its productions; and this relation ascends even into the world of man. As the monotonous plains and innutritious fruits of Australia reared the lowest savages; so the picturesque mountain scenery, and the rich nutritious grapes, pomegranates and olives of Palestine developed the noblest of the human races. Judæa was not only the true climate and primitive centre of the vine, it was also the cradle of civilization in Palestine; here were started the first germs of that highly-developed social life which the Israelites found among the aboriginal Canaanites at the conquest. It may seem degrading thus to connect human progress with physical causes; but the soul is not more dependent upon the body, than body and soul are dependent upon the outer body of natural circumstances. It is possible, by the administration of various medicinal substances, to awaken almost every emotion of which the human breast is capable—joy, sorrow, hatred, benevolence, exhilaration, despair. The mountain elevation of Jerusalem,—one of the highest cities in the world,—with its pure air and bracing genial climate, may have had much to do with the purity of its manners, and the sanctity that attached to everything in it; while, on the other hand, the profound depression in which Sodom and Gomorrah lay,—the deepest abyss on the face of the earth,—with its enervating tropical climate and its hot, stagnant air, may have had much to do with the awful corruption of morals which made these cities of the plain a proverb of wickedness.

Thus is the profound saying of Ruskin,—"The distinctions of species among plants seem appointed with more definite ethical address to the intelligence of man as their material products become more useful to him," illustrated in the case of the vine in Judæa. But besides its local suitableness, there were many obvious fitnesses to recommend our Lord's choice of the symbol in His last discourse in Jerusalem. He wished to represent outwardly the permanent spiritual union of His disciples with Himself; and therefore a perennial and not an annual plant must be selected, a dicotyledonous tree with branches, and not a monocotyledonous tree without branches. The image of the lily suited our Lord when His own personal loveliness, purity, and fragrance, and His own short-lived single life on earth were intended to be shadowed forth; and the image of the palm-tree, which has no branches, suited the disciples when their own individual excellence was portrayed:— "The righteous shall flourish like the palm-tree." But when the lasting union between Christ and His disciples is to be represented, these images are found inappropriate. A plant must be selected from another order of the vegetable kingdom altogether, whose characteristic it is to produce branches, and live, and grow year after year. Further, the fruitfulness of Christ and the fruitfulness of believers in Him, is an idea that has to be outwardly symbolised; and hence the plant that can do this adequately must be a cultivated one—not a mere herb of the field, like corn, yielding fruit only on the top of a stalk, but a tree yielding fruit all round, on every branch and twig. Further still, the subordinate relation to and dependence of Christ upon His Father in the days of His flesh, is another idea which must be expressed by the symbol; and this idea manifestly excludes all fruit-trees that are capable of standing alone and unsupported, such as the apple—the pomegranate, or the fig tree. The plant that is to convey this idea must be a trailing, climbing plant, which clings to some object of support, and is incapable of standing and growing up alone. Believers in Christ exhibit, with general features of resemblance to each other, considerable personal differences of character and experience; and the plant which is to represent this quality must admit of considerable variability within certain distinct and well-recognised limits. All these qualifications, and others which will be stated further on, required in the allegory, meet in the vine, and in the vine alone. It is a cultivated, fruitful, perennial, branching, climbing plant; it is extremely variable under cultivation, every country and province having a special form, and new varieties being produced every year; and hence it admirably symbolises the relations of our Lord to the Father on the one hand, and to the disciples on the other.

The vine does not belong to the earlier ages of the world's history. It is never found in the shape of fossil remains in geological strata, previous to the Upper Miocene. It belongs peculiarly to the human period, and was planted in the earth shortly before its occupancy by man. It came into the world along with the beautiful rose, and the fruitful apple, and the fragrant mint, and the honey-laden bee, to make an Eden of nature for man's use and enjoyment. The former ages were flowerless; green, monotonous tree-ferns and tree-mosses, destined to become fuel for man, alone covered the land.   But blossoms and fruits came with humanity, as outbirths and representatives of spiritual principles—thus testifying to the close correspondence between nature and the soul of man.   Prophesied by all previous vegetable forms, whose structure approached nearer and nearer to its type, the vine appeared in the fulness of the earth's time; just as He whom it shadowed forth was announced in type and prophecy from the foundation of the world, and by all His forerunners in typical personages back to Adam, and appeared in the fulness of human history when the world was ready for His reception.   And thus the symbol and the Person symbolised belong peculiarly to the human world, and were destined specially for human nourishment and satisfaction.

Fruit trees form a peculiar link between the ages and the zones—between the dead and the living; and this is another feature of the vine's fitness for representing human qualities.   They enlist our hopes and sympathies year after year; and their aged branches, like withered hands and arms, hold out their ripened produce—the best that they can give, to successive generations.   They are domesticated, and brought into relationship with each member of the family by their individual qualities.   They have grown humanized, as Hawthorne says, by receiving the care of man, and by contributing to his wants. They are associated in a remarkable manner with the history of the human race.   We can trace the gradual diffusion of mankind and their progressive advancement in civilization, by the distribution of certain favourite fruits over the surface of the globe, and the gradual improvement of them by cultivation. Wherever man has penetrated he has carried with him, and planted in the new soil, the fruits upon which he depended for food or luxury. Most of our own fruits mark the different revolutions in our national history, and the great changes in our social state. To the Roman invaders we are indebted for the cherry, which Lucullus brought to Rome from Pontus, as a memorial of his victory over Mithridates; and the peach, the plum, and the pear, introduced by them from Persia and Armenia, are evidences that our country was once a Roman colony. By the monks also, who accompanied the crusades to the Holy Land, many new and valuable fruit trees were brought from the East, and planted in the monastic gardens, from whence they gradually spread over the land. In the same manner, the Spanish priests caused almost all the fruits of temperate Europe to flourish amidst the productions of the torrid zone in South America. Missionaries have introduced European fruits into India, Southern Africa, and the islands of the South Seas. This historical connection of fruits with the progress of civilization, is in no case so striking as in that of the vine. From Asia it passed into Greece and thence into Sicily; the Phoceans carried it into the south of France; the Romans planted it in Spain and on the banks of the Rhine; while British enterprise introduced it into America, Madeira, Cape of Good Hope, and Australia, where it yields an abundant vintage. A strict correlation exists between the culture of the vine, and the intellectual and spiritual development of humanity. Wherever the grape ripens, there flourish all the arts that chiefly tend to make life nobler and more enjoyable. The spread of the Christian religion, as a general rule, has been co-extensive and synchronous with that of the vine. To almost every region where the Gospel has been preached the vine has extended, so that wherever the allegory of our Saviour is read, there the natural object may be seen to illustrate it.

In the symbol of the vine our Lord recognises the prefiguration in plants of animal forms and functions. This prefiguration opens up to us one of the most interesting and instructive fields of study, for it helps us to a right conception of the unity of nature. As a general rule, there is nothing to be found in the world of animals for which a parallel may not be found in the world of plants. The lower objects show distinctly and in detail what in the higher objects is obscured by their more complex organisation. We see in the trees and flowers around us interpreters of the mysteries of our own nature—mute prophecies of our own human form, character and actions. If we consider the lilies how they grow, we shall find in them, as in a picture, set forth all the incidents and experiences that make up our own life. They cease their work like us, close their eyelids and sleep every night when the sun sets, and awake to renewed activity, like us, when the morning comes Their snowy blossoms, with their stamens and pistils, prefigure the purity and beauty of our human marriage;

and their fragrance the sweetness of our human love. We have a foreshadowing of human birth in the bursting of the pod and the escape of the seed; and of the mother's bosom in the supply of milk-like nourishment stored up in the seed with the germ, from which the young plant draws its food till it is weaned, and able to cater from the soil for itself. How beautiful is the parallel between the life of leaves and that of man, unfolding in the delicate greenness of spring, maturing in the vigour of summer, and fading away in the languor and decay of autumn! In the stem, branches, and foliage of the vine, we discern the ideal plan or model on which our own bodies are constructed: the stem being the spinal column; the branches the ribs and members; the leaves the lungs; while the sap-vessels, filled with their nourishing fluid, correspond with the veins and their circulating blood. The functions, too, which all these parts and organs in the vine perform are precisely analogous to those which similar parts and organs perform in the economy of man. Indeed, we cannot speak in the most literal and matter-of-fact way of the vine, without implying the profound poetic truth of prefigurement,—without unconsciously philosophizing and using terms first framed to denote the members of our own bodies. Upon this wonderful resemblance of man to the flowers of the field and the trees of the forest every poetical mind has delighted to dwell, without knowing, perhaps, the reason. The Greeks of old pictured it in their beautiful fables of the Dryads, Daphnes, and Ariels. Jotham's parable of the trees, and our Saviour's parables from the vegetable kingdom, are examples of the same deep-seated feeling. Our modern language of flowers, with all its sentimental absurdities, is an unconscious recognition of it. How touchingly does Herrick describe it in the well-known verses on the daffodils! How it glows on almost every page of Wordsworth's poetry, who believed that flowers had feeling, and that man is a tree endowed with powers of self-knowledge and self-movement, or an "*arbor inversa,*" as the ancients called him! Shelley speaks of "a wood of sad sweet thoughts." Every one who has passed through a forest has felt what may be called its intense human feeling. Its shadow lies upon the hushed heart like the presence of some unknown being. In its dim perspectives, leading to deeper solitudes, there seem to lurk strange weird mysteries and speechless terrors, that keep eye and ear intent in vague expectancy, as if waiting for some one. The trunks of the trees, with their knotted bark covered with hoary lichens, seem like a solemn senate. How vividly, in the ballad of the Erl King, does Goethe describe this human feeling of the forest, which, as we have seen, is not all mere fancy! What a terrible use does Dante make of it in his description of the human forest in the infernal regions,—men metamorphosed into trees; branches, when broken, dripping blood and uttering a wild human wail! The conclusion to which these considerations lead us is, that when we employ the vine as a symbol of human qualities, the congruity between them is of a deeper and truer nature than that of mere poetical selection or arbitrary metaphor. It lies in the very nature of things. It is founded upon the plan of creation, upon the mutual structural and functional relations of plants and animals as parts of one great whole.

The vocabulary of St. John's gospel is eminently characteristic. It has several peculiar terms—such as the Word, the Light, the Life, the Truth, the World, Glory, Grace—which, perhaps more than all others, bear upon them the clear stamp of the Divine signet. They are key-words which open up new realms of thought to us; as suggestive as the streak of dawn along the eastern hills. Like the jewels in the breastplate of the Jewish high-priest, they glow among the commoner terms with a mystic radiance which dispels the shadows of earth and time, and reveals the unseen and eternal. To these peculiar words may be added the word "true," which occurs no less than twenty-two times in the Gospel of St. John, as against five times in all the rest of the New Testament. This word illustrates in a remarkable way the meditative simplicity of St. John's writings, in which all the ideas reduce themselves to a few comprehensive terms. The full meaning of the word "true," as Archbishop Trench says, is not commonly understood, owing to the fact that it is employed to represent, and so confound, two ideas which are most distinct; *viz.*, the true as opposed to the false, and the true as distinguished from the typical or subordinate realization. Our forefathers, wiser in this respect than we, recognised this distinction, and expressed the former idea by the word *true*, and the latter by the word *very*, which has now become obsolete in that sense. The man who fulfilled the promise of his lips was a *true* man; but the man who fulfilled the wider promise of his name was a *very* man, a man indeed. God is the *true* God, in the sense that He cannot lie—that He is the truth-speaking and the truth-loving God, whose every word is Yea and Amen; but He is much more than that; He is the true God, inasmuch as He is all that the name of God implies, in contradistinction to idols or false gods, which have no existence save in the dreams of diseased fancy or degraded superstition. He is, as the old phrase is still retained in the Nicene creed, "*very* God of *very* God." In Greek the distinction is clearly indicated by the use of two words, *alethes* true, and *alethinos* very, which are never used indiscriminately. The word translated in our version is *alethinos*, and should be rendered *very*, for it indicates the contrast, not between the true and the false, but between the imperfect and the perfect— between the shadowy and the substantial, the type and the archetype, the highest ideal and a subordinate realization or partial anticipation. This last is the sense in which St. John almost exclusively employs the term. Christ is declared to be " the true light,"* not thereby

---

* The seven-branched candlestick of the tabernacle may be said to have combined in itself the two emblems of the " true vine " and the " true light," just as they were united in the bush of the desert that burned with fire and was not consumed. The sacred candlestick was in the shape of a tree ; its ornaments were derived from the vegetable kingdom ; its knobs and bowls were almond

indicating that all other lights are false or have no real existence, but that He is the "Light which lighteth every man that cometh into the world," the central Sun whose light is reflected by every object and person as His satellites,—the Eye that made the eye, the Light that created the sun, the Light that shone in the pillar of fire, that made John the Baptist a burning and shining light, that walketh in the midst of the seven golden candlesticks, and holdeth the seven stars in His hand, and kindles all believers as lights in the world. Similarly, Christ is "the *true* bread"—not denying by this expression, that there was nourishing power in the manna in the wilderness, or that our daily bread is able to sustain our natural life, but merely indicating that these corrupted if kept, nourished only the body, and did not preserve those who partook of them from death; they were bread only in an inferior and subordinate degree—a shadow of Him who is bread in the highest and fullest sense of which if a man eat, he shall never hunger, and shall be nourished up into everlasting life. Thus we are able to enter into the full meaning of Christ's words, "I am the True Vine." And in this connection it is interesting to notice that the Saxon

blossoms and fruit. There is a close analogy between trees and flames, between the "true light" and the "true vine." The vine is concentrated solar light,—the seven-branched candlestick which exhibits the light kindled by the sun in the shape of leaves, flowers, and fruit. Like the flame of a candle, the vine is nothing more than a temporary state through which material substance is passing, because of some original physical impression made upon it, and the present operation of external circumstances.

word *tree* is etymologically cognate with *true*, signifying that which is firm, strong, or well-established.

"The vineyard of the Lord of Hosts is the house of Israel, and the men of Judah His pleasant plant." Israel was *a* vine,—the vine which God brought out of Egypt,* as an unsuitable soil and climate for its production—too tropical, enervating, and debasing—and planted in the rocky soil and temperate climate of Palestine, amid hardy conditions and changeable circumstances, fitted to train up a brave and God-fearing nation. But Israel was not the *true* vine of God.

* The vine cannot endure a tropical climate, ceasing to flourish productively whenever the mean temperature of the year approaches 22° centigrade or 71° 6" Fahrenheit. In Asia, Africa, and Europe it has never been cultivated, with the view of converting its fruit into wine, outside the zone comprised between the thirtieth and fiftieth degrees of north latitude. In the warm climate of the valley of the Jordan it was rare, if not unknown ; and it appears to have been unproductive on the low lands adjoining the Mediterranean. Spots that were favourable to the palm were unfavourable to the vine. It might therefore be expected to flourish on the mountains of Judæa, and to fail on the plains of Jericho. The region of Palestine is almost or quite the farthest south in that quarter of the globe where the vine is luxuriant and productive ; the elevation of the hills and table-lands of Judæa being, as already mentioned, its true climate. We read indeed in the Old Testament that the vine was used for vintaging purposes in Egypt ; and numerous hieroglyphics attest that this was not an exceptional, but a common practice. The wine of Antilles, grown near Alexandria, was the choicest at the banquet of Antony and Cleopatra. But in that country the vine was grown only in the north, and in places exceptionally cool and moist, where by sheltering it from the rays of the sun and other precautions, the injurious influence of climate was prevented. At Cairo, with a mean temperature of 72°, the culture is insignificant.

Though not altogether false and fraudulent, it was an inferior and subordinate realization, a partial and imperfect anticipation of the truth. It did not come up to God's ideal of a vine; it fulfilled very imperfectly and unsatisfactorily the purposes of its existence. It was carefully tended by God's gracious husbandry; but when the Husbandman came seeking fruit upon it, He found none, or only wild grapes. "Israel is an empty vine; he bringeth forth fruit unto himself." "Yet I had planted thee a noble vine, wholly a right seed, how then art thou turned into the degenerate plant of a strange vine unto me?" "For their vine is of the vine of Sodom and of the fields of Gomorrah; their grapes are grapes of gall; their clusters are bitter; their wine is the poison of dragons and the cruel venom of asps." But Christ was the *True* Vine of God; He fulfilled to the utmost the purposes of His existence. The vineyard of Israel was to be laid waste and destroyed. It was to be taken from the wicked husbandmen, and given to the husbandmen who should faithfully render the fruits in their season. But out of this Jewish vineyard was to grow one Vine, which should endure when all the peculiar institutions of Judaism had perished, and become the starting-point of a new and higher religious growth. He who was born and lived and died as a Jew, was to be known as the Son of man, in whom the horizon of humanity would be widened and ennobled. The human tree, which hitherto had propagated itself, generation after generation, by means of buds alone, inheriting the sins and corruptions of nature in a wearisome monotony and uniformity of sin, in Him blossomed and produced seed, by means of which a new variety of spiritual life and growth was introduced into the world. He realized the name of God's Vine in its highest form, in its ripest and completest development. Whatever that name implied, whatever, according to that name, He ought to be, that He was to the full. "The idea and the fact were in Him, what they never could be in any other, absolutely commensurate." While the Law was given by Moses, grace and *truth* came by Jesus Christ; the imperfect and the shadowy were given by the one, the perfect and the substantial by the other. Christ is *the* Truth in whom all types find their fullest realization, and reach their culminating glory.

Christ is also the "True Vine," as distinguished from the false or counterfeit vine. One natural object in Scripture is frequently employed to shadow forth two spiritual truths—is used in a good and in a bad sense. Leaven, for instance, is likened by our Saviour to the kingdom of heaven; it is also employed as the symbol of what is false and corrupting. So the vine, which is employed to denote Christ and His people, also denotes Antichrist and his confederates. "And the angel thrust in his sickle into the earth, and gathered the vine of the earth, and cast it into the great wine-press of the wrath of God." There are many species of vine, but there is only one grape-vine; so error is multiform, but truth is one. And just as the wheat is imitated by the tares —the poisonous darnel—which closely resemble it in every respect; so the True Vine is imitated by the vine of Sodom, with its poisonous fruit. Whatever we see in the kingdom of light is parodied and caricatured by the kingdom of darkness. The Christ of the one is the Antichrist of the other; the saints of the one are the hypocrites of the other. Whatever befalls the one in good is reflected by the other in evil.

But there is another aspect still in which the phrase "True Vine," as applied by Christ to Himself, may be viewed. The Greek word for "true" here, as I have already said, is *alethinos*. It is derived from the verb *lanthano*—to lie hid, to be concealed,—and from the particle *a*—being a contraction of *apo*—having a privative power; and therefore signifies, literally, *unconcealed*, —as if Christ had said, "I am the unconcealed Vine." This idea opens up a new set of relations. Israel was a *concealed* vine. Its full significance was not known until Christ, the True Vine, revealed it. It had a value, but, like a cipher, which means nothing until conjoined with a numeral, that value was indefinite until it was associated with Him who is the chiefest among ten thousand, and altogether lovely. The history of Christ sheds light upon the whole history of Israel. St. Matthew, in his opening chapter, draws our attention to the fact that the history of the type is repeated in that of the Archetype. Israel, the son of God as a nation, was rescued in its infancy from the bondage of Egypt. God's Only-Begotten Son had a similar destiny; for He too, in His infancy, was exposed to a tyrant's persecution, and, by Divine interposition, rescued from it. St.

Matthew quotes the words of Hosea, "Out of Egypt have I called my Son," as fulfilled in the fortunes of the infant Saviour.   And so was it with all the institutions of Israel.   The law that came by Moses was weak and unprofitable ; it accomplished nothing ; it was a symbol having a concealed meaning—a schoolmaster leading to Christ.   This was implied in the fact that, during prayer and the reading of the law in the synagogue, the priests always wore the *Tallith*, or veil, in commemoration of that with which Moses covered his shining face, and in order, as St. Paul explains to us, not merely to shroud the glory of the law from weak and awe-stricken eyes, but also to protect it from a too-penetrating scrutiny, which might have revealed, in the very history of its introduction, a higher object beyond itself.   "Moses put a veil over his face, that the children of Israel could not steadfastly look to the end of that which is abolished."   But the *aletheia*—the truth, the full meaning and purpose of the law—came by Jesus Christ, in whom were fulfilled the law and the prophets,—who is the end of the law for righteousness to all who believe. "When it"—that is, the heart of the people—"shall turn to the Lord, the veil shall be taken away."   So, too, the Jewish tabernacle was a shadow of Christ, the True Tabernacle, who assumed our nature, and dwelt in our world.   It had two coverings,—one of rams' skins dyed red, and another of badgers' skins,—not merely to protect it, on the march, from the sun or dust, but to indicate that it was a veiled or concealed symbol.   Its inner glory was hidden by its rough badger-skin exterior, just as its real design was hidden by its common appearance—a tent like the tents of Israel. All its sacred furniture and vessels, we find in the fourth chapter of Numbers, were also wrapped, for the same reason, in coverings or veils of blue, and scarlet, and purple, and badgers' skins. "And upon the table of showbread they shall spread a cloth of blue;" "and they shall take a cloth of blue and cover the candlestick of the light;" and "they shall take away the ashes from the altar, and spread a purple cloth thereon," etc. When Christ appeared, He disclosed the meaning of those symbols of human uses and associations which the structure and objects of the tabernacle had been indicating. He removed the covering from them, as it were; He Himself was the unconcealed tabernacle. What before had been seen in shadow now comes out clearly. The older saints had merely the shadow; but we, with open face, looking into the New Testament as into a glass, see the very image.

In a similar way the natural vine is a *concealed* vine. When created, as Dr. Balfour says, it had a symbolical meaning—a distinct reference to Christ. It was a living parable or riddle, speaking of Him age after age. But men could not understand its symbolical meaning; they misinterpreted its lessons; they thought that it had no higher uses than the mere material, utilitarian ones,—to delight their eye with its beauty, to refresh their palate with its fruit, or to minister to their depraved senses in the intoxicating draught. It was only when Christ appeared that the parable was explained, and the mystery, hid from ages and generations, revealed. When He said, "I am the True (or *unconcealed*) Vine," then men understood for the first time the meaning that had all along been concealed in the vine. Then articulate expression was given to the secret which the vine, from the beginning of the world, by its dumb language of signs, had been striving in vain to impart. Our Lord's first miracle at Cana of Galilee—the conversion of. water into wine—was effected by the direct and immediate agency of the True Vine. It revealed the power which enables the natural vine in the vineyard to change the rains and dews of every summer into wine in its grapes. Jesus lifted the veil from the natural form, and disclosed, once for all, the spiritual Presence always working behind it. And what is thus asserted of the vine is equally applicable to bread, to light, to water,—to every natural object. They all had a concealed meaning—a reference to Christ—from the beginning; so that when He appeared, the whole was unconcealed or revealed. We are placed, as it were, in the presence of an Isis—a veiled glory. The heavenly tabernacle is about us, but we know it not. We live, and move, and have our being in the midst of its eternal realities, but they are covered with the badger's skin of familiar uses and common-place enjoyments, veiled with the blue wrappings of sky and sea, and the purple and scarlet veils of mountain and flower. Our whole life is spent in the effort to see more of heaven in nature and in revelation. Now and then, while we work and pray, the covering is partially lifted, and we obtain a glimpse of the hidden effulgence. When we are conscientiously and earnestly endeavouring to find out the design and significance of creation, in the light given to us by Him who is the absolute Truth, we are attaining to the knowledge of *the truth*, or *the uncon-cealed;* we are sharing in the dignity of communion with God. "It is the glory of God *to conceal a thing;* but the honour of kings is to search out a matter."*

We are accustomed to call such language as our Lord employs in the text figurative language, thereby implying that there is nothing in it but a fanciful analogy. But we have seen that such language is not really metaphorical, but is our Lord's simple, literal explanation of His own creative purposes. The truest language is necessarily what we call figurative, and only false when the spiritual is interpreted by the physical, instead of the physical by the spiritual. Our Lord does not say, "I am *like* the vine." That would have been to use a mere metaphor, or figure of speech—to lay hold of a mere fanciful or arbitrary resemblance between Himself and the vine. But He says, "I *am* the True Vine;" and this declares that the vine is the

---

* Idolatry, instead of taking off the covering from the spiritual idea which nature contains, only darkens it by throwing over it an additional veil. The *eidolon*, or idol-image, instead of being a medium for the worship of the true or unconcealed God, hides Him more completely from the view. So, too, all ritualism obscures the significance of the truth by its symbols—deals with the truth as the Mahometans do with the sacred ark called the *kaaba* of Mecca, which they cover every year with a new *kesoua*, or silken covering. The only way to unveil the truth is by spirituality of mind and purity of heart.

actual shadow of His substance. He is not merely the ingenious Deviser and Designer, displaying in the vine His contrivances of skill, but its Archetype; He is the ideal, and the vine is the material representative. It is what we find it, not because God *willed* it to be so arbitrarily, as because of His containing in His own nature the first principles of its whole fabric and economy. It is one of the things that are made in which are clearly seen the invisible things of God,—one of the inert images or forms in time of spiritual and eternal facts. In common with every object of the physical world, it is derived from an anterior spiritual world, and is the effect of a spiritual cause, which gives it its formative force,—preserves in this peculiar pattern its matter, that would otherwise pass indifferently from mould to mould, without taking the shape of any,—enables it to select its materials from earth and air, and causes it to come back, and grow up, generation after generation, in its own peculiar and adopted form. This profound and interesting truth is expressly taught in the Mosaic account of creation :—"These are the generations of the heavens and the earth, and of every herb of the field *before it was in the earth,* and of every herb of the field *before it grew.*" These words tell us as plainly as language can, of the spiritual source of the physical world, —that before the earth was, green verdure already existed, though not visible,—that every herb of the field is an outbirth from the unseen universe. The model, or pattern of all created things existed in the spiritual world, in the mind of Him who calleth those things that be not as though they were, just as truly as the patterns of the tabernacle existed in the spiritual world, and were shown to Bezaleel on the mount. The tabernacle of nature, no less than the tabernacle of Israel, is an earthly copy of things which have a most real and glorious existence in heaven.

What qualities in Christ are adumbrated by the vine? What infinite reality in Him is indicated by the finite shadow? This we cannot fully unfold. We know only in part, and can prophesy only in part. We see through a glass darkly. But some of the resemblances are obvious. The vine, take it all in all, is the most perfect of plants. Some plants possess one part, or one quality, more highly developed; but for the harmonious development of every part and quality—for perfect balance of loveliness and usefulness, there are none to equal the vine. It belongs to the highest order of the vegetable kingdom, ranks in structure above the lily and the palm, occupies the same position among plants which man does among animals. Its stem and leaves are among the most elegant in shape and hue, its blossoms among the most modest and fragrant, while its fruit is botanically the most perfect; and, æsthetically, painters tell us, that to study the perfection of form, colour, light, and shade, united in one object, we must place before us a bunch of grapes. It is perfectly innocent, being one of the few climbing plants that do not injure the object of their support. It has no thorns —no noxious qualities; all its parts are useful. Its foliage affords a refreshing shade from the scorching

sunshine; its fruit was one of the first oblations to the
Divinity, and, along with bread, is one of the primary
and essential elements of human food.   It beautifies
the landscape wherever it is allowed to wreath the
trellised cottages with its garlands, and festoon the
trees with its luxuriant drapery.   In common with
other plants, it purifies the air—feeding upon what
we reject as poison, and returning it to us as wine
that maketh glad the heart, and in the process
maintaining the atmosphere in a fit condition for
our breathing.   In all these aspects the vine is the
shadow of Him who is altogether lovely—who unites
in Himself the extremes of perfection—who is continually doing good—who beautified our fallen world
by His presence, changed its wilderness into an
Eden, and made the polluted atmosphere of our life
purer by breathing it, and is now transforming our evil
into good, and our sorrow into a fruitful and strengthening joy.

The words "I am the True Vine," moreover, distinguish clearly between nature and that which is above it.
To Pantheism nature is all—nature is God, or God is
nature; but the phrase, "I am the True Vine" reveals
to us the existence of a Being who is distinct from, and
superior to, the works of His hands; traces the stream
of effect up to a living origin, and discriminates the
nature of that origin.   It is the satisfaction of true
reason, which, finding transitory beauty in the type,
turns by its own law to gaze on the eternal beauty
beyond,—which, hearing broken music in the echo,

yearns after the perfect harmony which caused the echo, —which, in short, will not be satisfied with any image, but cries after the Original. The pronoun "I" in it leads us up to the Personal Origin of all creation; shows to us that creation is not eternal, but springs from a Person. The fact that we ourselves are persons indicates that only a Personal cause could have created us. A thing cannot originate a person; only a person can create a thing. Physical causes possess no inherent power—are as incapable of maintaining, as of first producing, the system of the universe. Natural selection, evolution, development, cannot account for the origin and maintenance of nature; they are merely, supposing them to be true, the modes in which a personal Agent operates, and cannot be the cause of their own observance. The very genius of language, God's gift, and the indispensable medium of thought, recognises the fact that a person only can be really an agent—a mere thing not acting, but being acted upon. In the Greek and Latin language, as Dr. Whately remarks, "nouns of the neuter gender, considered as denoting things, and not persons, invariably have the nominative and accusative the same, or rather may be said to have an accusative only, employed as a nominative, when the grammatical construction requires it." Our Saviour, too, in *rebuking* the fever, and the winds and waves, did not use a mere oratorical personification, but traced the disorders of nature up to their source in a person— brought them back to Satan and to fallen man as their ultimate cause. When, therefore, he says, " I am the

True Vine," He reveals Himself as the personal Origin of all that the vine is and does.

If all this be really as I have said, how can any one expect to be able to interpret the meaning of the vine, without the personal knowledge of the Living Being who is working and speaking to us through its instrumentality? Its botanical structure and history, its æsthetic qualities and economical uses, we may know by the methods of science; but its higher significance —the object for which it truly exists, and which connects it with the spiritual world, by whose laws it is what it is, and does what it does,—that in it which appeals not to the intellect, but to the heart and the spirit—must be altogether unknown to him who does not enter within the veil of creation, and in the Holy Place above the mercy-seat, where there are the heavenly realities of earthly shadows, talk with God face to face as a man talketh with his friend. It is because many of our poets and scientific men have not been alone with God on the mount, receiving from Him the revelation of the laws of the universe, and beholding the patterns of earthly things in His book, that nature is as blank to them of spiritual meaning as the tables of stone before God's finger wrote upon them; that much of modern poetry is a mere reflex of humanity, and of modern science only a circle of continuous force continually returning upon itself. " If," as St. Paul says, " God has gathered together in one all things in Christ, both those which are in the heavens, and those which are on the earth, even in Him," then the highest generalizations of science that fall short of Him want the unit that completes them, and gives to their ciphers an infinite significance. Without the knowledge of His *person* we cannot have the knowledge of His *work* in its fulness. The secret of the Lord is not with us. But once united to Him by a living and loving faith, we have the proper view-point of the universe. The Sun of Righteousness, and not the earth itself, is the centre of the system of nature; and regarded from this helio-centric position, difficulties and mysteries, insoluble from the geocentric position, are cleared away. There is a very curious puzzle, which, when viewed in the ordinary way, is an utterly incomprehensible jumble of lines and forms; but when a polished cylindrical reflector is placed at a particular point, the reflected image becomes a perfect picture. In like manner does Jesus show, in its true order and beauty, what apart from Him appears hopeless confusion. In Him we have the Living Word that created and interprets all things. Creation and redemption are seen by eyes purged by His spiritual eye-salve, and hearts made pure and simple by His love, to be parts of one glorious system, which may not be disjoined, or unduly exalted the one above the other. The territory of nature is no more, as many still ignorantly and foolishly think, what Canaan was at first—a heathen land outside of the Gospel. Our Joshua or Jesus, has conquered it for His own Israel, and made it a Holy Land; and He now leads the Christian's thoughts and affections to dwell in it, and make it his home. The same great truths are seen to be imprinted upon nature that shine forth with clearest light in redemption. Communion with nature is a sacramental communion. Everything shows forth the glory of the Redeemer; His righteousness is manifested in the great mountains, and His judgments in the great deeps; the lilies of the field speak of His loveliness; the trees of the forest clap their hands to Him; and the very stones cry out " Hosannas ! "

> " Two worlds are ours ! 'tis only sin
>   Forbids us to descry
> The mystic heaven, and earth within,
>   Plain as the sea and sky.
>
> Thou who hast given me eyes to see,
>   And love this sight so fair,
> Give me a heart to find out Thee,
>   And read Thee everywhere."

CHAPTER II.

THE HUSBANDMAN.

"And my Father is the Husbandman."—JOHN xv. 1.

IT is a remarkable example of providential pre-arrangement, that the book which is most human and most Divine should have been written in circumstances and languages the best adapted to convey its truth to men. The Divine revelation was given first in the deserts and mountains of the unchanging East, amid stereotyped customs and calm unvarying scenery; then it passed to the busy cities of the West, and took its place as a heavenly leaven among ever-varying scenes of life, and continually-changing conditions of society. It was given first in oracles, proclaimed by prophets to the people, standing aloof and at a great moral height above them, and silencing the doubts and questionings of men's hearts by the unanswerable formula: "Thus saith the Lord." It then passed into the form of epistles, or familiar letters, written by apostles to brethren with whom they had intimate fellowship in the Divine truth, and who were placed on the same level with them, to meet a special occasion, and in immediate contact with actual life. The first part of it spreads over the long period of four thousand years, like a perennial plant repeating, generation after generation, the same parts of stem and foliage, but slowly preparing for, and progressing all the time towards, a great and definite crisis. The last part is completed in the short space of less than forty years, and is like the sudden blossoming of the plant, in which leaves, wound spirally round the stem at distant intervals, are compressed into the close rows of the petals of the flower, and brilliantly coloured by the intenser action of life. The Old Testament Scriptures were given in the Hebrew tongue, whose words, though few and simple, are many-sided, contain depth below depth of meaning, and are capable of the widest range and application. The New Testament Scriptures were given in the Greek tongue, whose extraordinary wealth of inflexions, flexibility of expression, and boundless opportunity of style, translated the grand old Hebrew words of Divine truth into an easy and practical medium between man and man in the every-day intercourse and business of life. The Old Testament is a rich, ripe capsule, full of seeds of thought; the New Testament is the sowing and the germinating of these seeds in the field which man tills and tends. The Hebrew language of the one is like the rod in the prophet's hand,—stiff and unbending in its stateliness; the Greek language of the other is like the rod cast upon the ground, and changed into a serpent instinct with life, and bending in all directions.

In the one we have the general comprehensive precepts; in the other, the specific and practical applications of them. In the writers of the later Scriptures we have the necessary combination of Hebrew thought and life and Greek life and culture; and in that peculiar Hellenistic dialect which they employed, the necessary transition from the language of the East to the language of the West—the wedding of the most exact form of expression with the most spiritual mode of conception.

These thoughts are suggested by the original names in Scripture for the vine. In Hebrew there are two words—*gephen* and *sorek*, or *sorekah*—employed to denote this plant. The word *gephen* is of frequent occurrence in the Bible, and is used, in a general sense, to signify a plant that resembles the vine in the habit of climbing or trailing by means of tendrils, although in other respects it may be very different. For instance, the gourd or colocynth plant, whose fruit is disagreeable to the taste, and poisonous, is called *gephen sâdeh*, translated in our version *wild vine*, because its leaves and tendrils bear a resemblance to those of the true vine. This plant is, beyond doubt, the *gephen Sedom*— the vine of Sodom, yielding the famous apples that tempt the eye with their beautiful appearance, and turn to ashes on the lips. By the Jews the word always specially applied to the cultivated or grape-vine was *sorek* or *sorekah*,—the name of the Philistine valley of Sorek where Delilah dwelt, being derived from a peculiarly choice kind of vine cultivated there, with purple grapes and minute soft pips, yielding a highly-esteemed red wine. We find in the Greek language also two terms employed to distinguish between the vine as a climbing creeper and the vine as a cultivated fruit-bearing plant. In classic Greek, the word corresponding to the Hebrew *sorek*—most frequently used to signify the grape-vine—was *oine*, from whence comes our common word *wine*. But in the Hellenistic Greek of the New Testament, as in the text of this chapter, the word is *ampelos*—from *amphi*, round about, corresponding with the Hebrew *gephen*, and signifying, like it, any plant with the peculiar appearance and habit of the vine, however botanically different. By Theophrastus, for instance, the term *ampelos* was applied to the bryony— a climbing plant which twines round our own English hedges; and the Virginian creeper is known to botanists by the generic name of Ampelopsis, derived from its vine-like habit of growth. It is not, I believe, without deep significance, that the word *ampelos* should be applied by Christ to Himself in the text, instead of *oine*. It is to the twining habit of the vine, rather than to its fruit-bearing property, that He directs attention, in the first place, as a symbol of Himself in His relation to the Father. An independent tree, like a palm, an apple, or a fig tree, capable of standing and growing erect without any help from any other plant, as I have said already, would not have expressed the dependence of the Son upon the Father; and therefore a trailing, twining plant that needs support, like the vine, must be chosen to symbolize this idea. And it is·this dependent habit of the vine which forms the nexus of thought joining the two parts of the verse together—the phrase, " I am the True Vine," with the phrase, "and my Father is the Husbandman."   Indeed, the conjunction *and* might not inaptly be compared to a tendril of the True Vine, by which He is connected with, and clings to, His Father the Husbandman.

1. There are two ideas conveyed to us by the symbol of the True Vine in connection with the Husbandman, viz., *dependence* and *cultivation.*   Let us look, in the first place, at the figurative representation of our Lord's dependent position in the days of His flesh.   The vine cannot, as I have said, stand erect of itself like the oak or palm.   It cannot grow independently; it requires to be held up and sustained in its place by a prop.   It is furnished with long delicate tendrils, which twine round and cling to the object of support, and thus raise it from the ground, sustain it in its rapid and extensive climbing, and support its heavy clusters of grapes, which would otherwise break, or helplessly weigh down the branches on which they grow.   The ancient Jews fastened their vines to strong stakes, as is the modern custom in France and Germany; and this mode of cultivation appears to be alluded to by Ezekiel: " Thy mother is like a vine in thy blood, planted by the waters : she was fruitful and full of branches, by reason of many waters; and she had strong rods for the sceptres of them that bare rule ; and her stature was exalted among the thick branches, and she appeared in her height with the multitude of her branches."   But though a twining plant, the vine is no parasite—subsisting upon

the juices of the plant to which it clings, or strangling it in its deadly embrace. Creepers, as a rule, have acquired this evil reputation. Most of the plants in the dense forests of Brazil are creepers: species of genera not given to climbing assume the habit in that region. There is even a Jacitara, or climbing palm. Parasitic plants are seen in every direction fastening with choking grip upon others, and making use of them with reckless indifference, in their selfish struggling upwards towards light and air. A painful impression is produced upon the mind by this keen competition of vegetable forces on a grand scale, especially when the moral character of the native population is seen reflected in it. How different, and how much more pleasing, is the aspect of calm repose and mutual helpfulness of European woods, where there are almost no parasites? How significant are their ivy, clematis, and honey-suckle, of the superior moral character of European nations?

The twining of the vine round its support is one of the most engaging sights in nature. It is a mimicry in the vegetable world of the çlinging of weak human beings to the strong, of the wife to the husband. It prefigures the tender yearning impulse of the human heart to seek protection and sympathy in the cherishing love of relatives and friends. In return for the support which it receives, the vine adorns the object round which it twines with its beautiful foliage and graceful shoots. Nothing can be more charming than a tree festooned with the many-tendrilled vine, every leaf a model of elegance in form, and every bunch of grapes the beau-ideal of a fruit. In Italy it is commonly trained round the homely elm, roofing the boughs with verdure, producing a profuse and varied mass of the richest green tints, the intense light shining through the transparent leaves, and investing the tree with the most exquisite beauty that art can superadd. As an ornament in architecture the vine wreath has been even more popular than the lotus of the Egyptian pillar, the palm-tree of the Indian shrine, or the ivy which forms the stone foliage of the Gothic cathedral. In art, *vignettes* are so called because all such little pictures were at one time surrounded by an engraved vine wreath.

This feature of the vine applies in a most interesting manner to Christ. Self-existent and self-sustained as an independent palm-tree in the bosom of the Father, in the days of His flesh He became dependent as a clinging vine. The equal and fellow of God from all eternity, He became in the fulness of time God's minister and servant. Throughout the whole course of His earthly life, He emptied Himself of His glory; maintained this subordinate position, and employed language regarding it which has been perverted by the enemies of the truth to prove His absolute and eternal, and not His mere relative and temporary, inferiority to God. He appeared among men in the character of the perfect Son; and therefore the chief feature of gospel teaching is found in the relation between Himself and His Father. The first recorded words which he uttered implied the consciousness of that relation, " Wist ye not that I must be about my Father's business;" the first

words from heaven by which He was introduced to
men ratified that consciousness, "This is my beloved
Son, in whom I am well pleased." It was the will of
the Father that He obeyed, it was the works of the
Father that He wrought, it was the doctrine of the
Father that He taught, it was the nature of the Father
that He revealed. It was not His own glory but the
Father's that He sought. Devotion to His Father's will
was not merely one principle or law, or obligation of
His life; it was the root of His whole being, blossoming
out at every point and period of His life in acts of submission and self-sacrifice. It was this obedience, as it
has been justly said by an eminent writer, rooted in the
will and in love, and based on the closest spiritual
unity, that distinguished Jesus among men. His
mighty works might have been done, and His
words of wisdom might have been uttered, by other
men. Similar works were actually done by St. Peter
and St. Paul in His name; similar words of wisdom
were uttered by the apostles through the inspiration of
His Spirit. But no mortal man, however supernaturally
assisted and inspired, has ever approached the Lord
Jesus in the perfection of His submission to His Father's
will. We cannot imagine a more complete subordina-
tion. "Verily, verily I say unto you, the Son can do
nothing of Himself, but what He seeth the Father do."
"My doctrine is not Mine, but His that sent Me." "But
of that day and that hour knoweth no man, neither
the angels in heaven, nor the Son, but the Father."
Before bidding Lazarus come forth from the tomb,

He said, "Father, I thank Thee that Thou hast heard Me." In His last prayer in the upper chamber He said, "Father, the hour is come, glorify Thy Son, that Thy Son also may glorify Thee." In the agony of the garden He said, "Father, if it be possible let this cup pass from Me, nevertheless not My will, but Thine be done." On the cross He said, "Father, forgive them for they know not what they do;" "Father, into Thy hands I commit My spirit." Many other passages might be quoted to show how completely Jesus denuded Himself in the days of His flesh, of that independence which belonged to Him as the equal and fellow of God. Well then could He say, "I am the True Vine, and My Father is the Husbandman." He trusted in His Father, twined round Him like a wreathing vine throughout the whole course of His life on earth; and in the last bitter cry of the cross, in which all suffering culminated, "My God, My God, why hast thou forsaken Me!" He expressed most fully what His Father's aid had been to Him, and how dreadful was the loss of it.

As a vine wreath adorns the prop to which it clings, invests it with new or superadded beauty, so Christ, in His perfect dependence upon the Father, glorified Him, revealed His character in greater beauty to men, unfolded His perfections in such an engaging way as to attract the love and devotion of human hearts. In the form of a perfect, sinless human being, in all points made like unto His brethren, in all points tempted as they are tempted, consorting for three-and-thirty years with men, He revealed the love, holiness, truth, wisdom and power of the Father, so that He could say, "He that hath seen Me hath seen the Father." The blazing, burning effulgence of the Father's glory, shining through the transparent leaves of the True Vine, reaches us in a soft and mild radiance which our feeble human powers can bear. The otherwise irreconcilable attributes of God, as manifested in His dealings with us, are linked together and harmonized by the twining around them of the tendrils of the True Vine; so that we now see mercy and truth meeting together, righteousness and peace embracing each other. And not only does He reconcile the attributes of God to each other by His dependence upon them, but He brings us who were far off nigh by the power of the same holy submission. The tendrils with which He clings to God Himself, embrace us and bring us into the same harmonious union—into the same blessed dependence. In right of His own relation He straightway associates in it those who receive Him. The whole course of His teaching tended to that intertwining of His own relation to God with that of the disciples, which is finally expressed on the eve of His departure:—"My Father and your Father, My God and your God;" and which was so fully accomplished in the disciples that they could say, "Truly our fellowship is with the Father, and with His Son Jesus Christ." The consciousness predicted by Christ in the days of His flesh had been attained by the disciples after His departure. "At that day ye shall know that I am in My Father, and ye in Me, and I in you." Well then might Isaiah, in proclaiming the grand roll of the titles of Jesus, declare Him to be "Wonderful, Counsellor, the mighty God, the everlasting *Father*." The last title is an apparent paradox, but its meaning is clearly unfolded in these words, "To as many as received Him, to them gave He *power* to become the sons of God."

And just as our Lord was dependent during His earthly life upon His Father, so was He dependent upon human beings and earthly things. He was a branch of the tree of humanity, budding and blossoming with all beautiful human affections, clinging with tendrils of human feelings to all that the heart of man clings to. He was born into our world of a human mother, accepted the feebleness and peculiar humiliation of human infancy. He lay upon the breast of a human mother, and depended upon her care and love in natural helplessness. He subjected Himself to all the limitations and privations of human existence—to its slowly-opening intellect and gradually-acquired experience. He grew in wisdom and in stature, and in favour with God and man, by the very same natural and social influences which develop our childhood. He was not "too bright and good for human nature's daily food." And though He was a lonely man, so far as the deeper things of His spirit and the peculiar character of His work were concerned, finding none to understand or sympathize with Him, yet in His daily life He was not an isolated, independent Being, living by and for Himself, like a solitary palm-tree in a desert. On

the contrary, like a vine in a vineyard, He twined Himself round every innocent human experience. He was
pre-eminently social. He had intercourse with many in
the common walks of life, in the streets, in the market-
places, in the synagogues, in the homes, and at the
tables of men. How closely were the tendrils of His
affections twined round St. John, round each of His
disciples, round each member of the family at Bethany,
round all whom He admitted into friendship and fellowship with Him! " He loved Martha and her sister and
Lazarus." They all had their own place in His heart,
which thoroughly understood and sympathized with all
our human relationships. How dependent was He upon
human help; for the women that followed Him ministered to Him of their substance! How He longed for
human sympathy; for in the agony of the garden He
said to the sleepy disciples, " Could ye not watch with
Me one hour!" We observe even a human touch of
resentment and quick sense of disgrace in His expostu-
lation, "Be ye come out *as against a thief* with swords
and staves?" Then, too, how completely were all the
actions of His life referred to the same letter of the law
given for the guidance of ignorant and fallible creatures
like us! He twined round the same narrow rule which
supports us in our moral weakness. He repelled the
temptations of Satan by the same word of Scripture
which we possess, and defended the conduct of the
disciples in plucking and eating the ears of corn, not
by the assertion of His own authority as Lord of the
Sabbath, but by quoting the example of what David

D

did on a similar occasion when he was an hungered. Though He had all power, He consented to become weak as other men; wrought miracles for the benefit of others, never for His own. And how strikingly was the dependence of His whole earthly life shown in the incidents of His Passion! He was betrayed by Judas, judged by Caiaphas and Pilate, and nailed by the Roman soldiers to the accursed tree; and all in unresisting silence and complete self-abnegation. Contemplate the True Vine clinging to that fatal prop, lifted up by that awful support! He could have accomplished the redemption of the world by a word, and yet He needed the aid of a shameful and painful cross to do it. "As Moses lifted up the serpent in the wilderness, even so must the Son of Man *be lifted up*, that whosoever believeth in Him should not perish, but have everlasting life." "I, if I *be lifted up*, will draw all men unto me."

And thus clinging, like a vine, to the support of human persons and earthly things, how marvellously has He exalted and beautified them by His own experience. Every relation of human life is dignified and hallowed by having been manifested in Him. The mother's love for her child—the purest and most unselfish of all natural affections—is ennobled by the love of Mary for the Holy Child. "The blessing of the Son of Mary is shed on every Christian household—on every domestic tie and duty." His childhood and boyhood sanctify the weakness and dependence of life's earliest years. He passed through all that is common to pure humanity in each stage and relation of life, and claimed all that is best and sweetest in it for God. He made the real, by His experience, the ideal, and connected the lowest offices, the humblest work and duty, with the highest imagination of man's spirit, and his loftiest vision of perfection. He condemned the unnecessary mortifications and self-denials of the Pharisee, and vindicated the common affections of our nature from the charge of grossness and carnality, which an unreal asceticism had foolishly and wickedly fastened upon them. He showed, by His own example, that the highest type of perfection is formed, not by the voluntary desertion of society, the renunciation of the joys, cares, and duties of friendship and love, the mortification of the innocent and natural instincts of the heart, in order that the soul may freely indulge in the raptures of an imaginary devotion; but, on the contrary, by the living of a pure and heavenly life in the ordinary moulds of human nature, and in the ordinary walks of society. He breathed a fresh spirit through our common life, invested the whole of it with a divine aureola, and showed that every part of it contains some spiritual capacity and power—that the same blue sky of God bends over and harmonizes the common and the sacred, the house of prayer and the market-place. And in His ascension to heaven, He carried up with Him, in a transfigured and glorified form, the whole of His human nature and life-work on earth—the fruits of His submission to His parents and His obscure toil in Nazareth, as well as the results of His miracles on nature, and man, and the spirit-world, and His victory over death and the grave, —in token of the essential unity in the experience of those who are quickened and raised up in Him, of the seen and the unseen, of earth and heaven, of the conventionally secular and the conventionally religious,— in token that all life in Him is *one.*

By twining round the law, He magnified it, and made it honourable. He showed that it is not a proof of intellectual greatness, on the part of ignorant, erring creatures like us, to subject that law to our own judgment and experience, and receive or reject it as we please; but, on the contrary, that it is a token of real nobility of soul to fulfil all righteousness under its authoritative decisions. He proved, by His own experience, that the law is a transcript of God's nature, and the commandment holy, and just, and good, in all its relations to men. By twining round the cross, the True Vine, by its wonderful beauty there displayed, has made the instrument of torture and shame no more an object of offence, but an object of glorying. The bare, hard, angular cross of humiliation, suffering, defeat, and death, invested with the beauties of Christ's holiness, with the grandeur of His self-sacrifice, with the rich fruits of His righteousness, has become haloed with the highest honour and victory. The foremost man of all the world in his time said, "God forbid that I should glory, save in the cross of our Lord Jesus Christ, by whom the world is crucified unto me, and I unto the world!" And these noble words since then, have found an echo in myriads of human hearts. The cross wreathed with the True Vine is now the most beautiful object, the mightiest power of attraction in the universe. By the exhibition of Divine self-sacrificing love which it presents, it draws all hearts to God. It has affected many whom the terrors of judgment could never have reached—has brought them home, like prodigal sons to a forgiving Father,—has brought them to repentance instead of remorse, and to loving submission instead of stubborn despair.

But further, the True Vine, by His tendrils of self-sacrificing love, not only draws us to the Father and to Himself, but also to one another. Vines not only cling to their own support, but often twine round one another, and thus make of the whole vineyard one great bower of mutually-interlacing leaves. And so the True Vine twines His tendrils round men, and unites them to Himself and to one another. He is the Son of Man, in whom all humanity centres and becomes conscious of its unity. He gives to all who are His by faith and love a corporate existence—makes them members of one body—one great brotherhood and commonwealth. In claiming them as related to Himself, He declares them to be all related to one another. By the eye of faith we see in Him the nobler affinities of our human nature; and in the heart of love we feel the power of the heavenly bonds which unite us to our fellow-Christians.

But another interesting point of analogy requires to be noticed before we pass from this head. The tendril of the vine is a transformed terminal bud—a modified flower peduncle or footstalk.* It is of great size and thickness, sometimes sixteen inches in length. It is divided into two branches, which diverge equally from the common stalk, like the letter **Y.** One of these branches bears blossoms and fruit, and, in so doing, loses its sensitiveness, and ceases to contract spirally and curl round an object of support; while the other becomes barren, acquires increased sensitiveness, and, by twining round its prop, gives support to the bunch of grapes on the other branch of the tendril. Either branch of the tendril may bear fruit at the expense of its spontaneous movement and clasping power, when

---

* Tendrils are extremely interesting parts of a plant. They are modifications of the leaf—the stipule, the branch, or the flower-stalk. When they are modifications of the leaf,—prolongations of its mid-rib, their origin is betrayed by the occasional presence of small leaflets upon them. When they are modifications of the branch, their axial nature is revealed by the not unfrequent presence of flowers or berries upon them. Sometimes they are produced abnormally from the calyx or corolla; the sepal or petal being lengthened out into a tendril; which thing happens normally in several genera of plants, as for instance *Hodgsonia, Strophanthus.* In some plants the tendrils turn away from the light and crawl like roots into crevices, where they form cellular masses, and secrete an adhesive cement,—peculiarities differing in a most remarkable manner from the habits of leaves, out of which they are metamorphosed, and yet showing the unity of all parts of the plant. The root that seeks the darkness is thus seen to be of the same nature as the leaf that seeks the light, the tendril in this case reconciling the two. So sensitive are the tendrils of the Passion-flower that Mr. Darwin found that the slightest contact of a twig, or even of a thread weighing no more than the thirty-second part of a grain, caused them to bend; and yet they remained insensible to the harder contact and pressure of each other, and of the falling drops of rain.

the other branch that remains barren is compensated by the possession of greater vital force, and has the vicarious privilege of supporting its neighbour in its burdened helplessness. And is it not thus with the tendrils of the True Vine? They are the flowerstalks, so to speak, of the glory which He had with the Father before the world was, transformed into means of support for us. He who was rich, yet for our sakes became poor, that we through His poverty might become rich. He came not to be ministered unto, but to minister, and to give His life a ransom for many. He was among us as one that serveth. Instead of bearing blossoms and fruit for Himself, He denied Himself the common blessings of life, and had not where to lay His head. His glory was manifested in suffering; His love was seen in lowly service. "Jesus, knowing that the Father had given all things into His hands, and that He was come from God, and went to God; He riseth from supper, and laid aside His garment, and took a towel, and girded Himself. After that He poureth water into a basin, and began to wash the disciples' feet, and to wipe them with the towel wherewith He was girded." The miraculous power, which might have produced all wealth and comfort for Himself, He employed solely in ministering to the necessities of the weary and the heavy-laden. And just as the vine-tendril divides into two branches—the one bearing fruit, and the other serving for support—so, from His dependence upon God and upon men, sprang up the rich fruits of His redemptive work. His victory over sin and death grew from the same self-denying, self-sacrificing love which made Him a servant of servants on earth. " He humbled Himself, and became obedient unto death, even the death of the cross. Wherefore God also hath highly exalted Him, and given Him a name which is above every name."

2. I come now to the consideration of the second idea conveyed by the symbol of the vine in connection with the husbandman, viz., *cultivation;* "and my Father is the Husbandman." We notice here a peculiarity observable in all our Saviour's references to His relationship to the Father. He never confounded the peculiar relationship in which He Himself stood to God with that in which men stood to God. He says not "Our Father," but "My Father;" and even when He seeks to embrace the disciples within the same circle of filial love, He still maintains the distinction between them, as in the words "My Father *and* your Father, My God *and* your God." The only occasion on which He used the expression "Our Father," was in the prayer which He composed not for Himself, but for His disciples. God is our Father by creation and adoption, but He is the Father of our Lord and Saviour Jesus Christ by eternal generation, by affiliation distinct and unique. Christ is the *only-begotten* Son of the Father. Into this peculiar relation no human being can possibly be brought. He who assumed our nature, and thus became our elder brother, united to us by blood relationship, has drawn us into closer union with God than any angel or archangel can enjoy; but still we cannot share in the

peculiar glories of His Sonship. We may drink of His cup, and be baptized with His baptism, but to be sons of God in the sense in which He is the Son of God, is an impossibility in the very nature of things. God is more properly and peculiarly a Father, and Christ more properly and perfectly a Son than any creature-fathers or sons can be. The human relation is the feeble and imperfect type of the Divine.

The Father is represented, under the symbol of the vine in the text, as standing to the Son in the same relation in which a husbandman stands to the plant which he cultivates. The word husbandman implies, in the original, ownership as well as cultivation. God is no hireling vine-dresser, having no property in the object of His solicitude. He is the householder in the parable who planted the vineyard and let it out to certain husbandmen, and demanded the fruit thereof. He is the possessor as well as the cultivator of the True Vine, and therefore feels the deepest interest in its growth and fruitfulness. The Son in a peculiar sense belongs to the Father for redemptive purposes. He is God's unspeakable gift. God gave the Son to be the source of blessings to man, that all grace might descend through Him. The Father is the proprietor of the universe; "the earth is the Lord's and the fulness thereof." He is the great "earth-worker," as the original word for husbandman should be rendered. "The Father worketh hitherto and the Son worketh." "The Son can do nothing of Himself, but what He seeth the Father do." The work which Christ did for men was not His own work only, it was primarily His Father's business. In doing His own work He was doing His Father's work. It was a united work done as if by one will. "I have glorified Thee upon the earth; I have finished the work which Thou gavest me to do." "If I do not the work of my Father believe me not. But if I do, though ye believe not me, believe the works, that ye may know and believe that the Father is in me and I in Him." The thoughts and purposes of our hearts assume a definite form, and are revealed to our fellow-men in words; and the Son is the Word of God. A luminous body is perceived by the light which streams forth from it; and the Son is the ray or "the brightness of the Father's glory." A vine is a delicate and complicated machinery of Providence, by which the surrounding elements of earth, air, and water are fashioned into leaf, and flower, and fruit; and the Son is the True Vine by which all the elements of the spiritual world are assimilated and presented to us in the form of a lovely and fruitful earthly life.

This image of the Father as the Husbandman—the proprietor and cultivator of the True Vine—is very significant. It disabuses our minds of the idea that the work of grace is all Christ's, and that the Father has no share in it, save the somewhat cold and distant one of pardoning and receiving the sinners whom Christ's sacrifice has won. It shows us that as the existence of the husbandman must necessarily precede the planting and cultivation of the vine, so God, as the

Husbandman of the True Vine, must necessarily have taken the initiative in the work of redemption. It was Jehovah Himself who inspired the purpose and planned the method of redemption. The marvellous plan of mercy sprang from His own bosom, not only before repentance or sorrow for sin had been displayed by man, but even before he fell, yea, even before he was formed, or the earth he treads upon was created. The Father, in the mysterious counsels of the eternal Trinity, is represented as devising means whereby His lost creatures might be saved; and it is in answer to His request that the only-begotten Son, who was from eternity in the bosom of the Father, is represented as offering Himself as man's Redeemer. "Lo, I come to do Thy will! In the volume of the Book it is written of Me." It was God who so loved the world that He gave His only-begotten Son, that whosoever believeth in Him should not perish, but have everlasting life. The whole work of grace, from the first promise to the last consummation, is the Father's. This is the great doctrine of the written Word—the great revelation of the Incarnate Word. And it is a feature in the Gospel unspeakably precious to every believer. It shows to us that the Father Himself loveth us,—that this love is from everlasting to everlasting. It declares that the function of Husbandman was not suddenly assumed by Him, or for a temporary purpose. We can never conceive of God except as a Husbandman, and of Christ except as a cultivated Vine. For the cultivation found place in the purpose of Him who ordained it, and of Him who was subjected to it from the very beginning. And as Christ was foreordained *before* the foundation of the world,—slain *from* the foundation of the world,—so He who beholds the end from the beginning had beheld us from the first as chosen, reconciled, and reconstituted in Christ.

As a vine is taken from the wilds of nature—from the uncultivated woods, and planted in a prepared and enclosed vineyard, so the Divine Husbandman took the True Vine from the boundless and glorious fields of heaven, and· planted it amid all the limitations and pre-arrangements of that earth which was fitted up to be the theatre of redemption. God sent forth His Son made of a woman; a body was prepared for Him; He became man, and dwelt on our earth. His cultivation by the Father began from the very beginning—from the very seed. He entered human life by the ordinary portals of human birth. The natural vine is planted not in rich, but in poor and rocky soil. Waste places that yield nothing else, often produce the finest grapes; and the barren hill-sides, where the rock protrudes, and but a thin coating of mould covers it, are often clothed with the most luxuriant vineyards. The Stein wine of Germany is produced—as its name implies—on rocky soil that is not fit for growing anything else. And does not this feature of the vine's cultivation correspond with the Father's husbandry of the Son? Not amid luxurious and pleasant earthly conditions—in an Eden of beauty and plenty—was the True Vine planted. It was in the waste wilderness which man's sin had made,—the bare, barren, rocky soil which Adam's fall had covered with the thorns and thistles of the curse. Our Lord's circumstances in life were typical of the miserable destitution into which the fall had brought us. He took up our condition at that low, wretched point to which our first parents by their sin had humbled it. He came in a poor and mean condition, not because He chose poverty and meanness for their own sake, as if there was a special and peculiar merit in them; not simply because He knew that a poor and mean condition would be the state in which He could best subserve His Father's purposes; but because meanness and poverty was the condition to which Adam by his fall had reduced man. He, as the second Adam, took upon Him not a favourable but a representative condition; not the condition of the few exceptionally rich and prosperous favourites of fortune, in whose case—so far at least as outward circumstances are concerned—the effects of the curse have been modified; but the condition of the great bulk of mankind, in which the effects of the curse are most vividly seen—of the many poor who are always with us. The first Adam was a dresser and keeper of the trees in the garden of Eden, helping their natural, spontaneous growth by light and easy labour, and eating the ripe fruit from them as it fell into his lap; the second Adam, suffering the consequences of sin, was a carpenter lifting up his axe upon the thick trees, and converting them, *in the sweat of his brow*, to human uses, and thus earning toilsomely his daily bread;—surely an instructive picture illustrating the promise and the conditions of the restored paradise. " To *him that overcometh* will I give to eat of the tree of life, which is in the midst of the paradise of God." .

And not only was He planted in such hard and stony soil of circumstances, His whole earthly lot was one of sorrow and suffering. God spared not His Son in giving Him to us; and He spared Him not in discipling Him for us. It pleased the Father to bruise Him, and to put Him to grief. He dug about His roots, and pruned His branches with the chastisement of our peace. Though He were a Son, yet learned He obedience through the things which He suffered. Though a partaker of the Divine nature, yet, in His humiliation as man, He was not in anywise exempted from man's earthly lot, or from the conditions under which man's obedience has to be rendered. His soul was made an offering for sin. He endured whatever might be its penalty. All that we ought to have suffered throughout eternity was imposed upon Him. Who can tell the full extent of the Father's discipline of the Son—the real nature of the Husbandman's cultivation of the True Vine! Once and again the veil is lifted in the gospel narrative, and we see the painfulness of the process. We see the Man of Sorrows and acquainted with grief, in a world of misery, standing alone in an awful supremacy of woe—marked by the crown of thorns as the very King of a suffering race. We see Him sinking into a deeper darkness than ever made us tremble, and realizing the awful burden of human wretchedness as we have never realized it. We see Him tempted in all points like as we are,—tempted by human weariness and weakness, by want of success, by the treachery of His friends, by the malice of His foes. There was a time when His soul was exceeding sorrowful, even unto death; "when all the forces of His human nature, though rooted immovably in a Divine steadfastness, were straining and bending like the trees of the forest under the stress of a vehement storm." There was a mysterious agony—a bloody sweat; an earnest prayer, thrice repeated, that, if it were possible, the cup might pass from Him; a horror of great darkness and loneliness on the cross, and an awful, heart-broken cry, "My God! my God! why hast Thou forsaken Me?"

And if the True Vine thus suffered under this dreadful spiritual husbandry, let us not imagine that the Husbandman who inflicted it was callous and indifferent. We should not separate the Father from the Son in this sublime work of self-sacrifice. It was the Father's love—the Father's suffering, which the Son was revealing through His own. He and the Father were one in the deepest depth of His humiliation and sorrow. "Alone, yet not alone, for the Father is with Me;" with Him, not merely comforting Him, as we commonly suppose, but suffering with Him—suffering through Him. The pangs that rent the heart of the Son pierced the Father's bosom; the hilt of the sword with which He smote the Shepherd of the sheep cut through His own hand; the hilt was sharper than the blade. No human or angelic thought can ever fathom the depth of God's suffering when He listened to the agonizing appeal of the beloved Son who had dwelt in His bosom from all eternity,—"Father, if it be possible let this cup pass from Me!"—and yet held the flaming cup to the unresisting Sufferer's lips. It is surely an unspeakable love that the Father bears to us, when, for the sake of our redemption, He subjected Himself and His Son to such unspeakable agony!

The True Vine is, indeed, a true Passion flower. What the eyes of superstition saw in that natural plant is represented in Him in truth. The Spanish Jesuits, in their zeal for the propagation of Christianity among the untutored Indians of South America, appealed to the Passion flower, growing in the woods, as exhibiting signs and symbols of the passion of our Lord. The five anthers resembled the five wounds; the triple style the three nails—two for the hands and one for the feet; the central gynophore, bearing the stamens and pistil, was the pillar of the cross; the showy coronet of the blossom corresponded to the halo or nimbus of glory round the sacred head of Jesus; the climbing habit of the plant indicated the crucifixion; the tendrils symbolized the scourge; and the sepals and petals typified the apostles—two of whom, viz., Peter who denied Him, and Judas who betrayed Him, are absent, and hence there are only ten segments to this part of the flower— five sepals and five petals. These fanciful comparisons have a meaning only when applied to the True Vine. Jesus exhibited in Himself all the signs and symbols of the Cross. When He blossomed into marvellous superhuman beauty on the mount of transfiguration, that flower of glory which He bore exhibited the shadows of the crucifixion. In that most ecstatic moment of His earthly life, we hear Him speaking with the celestial visitants of the decease which He should accomplish at Jerusalem—of the hour of His greatest pain. We find the same strange intermingling of experiences when the Greeks sought to see Him, and He said, "Now is my soul troubled, and what shall I say? Father, save Me from this hour;" and during His triumphal entry into Jerusalem, when He wept over the doomed city. We see the signs of the cross in every part of His life, but most conspicuously, as in the Passion flower, when that life, at rare and transient intervals, opened out into lovely blossoms of glory and joy.

And what is the result of this marvellous cultivation of the True Vine by the Divine Husbandman? The typical vines all proved unsuccessful, and, in spite of everything Divine skill and power could do, brought forth only wild grapes. Adam was God's vine, planted in the bright garden of Eden. But he failed to fulfil the purpose of his cultivation, and, in his own blight and withering, changed Eden into a wilderness. God repeated the experiment—chose another vine in Israel, and planted it in another Eden in Palestine. The possession of the Promised Land was a kind of renewal of the basis of paradise. But Israel, too, failed in its cultivation, and in its decay changed the land flowing with milk and honey into a desert. The wild boar out of the woods wasted the vineyard of the Lord, and the curse of thorns and thistles came upon it. Man repeating the sin of Eden renewed the curse—"cursed is the ground for thy sake." The Jews hanged upon a tree Him who would have saved them, and in consequence the trees of the land were all cut down by the Romans, to make crosses on which to crucify themselves. So, too, the seven churches of Asia were vines that did not serve God's purposes, and which, in their withering, desolated the Edens in the midst of which they were planted. No parts of the' ancient world were more beautiful and prosperous than the regions around Ephesus, Pergamos, and Sardis. God gave them all, in some measure, in a physical sense, what He had promised spiritually to one—" to eat of the tree of life which is in the midst of the paradise of God." But when their candlestick was removed out of its place, by reason of their unfaithfulness, then blight and desolation came upon the face of nature around them, so that now they are among the dreariest regions on the face of the earth. Man's sin has everywhere turned nature into a waste. The true deserts of the world, as it has been well said, are not those wide expanses of sand or rock, like Sahara or Arabia Deserta, which man has never tenanted. These are "the lungs of the world," by which its air is purified, and its climates properly balanced. "The white snow wreaths are withdrawn from the fields of the Swiss peasant by the glow of Libyan rock." Our life depends more upon the moorlands and the sandy barrens, than upon the finest arable land. The true deserts of the world, on the contrary, are places like the Campagna of Rome, and the solitary marshy tracts of Asia Minor, in whose drear expanse ages of civilization are engulfed, and where nothing is beautiful but the sky—places which nature did not create, but which are the results of man's sin, and whose poisonous miasma is like the memory of his violence and crimes.

The True Vine came into this wilderness, which man's sin had made, and by the discipline of His life there, by submission to the sentence of toil, and obedience to the law of God, brought back the beauty and the bounty of the primeval state of innocence—made the wilderness to rejoice and blossom as the rose. It is in the toil and the discipline of Christ on earth that all the marvels of our modern Christian civilization originate—its power over the elements of nature; its beautifying and enriching of waste places; its equalising of harvests; its rebuking of fevers; its calming of storms. The sorrow of the True Vine changes into a fruitful joy for all the world. What transcendent beauty did that sorrow develop in Christ! The Captain of our salvation was made *perfect* through sufferings. Not that there was any imperfection in Him to perfect; for, from first to last, He was holy, harmless, undefiled, and separate from sinners; but the perfection of His obedience was illustriously displayed against the dark back-ground of his sufferings. In the midst of man's rebellion, the Son of Man, sharing in the consequences of that rebellion, revealed, by His perfect obedience, the perfect beauty and goodness of the Divine will. His sympathy was made perfect by suffering; having passed through our sorrowful history, He must needs be touched with a fellow-feeling of our infirmities, in a way that, without that experience, He could never have known. Between ourselves and Him now an immortal sympathy is established. "We can speak to Him of our sorrow with greater freedom, remembering His own; we can invoke His aid with greater confidence, remembering His strong crying and tears; we feel the surer of His pity and merciful help, because, by personal experience, and not merely as our Creator, "He knoweth our frame, and remembereth that we are dust."

His miracles of power and love on earth were the fruit of the cultivation of Him by the Father. He removed the effects of the curse in disease and storm and poverty, by bearing the curse. He cast out devils by fasting and prayer. He healed the sick and raised the dead, by Himself taking our infirmities and bearing our sicknesses. Through death He destroyed him that had the power of death. He took no path of His own into the domain of the King of terrors. The gate He went through was that appointed for all flesh. He, before whom the everlasting doors had to be lifted up, stooped beneath that low arch of darkness; and as He emerged on the other side, He dragged captivity captive, and carried the gates of the grave up the hill of God. His miracles of grace now in heaven are the fruit of His obedience, suffering, and death on earth. That same deathless life, so strange and brief a miracle of beauty here, which shed its healing influence over the sick and the sinful in Galilee and Judæa, is now at the right hand of God, fostering the true Divine nature beneath the falsehoods of all actual life, and working mightily in us both to will and to do of His good pleasure. To the boughs, once sorely pruned, now cling the rich clusters of righteousness—hanging over the wall, ready for the passer-by to pluck and eat. Trodden in the wine-press of God's wrath, the grapes of His love now fill the cup of salvation with the true *Lachryma Christi*, the wine of grace, for the dry and parched lips of humanity. Every time that we drink of the sacramental cup we are reminded of the words, "I am the True Vine, and my Father is the Husbandman." It is the New Testament in His blood shed for the remission of sins. Every drop of it speaks of the suffering by which He was perfected. It is ever blushing for the shedding of His blood. The feast itself, consisting of the simplest means of nourishment—a vegetable, and not an animal feast—the. Passover, with its bleeding Lamb, passing into the Lord's Supper, with its bread and wine, is the link through the death of Christ which connects. the food of Eden with the food of heaven.* Through the culture of the Husband-

---

* It is very interesting to notice that our Saviour, in the sixth chapter of St. John's Gospel, uses two Greek synonyms, *phago* and *trogo*, to express the act of eating as applied to Himself. When speaking of Himself as the True Bread, the archetype of the manna in the wilderness, He invariably employs *phago*, which is a general term, meaning to eat any kind of substance, and in any way. But when speaking of His own flesh He suddenly uses the word *trogo*, which is a specific term, and means to chew food like a ruminating animal, to eat vegetable substances alone. It is one of those delicate refinements of the Greek text which we lose in our English version, and which seems to have been intended by Him who is

man, the True Vine converts the water of the common blessings of life—the dews and showers of ordinary enjoyments—into wine that maketh glad the heart of man, sanctifies all life's sorrows, and makes covenant mercies of all life's blessings. And, finally, as the result of the cultivation of the True Vine, all who are His disciples will drink of the fruit of the Vine in the kingdom of their heavenly Father, and will say at the marriage supper of the Lamb, where all the water is changed into wine, and every beaming chalice is brimming over with bliss, "Thou hast kept the good wine until now."

There are some who see no spiritual significance in this wonderful Vine that has been cultivated by the Divine Husbandman in the world. They admire and enjoy the physical and social benefits of Christianity; but Christ Himself is to them a root out of a dry ground, without form or comeliness. They have no saving knowledge of Him, no susceptibility to His love in their hearts. . Their attitude towards the True Vine is like that of many towards the natural vine. The natural vine suggests nothing spiritual to them; its growth appears to them the dullest of all phenomena;

the Word, to connect more closely His flesh and blood with the manna and the bread. He limits the general term, applied to animal and vegetable food indiscriminately, to the manna and the bread; He enlarges the specific term applied exclusively to vegetable food, so as to embrace His flesh and blood. His flesh is bread, and bread is His flesh. The broken bread of the Supper is His broken body; and we are to eat of it in both the senses signified by *phago* and *trogo*.

they are interested in it only so far as it supplies an agreeable fruit to minister to their palate. They estimate it solely by a utilitarian standard. Seeing they see, but do not perceive its parabolic significance—its witness-bearing of that which is nearest to them, of that which it most concerns them to know, of the mysteries of their own life and of God's relation to them. And in the same way they regard the True Vine. They admire the beautiful system of morality which Christ taught, and appreciate the perfect example of patience, devotion, and self-sacrificing love which He gave in His life and in His death; but they have no personal interest in Him as their Redeemer. They do not realize that the cultivation of Christ was for them, that He who died for their sins rose again for their justification, and ever liveth to make intercession for them. And therefore all the benefits they get from His culture are only the amenities of modern life, the good things of an outward civilization, that perish in the using, and leave conscience unappeased, the soul unsatisfied, and eternity without provision. Others there are who are guilty of a still deadlier sin. Like the man who perverts the juice of the grape into a means of intoxication, they change the cup of salvation into the cup of devils. The cultivation of the True Vine only yields what proves to them a savour of death unto death. Not discerning the Lord's body, they eat and drink of the benefits of the Gospel judgment to themselves. The love that is better than wine, instead of raising and purifying them, only degrades and destroys them.

Christ Himself becomes the minister of sin and condemnation, and that which was ordained unto life, proves unto death. " Of how much sorer punishment, suppose ye, shall he be thought worthy who hath trodden under foot the Son of God, and hath counted the blood of the covenant wherewith he was sanctified an unholy thing, and hath done despite unto the Spirit of Grace?" But blessed are they who, from all their intercourse with Christ in the closet and in the sanctuary, bring back clusters like those of Eshcol—specimens of the fulness that is in Him—foretastes of the richness of the heavenly inheritance; and who, in the daily business and intercourse of life, link the most common actions with the most sacred feelings,—"bind their foal unto the vine, and their ass's colt unto the choice vine; wash their garments in wine, and their clothes in the blood of grapes!"

CHAPTER III.

THE BRANCHES.

"I am the Vine, ye are the branches."—JOHN xv. 5.

MANY of the correspondences between natural and spiritual things are often called fanciful, and are therefore put aside as unworthy of serious attention. This arises from the fact that natural objects are regarded solely from the utilitarian point of view. Things that are looked at in this way are seen at so uniform, or featureless a part, that they seem to have no meaning or reference beyond themselves. They are, to use an illustration I have met somewhere, like the white marks embedded in the black polished marble of a mantelpiece, that present no appearance of organization, but look like mere mineral veins or discolourations, because the plane in which they are laid open to view does not coincide with the outline of their structure, but passes unconformably through it. The object of the sculptor was not to lay bare the real character of these marks, but to make a smooth and polished slab to adorn the fire-place; but the geologist, who has not a utilitarian, but a scientific purpose to serve, takes the original mass of marble, and, regardless of appearances, breaks it open in the plane of the white marks, and thus reveals their true form and character—shows them to be shells of delicate structure, and corallines of exquisite shape, whose history opens up a wide vista into the mysterious past life of the globe. And so in converting the objects of nature to human uses, many drive their utilitarian chisel right through them, as it were, and thus reduce them to a uniform level of earthliness, polished by a familiarity in which the outlines of their spiritual significance are completely obscured. They keep the vineyard, and tend the corn-field, solely with an eye to the table or the market; but the growth of the vine and the corn is not in the least interesting to them as a fact of meditation. They are ignorant that there is any wonder in it. It suggests nothing to them. It is altogether *insignificant*—without spiritual purpose. But the Christian poet looks at the objects of nature from the plane of sanctified imagination, which coincides with their spiritual outlines, and to him their true character is revealed as figures of another world, articulate with heavenly meaning and beauty. What is fanciful to others who have not his key of interpretation, is to him intensely real and absolutely truthful; and often he has the satisfaction of finding that "the first glance of the imagination is abreast of, and in a line with the last decision of the reason."

These remarks will serve as a fit introduction to the following pages, in which the relations between natural and spiritual things, alluded to in general terms in the opening chapter, will be particularly applied. In the previous chapter, the connection between Christ and the Father as symbolised by the Vine and the Husbandman was considered. In this chapter falls to be considered, as next in order, the relation between Christ and His disciples, as typified by the vine and its branches. This relation is much closer than that indicated in the previous allegory of the Shepherd and the sheep. The shepherd guides, guards, and feeds his sheep, but he is distinct from them; he forms a world of his own, into which they cannot enter. Their natures are different, not only in degree, but in kind; and there can be no intelligent sympathy between them—no connection, save providence on the one hand and dependence on the other. But in the allegory of the Vine, the relation between Christ and His disciples is compared to the relation between a vine and its branches—which is one of kind, of equality, of the utmost closeness and intimacy, the nearest we can possibly imagine. He is not merely the Lord of the vineyard, and they the vines which He tends; He is the Vine, and they are the branches. Here the beautiful appropriateness of the image will be seen at once. There are two great, strictly natural orders of plants—the exogenous or dicotyledonous, and the endogenous or monocotyledonous. Of these the first is the most perfectly developed. Every part of an exogenous plant is moulded in the same complex and highly-organised pattern; the wood is deposited in consecutive layers; the stem is branched; the veins of the leaves are netted or branched; and the embryo of the seed is provided with two seed-lobes. Every part of an endogenous plant, on the other hand, is formed on an exceedingly simple type; the wood has dots instead of rings; the stem is destitute of branches;* the veins of the leaves are parallel; and the embryo has a solitary seed-lobe. Thus, it will be seen that the peculiarity of the exogen is to produce branches in all its parts; whereas the peculiarity of the endogen is to be simple and unbranched in all its parts. As examples of exogenous plants may be mentioned the oak, which is the most perfect representation of a forest tree; the apple, which is the highest realisation of a fruit; and the rose, which is the loveliest and most perfect of flowers. As examples of endogenous plants may be mentioned the palm, the grass, and the lily, which, however stately, useful, or beautiful, are constructed on a humbler type of organisation. Now to these two great orders of the vegetable kingdom correspond most closely the two great orders of the animal kingdom—the vertebrate and the invertebrate. Exogenous plants are the vegetable analogues of the vertebrata, as the endogenous of the invertebrata. The vine is an exogens, and belongs to the highest order of plant life; the beauty of its

---

* The Greek word for "branches" in the Gospel of St. John—xii. 13—"Took *branches* of palm trees and went forth to meet Him"—is not *klema*, as in the text of this chapter, but *baia*, derived from a Coptic root, and applied to the palm tree exclusively. It does not signify branches properly—for the palm tree, as above mentioned, has no branches like the vine—but the huge fibrous leaves which form the crown on the top of the stem.

appearance and the usefulness of its properties corresponding with the perfection of its structure. It, therefore, fitly represents man, the highest type of animal life, and particularly the Son of Man, in whom human nature is sublimated. Christ is not an endogens—a palm that grows in stately majesty alone in the desert, rearing its branchless trunk, like a Corinthian pillar, graceful but solitary, and drinking in, by means of its beautiful crown of foliage, all the fervid sunshine and the rich dews of heaven for its own selfish individual use. He is, on the contrary, an exogens—a vine growing in a crowded vineyard, sending out branches on every side, repeating the general type in numberless miniature copies of its own form and structure, and converting all the influences of heaven and earth into means of nourishment and growth for its whole social economy.

A vine, like any other tree of the same order of vegetation, is not a single individual in the sense in which a man is an individual. It is not one object, all its parts making up one and the self-same plant, as the bones and flesh, the nerves and blood-vessels, the body and members of a man make up one and the self-same person. It is, on the contrary, a body corporate, an aggregation or collection of living and growing, but separate and distinct plants, the production of the present year, and also of the dead remains of a still larger number of individual plants, the production of a series of bygone years. It is a colony of plants growing *vertically* in the air, and uniting their

stems and roots into one, living and dying on the
undecaying soil of their ancestors; instead of growing
like annual plants, horizontally, on the ground, and
living and dying on the soil, without any organic connection with one another. A plot of strawberry plants,
with its runners and buds connecting the whole together,
is just a tree spread out horizontally. We can conceive
of the stem growing perpendicularly, the runners
enduring instead of decaying, and creeping alongside
of it, and becoming incorporated with it, and the buds
becoming branches; and so, a strawberry tree, or at
least a shrub, like the currant or rasp, be produced.
We cannot, it is true, cause the strawberry to grow after
the manner of a tree; but we can cause the individual
plants composing the tree to grow after the manner of the
strawberry. We can plant the willow and the vine as
we do the strawberry, and with like results. A vine is
in the vegetable kingdom what a cluster of coral is in
the animal, which it is well known is composed of one
living generation of polyps, and of the remains and
labours of many generations of dead, built up into one
uniform organic structure. In a word, a vine is just a
vegetable genealogical tree, containing all its ancestors
and descendants in itself, having one generation of
living plants growing on its extremities, and many
generations of dead sealed up in its inner tissues,
and thus preserved from decay, the whole making
up one uniform vegetable organism. Every branch
in it of one year old, with the woody matter which
it has passed into the parent stock, is exactly

equal to an entire annual plant growing on the ground—is only a repetition of the first year's shoot; and such a branch has a distinct individuality, and is capable of independent existence, as is shown by "cuttings." Every vine is "struck" by employing one of these cuttings, or annual branches taken from the parent plant. The great difference between an animal and a tree is this,—that an animal is an absolute unity, all whose parts are mutually dependent upon each other, and whose springs of life are centralized; it has only one heart, one mouth, one set of limbs, and one system of bones; and not one of its vital organs can be removed without causing death to the whole fabric. Whereas a tree, on the other hand, has no centralization of its life; it has as many lungs as it has leaves, and as many reproductive parts as flowers; each branch is a little plant in itself, associated with the others, but still independent of them, sharing in the general organic life of the tree, but having its own autonomy,—feeding, growing, and propagating as an individual.

From this point of view, the vine beautifully symbolises the union of believers with Christ. He is the true mystical Vine, composed of all who believe in Him,—every member having a separate individuality, and yet sharing with all the branches a common corporate existence, so sensitive that the welfare of each is the welfare of all. The annual plants growing around upon the face of the earth, each separate from the other, having no common life, no bond of unity, dying and decaying into the mould, represent the ungodly, who have no part or lot in Christ,—no love to Him, and therefore no love to one another,—grovelling in worldly-mindedness and sordid pursuits, and at last decaying in death—their very thoughts perishing. But the perennial plants, on the other hand, that are gathered up into the living organism of the vine, and thus kept from all decay, and endowed with an un-limited existence, represent believers, who are rooted in the love of Christ, and united more closely to one another in Him—lifted above the world by the attrac-tion of His resurrection,—partakers of His eternal life, and kept by His power, through faith, unto the day of salvation. Each individual Christian of the present age is linked to the innumerable Christians who have gone before, and to the vast company who are to follow after. The Vine has visible and invisible branches. The first disciples are to us still fellow-branches, hid far down in its earlier growth. We grow upon the foundation of the apostles and prophets, as others will grow upon our foundation. In every generation the True Vine has a seed that serves Him; and all the past generations of the blessed dead that have died in the Lord are asleep in Him, and their works have followed them; just as the wood which each annual growth of a tree forms, is sealed up with it in the structure of the tree. Living and dead believers are bound up in the same gracious covenant, and make but one great com-munion in Christ. The living have their active life hid with Christ in God by faith; the dead have fallen asleep through faith in Christ, and their passive life is also hid with Christ in God; and thus nothing can separate them from the love of God which is in Christ Jesus our Lord, or from the love of one another in Him—neither life, nor death, nor things present, nor things to come.

How beautifully is this great truth revealed to us in the loving words of Jesus to Martha—not merely answering the longing that lay on the surface of her heart, but going down to the very deepest need of her soul,—"I am the Resurrection and the Life; he that believeth in Me, though he were dead yet shall he live; and whosoever liveth and believeth in Me shall never die." Receiving her brother back from the grave as a mortal man would have profited her little, for, as such, she would soon lose him again; death would again come and snatch him from her or her from him. Hence it was needful, before granting her heart's wish, to lift her into that higher region of life in Himself, in which death is destroyed, and all human love becomes immortal. In Him alone could she obtain the perfect remedy against death; in the present Saviour alone could the departed brother be found, and found in such a way as that it would be impossible to lose him any more; in Him they should both be rooted in the element of imperishableness, and possess one another fully and for ever. It is an unspeakably precious thought, that Christ is the living link that connects the living and the dead, and makes them inseparably one in Him. Like a father walking between his two children, He holds the dead by one hand and the living by the other, and never loses his hold of either. He is not the God of the dead, but of the living; and that friend of ours, whose fair companionship with us on earth is broken, still lives in God. In Christ we find him whom we have loved and lost. He and we are both in Christ—he in the peaceful sleep of faith, we in the useful life of faith—still undivided; like the family of Bethany, of whom it was never more touchingly and tenderly true than when the shadow of death tried to come between them and Christ, and between them and one another, " Now Jesus loved Martha, and her sister, and Lazarus."

This sharing of Christ's own life with others—having others bound up in corporate unity with Him—is wonderfully characteristic of the Divine Nature. He is not a solitary God, as Deists picture Him, living in isolated glory, far above the reach of the creatures He has formed; caring nothing for them, independent of humanity. He is not surrounded with a vast zero, an all-absorbing negation, summing up everything out of Himself, to use Fichte's famous word, as *Nicht-ich* or *Not I.* He is not a selfish God, as He is too often represented even by Christians,—doing things arbitrarily—acting, thinking, living for Himself, for His own glory alone. He has no *autarkia*, or self-sufficingness—no *ichheit*, or *I-hood*, as the Germans would say—no self-life; but realises His own life in the life of all; and " in giving Himself away, becomes the life of all." In all the personal conceptions we can form of Deity the *I* is inseparable from the *Thou* and the *He*. In other words, there can be no first person in Him to whom there is no

second, and *of* whom, and *by* whom, there is no third.
The very personality of God, it may reverently be said,
is involved in the fact of His having branches.   In
plants which possess terminal flowers—that is, in which
the main sprout terminates in a flower—all the lateral
sprouts, however numerous and regular, are *inessential.*
They are only repetitions of the main sprout; they
lie outside the straight line towards the flower and
fruit.   Their presence or absence appears as something accidental and indifferent to the plant.   It
would not matter to a tulip stem, for instance, whether
it acquired a branch by a lateral flower or not, for
in its singleness and simplicity it is perfect in form
and function already.   But though thus *inessential,* so
far as the free carrying out of the series of formations
up to the blossom and fruit are concerned, branches are
essential to the characterization and to the economy of
plants.   They give to them their peculiar form and
habit; they furnish them with the means of persisting
amid the most varied conditions, and guarding against
death in all cases of frustrated seed-formation.   The
bud and the branch are immensely significant, not
only in the vegetable kingdom, but in the whole
history of the earth and of man.   They form the
basis of timber.   Without them there could be no
wood, no coal; and hence, no civilization, no replenishing and subduing the earth.   Were plants merely
individuals—without branches, they would be annuals,
and would decay every year, lose all the material they
had organised, and scatter all the elements of their

summer growth to the winds of heaven. But putting forth branches, they become perennial colonies, capable, of storing up vegetable matter—retaining what they have acquired by their summer growth. They grow while we sleep, and summer and winter, year after year, stack up timber for us, independently of our toil and care. And the wood thus formed and organised has in past ages been changed into coal, and stored up as fuel for us in the bowels of the earth.* In like manner, branches

---

* The formation of branches is physically caused by the law of continuity or assimilation, whereby, through the instrumentality of the plant, on the one hand, the particles of the earth are lifted into the air, and ramified and sublimated; and on the other, the particles of the atmosphere are carried down to the surface, and into the earth, as concrete matter. Owing to this law, the hollow sphere in which all plants originate, and which is the permanent form of the simplest plants, tends to become more and more differentiated as it rises into the air—to separate and expand in branches, twigs, leaves, and blossoms—structures more and more aërial. For the same reason, all plants are thicker and more solid below, and lighter and more delicate above. We see, in the tendency of the plant to ramification, and in its tendency to preserve a rounded contour, the struggle between the law of sphericity and the law of continuity or assimilation; and the more successfully the plant maintains its circular form and at the same time ramifies, and subdivides, and multiplies its parts and organs, the more perfect a plant it is. This explanation of the cause of branches is satisfactory so far as it goes; but it does not go to the root of the matter. There is a higher spiritual reason, I believe, behind this physical reason. Special uses and individual advantages in nature are secured in the fulfilment of a grand principle--an all-embracing law—in the framing of which these were provided for. Before the creation of our world, all created life was individual—isolated; the angels were mere separate units. When God united dead matter to vegetable vitality, why did He not proceed upon

may be regarded, in one sense, as inessential to the True Vine. God is self-contained and self-satisfied. He needs no creature help or sympathy. And yet, in another sense, He is a Great Vine of which His creatures are the branches; and in this multiplication and diffusion of His own life by branches, His happiness and glory consist. He created the angels for the purpose of surrounding Himself with pure and holy beings to hold communion with Him. He created our world, and peopled it with human beings, made in His own image, that He might walk and converse with them among the trees of the garden.

the same plan of creation, and make all plants separate units, having no corporate existence, each living and dying in itself and for itself? Why should He have departed so widely from the angelic type of life, as to form a perennial, branched, social organism, such as a shrub or a tree? We have, in the formation of the first tree, an entirely new thing in the universe, an inconceivable idea to even the profound apprehension of an angel. What was the significance of a structure so peculiar, so unique? If we believe, that without Christ "was not anything made that was made," that He is the "First-born of every creature," that the world was fitted up, as to all its objects and arrangements, for redemptive purposes, then we have a glimpse of the ultimate reason why branches were created. We see, in the first tree, in the first branched plant, a dim material image of that glorious Trinity in whose brightness man was created, in whose fulness the Son of man came into our world: we see the first faint dawning of that great truth of a corporate life realised in man's social condition, in the covenant of grace, in the union of believers with Jesus, and in the communion of the Church. The first plant that ramified on this earth contained a mute type or prophecy, which was only explained and fulfilled in its highest form when our Lord said to His disciples, "I am the Vine, ye are the branches."

He formed the Church that He might have a redeemed and sanctified society, with His own image restored in them, capable once more of knowing and loving Him, and, amid the higher and holier scenes of the Transfiguration Mount, Gethsemane, and Calvary, talking with Him of the decease which He accomplished at Jerusalem. It was for the purpose of multiplying branches, and making the goodly Vine to overshadow the whole earth, that the Heavenly Husbandman cultivated it in this life. It was in order that many sons and daughters might be born unto God that Christ was born into this world. It was in order that many might be added daily to the Church of such as should be saved, that Jesus suffered and died. For this great object He pleased not Himself. He gave up His whole life to the service of men. He saved others ; Himself He could not save. He lost His own individual life by self-denial and self-sacrifice, in order that His individuality might become universal, His personality unlimited. The life of all for whom He gave His life thus becomes part of Him by faith and love. He is the Son of man—not an individual man, but humanity gathered up, born anew, sanctified and saved. He lives not in Himself, but in all His people. "I in you, and ye in Me," is the wonderful language so often repeated in the New Testament to express the transfusion of Christ's being by love into the being of each of His people—the absorption of their individuality in His individuality—and thus gaining a higher individuality than before.

Most strikingly does Jesus Himself express this truth in the Johanean parable : " Except a corn of wheat fall into the ground, and die, it abideth alone ; but if it die, it bringeth forth much fruit. He that loveth his life shall lose it, and he that hateth his life shall keep it unto life eternal." The seed that is kept out of the ground abideth alone—it produces no branches, no representatives of itself. But if it is sown in the ground, and thus yields up its own selfish life, it bringeth forth much fruit. It sends up several stalks from the same germinating embryo, and these, in the harvest-time produce the full corn in the ear—in some thirty, in some sixty, and in some an hundredfold. And so, in selfishly loving His life, Jesus would have remained alone. But in giving Himself a ransom for many, in dying for men, He multiplied Himself; it pleased the Father that all fulness should dwell in Him bodily : He spread His being over all the spiritual universe. The vine grown from the seed forms branches from the very beginning. Its dicotyledonous seed expands in germinating into two lobes ; the stem which it afterwards produces begins almost immediately to develop lateral buds and branches, and every year it goes on developing new buds and branches. From first to last, the natural vine lives by a process of self-multiplication—by the constant repetition of its own type. And is not this pre-eminently the case with the True Vine ? Even when sown as a seed in the ground, and dying there, He produced branches of Himself. The salvation of the dying thief on the cross was a proof of His power of self-multiplication in the act of germination, as it were; and the resurrection of those who came out of their graves at Jerusalem, and appeared unto many, showed the wonderful working of the same Divine power, even when the seed of eternal life was sown in the soil and lay buried in the solitude and darkness of the tomb. And ever since, a multitude which no man can number, who have lived and died in the faith and love of His name, have proclaimed to us, age after age, that there is no self-life in Jesus,—that, "while no personality is so unique as His, none is, at the same time, so universal,—while no individuality is so individual, none is at the same time so blended up with others."

It is a most interesting thought, that the basis of our relations to Christ as branches in the vine, is to be found in the duality of our nature, the mysterious union in us of mind and matter. In our creation as body, soul, and spirit, God exhibited the tri-personal aspect of His nature. God said—that is, the Three Persons of the Glorious Trinity—"Let *us* make man in our image, after *our* likeness;" and it is this great fact which renders our redemption from sin possible. The Divine image was imparted to man as a meet preparation for God's after assumption of the form of man. The incarnation was but the consequence of the presence of the Divine element in created man. Stock and graft thus possessed the necessary affinity, and were made capable of being united in a single Person,— the Son of God and the Son of man. In the creation of angels God manifested the glory of the unity of

His essence. They were formed separately. They have no mutual relationship. As pure spirits, they are isolated individuals, incapable of forming a race, a society, united by ties of blood, and accumulating a general experience. They cannot be branches of one vine; they have no common stock and root of their being; and hence, when they sinned and fell, there was no possibility of restoring them. There could be no natural link of unity between them and a Redeemer. The Son of God could not become incarnate in their nature, for their nature is incommunicable by generation, and, in the very simplicity and unity of its essence, affords no inlet, no room, for the indwelling of the Godhead. The Saviour could not expose the nature and consequences of sin objectively in an outward form to them; for they have no body in which His sacrifice in their room and stead could be offered up, and in which the separation of the fallen and rebellious will from its own perverseness, as the result of that sacrifice, could be effected. Having no connection with each other by relationship, there could be no common salvation, no covenant engagement, no corporate life, no intercessory faith. Each would require to be dealt with, in the matter of redemption, as a solitary unit. Their sin also remains unknown and unrepented of, owing to its being hid as a spiritual thing in the simplicity of a spiritual being. Their pride is unhumbled by the changes of a decaying body. The very immortality of their being perpetuates their evil, and seals them down forever in their guilt.

Hence Jesus took not on Him the nature of angels, but the seed of Abraham. Forasmuch as the children were partakers of flesh and blood He also Himself likewise took part of the same, and in that human nature linked Himself with the whole human race, and made atonement for human sin. He becomes the Redeemer of our several persons, because He is already the Redeemer of our common nature, which He has made forever His own. In our body we see projected the hidden spiritual evil of our nature,—what is impalpable is made visible. The disease of the sinful thought and purpose is forced out into full development in the body—breaks out in physical disease, degradation, and deformity; so that we see its true character, and are induced to hate and repent of it. By the fulcrum of our bodily organisation the soul can gradually expel its spiritual evil—has purchase in carrying on the contest against sin. By the crucifying of the flesh the lust within is crucified, and the whole internal process of redemption is aided. By the sex of the body, and the various human relations which spring from this duality of our nature, the simple emotion of creature-love is refracted into the various natural affections—parental, filial, fraternal, friendly; and man becomes mankind—society—one great brotherhood, giving mutual help, and sharing in the general experience. By sex, man fulfils his twofold mission of replenishing and subduing the earth. When created, Adam fulfilled these two purposes singly. It was to Adam alone, and not to Adam and Eve, that God said, " Be fruitful and multiply and replenish the earth and subdue it." He dressed the garden of Eden alone, and from a rib in his side reproduced the species in Eve, as a tree reproduces itself from the bud. This mode of reproduction by bud and branch might have been continued, and become the normal mode; but God had higher moral purposes to serve in the case of man, and therefore ordained that the human race should henceforth be perpetuated by marriage, just as a tree propagates itself by flower and fruit and seed. By this marriage union, the man has been left free to fulfil one part of the mission of the race, viz., to subdue the earth; while the woman is left free to fulfil the other part, "to replenish it," and to exercise a mother's purifying and elevating influence over their common offspring. By sex, too, man is endowed with "a passive infinity," a capacity of boundless and illimitable increase—has a resemblance to the life-imparting power of the Creator—is associated with God in a peculiarly wonderful manner in the eternal generation of His own Son, of which human generation is a type, and in the multitude which no man can number which shall be born again of the Son. By the changes of the body, man's discipline on earth is accomplished, pride is humbled, patience cultivated. And, finally, by the death of the body, sin is defecated, and that which is sown in weakness and corruption is raised in immortal power and glory. Thus, through the threefold constitution of our nature, the image of God in which we were made and which was ruined and defaced by the Fall is restored in us; we are united to God and to our fellow-creatures in the economy of salvation, and made branches in the True Vine. And in this respect we are a spectacle to angels; and to the principalities in heaven is revealed by the Church the manifold wisdom of God.

It is the branches that make up the form, outline and substance of the natural vine; without branches it would be a bare solitary axis, a mere vegetable staff, dry and leafless, without beauty or use. And so, it is believers who make up as branches the form and substance and outline of the True Vine. The redeemed Church, consisting of all the redeemed members, and yet more than all the believers together, the individuals deriving their life from the life of the whole, is the body of Christ, the *fulness* of Him that filleth all in all. Without His people He represents Himself as a root out of a dry ground without form or comeliness, as empty and imperfect. Were a single saint awanting, though the least in the kingdom of God, His body would be incomplete. The poorest, weakest member cannot be overlooked. He knoweth His own sheep by name, and leadeth them out; their names are engraved on the palms of His hands and their walls are continually before Him. The new-born babe in Christ, in whose heart the faintest pulse of spiritual life is beating, will form part of His fulness, as truly as the strong man who runs in the way of God's commandments and is not weary, who walks and is not faint. The door-keeper in the sanctuary cannot be wanted any more than the priest at the shrine. The beggar at the gate shares the honour and privilege

with the king on the throne. Lazarus has his
own place in the bosom of Jesus as truly as David.
In this sense the fulness of Christ is as yet imperfect,
for all saints are not yet gathered into Christ. Many
are still in the highways and hedges of paganism, and
in the streets and lanes of Christian civilization; and
though an innumerable company is already assembled
in the banqueting-house, the cry is "yet there is room."
During these nineteen Christian centuries, He has but
received the earnest of His joy, the gleanings and the
first-fruits of the human generations. He has not yet
seen of the travail of His soul and been satisfied.
For the ingathering of all possible saints into Him he
waits as for the outshining of that glory to which He
was exalted because of His humiliation, and the fulfilling
of that joy for which He endured the cross despising
the shame. His grace can no more endure a vacuum
than nature. When He sees a sinner converted, He
rejoices as one branch more added to the Vine,
as one more nearer the fulness of his perfection.
When He sees a saint growing in knowledge and in
grace, becoming more conformed to His own image,
He rejoices, for thus is His body completed and
glorified.

And just as Christ is incomplete without His people;
so the converse is true, His people are incomplete
without Him. The branches depend npon the Vine
in the same way that the Vine depends upon the
branches. Separate from Christ, who only hath life,
man has no spiritual vitality. He is like a branch cut

off from its parent tree, having no independent life, and therefore speedily withering and perishing in the very circumstances which would have promoted its well-being had it been united to the stock ; or, like a rootless plant, having no power of drawing nourishment from the surrounding elements, dried up by the sun and blown about by the wind. There is a great want about a man who is not a Christian, no matter what his gifts and attainments may be. He is restless, for he is not rooted in the love of Christ; he is dissatisfied, because Christ is not the portion of his soul. He has no fixedness of principle, no true individuality of character; he is the slave of circumstances ; and, destitute of spiritual life, he cannot obtain the formative material which will develop the highest capabilities of his nature. But, united to Christ, all the fulness of the Godhead is his to make him complete, wanting nothing. Whatever is in the Divine root he can draw out for his own nourishment and growth in grace ; from that root he can develop the fairest flowers and richest fruits of humanity. This is the true scripture pantheism, which, while it says that "in Him we live and move and have our being," recognises His personality and ours as all the more distinct from the very fact of the inter-dependence. "*I* am the Vine, *ye* are the branches," thus indicates the distinct personality, and yet the inseparable intersubsistence between Christ and His people, which, in the corresponding formula, "As Jehovah liveth, and as thy soul liveth," is made the ground of appeal, as the clearest fact on which to establish the immutability of an oath. " Because *I* live *ye* shall live also," Jesus says to His disciples; these words *I* and *ye* retaining all their measureless significance.

The branches are also incomplete without each other. The poet says that " we are greater as children than as brothers ;" and the creed of many is that religious experience is always a lonely thing—that our deepest spiritual life cannot include any human sympathy and social unity, but is lived solely under the eye of the Father who seeth in secret. But we cannot come into the presence of God without carrying with us the sympathies of our race. We cannot let go our fellowship with our fellowmen, when we hold communion with our God. We cannot be children without at the same time being brothers. The social state is not an accident or a circumstance but a law; not an economy which man himself has organised, but a principle, an inherent want and fact in his complex constitution from the very first. The human face, so facile and efficient a means of communion between man and man, implies society; the law of society is written upon the individual conscience, and reaches to the lowest depth of our most solitary life. Absolutely isolated from the other members of that living body of which we form a part, by whose intellectual vision and moral experience we profit so largely and continuously—and through whom more than through ourselves we perceive all complete and perfect truth—the very spring of piety would be dried up, and we should shrink into absolute individuality, which is spiritual death. Even God could not be understood or loved by the solitary worshipper, apart from those channels of human influence, through which alone spiritual perception and emotion flow; and spiritual life is not possible to individuals, if the social conditions under which it is invariably produced, are erased. God Himself recognised the necessity of this human association when He said, "it is not good for man to be alone" —even although man had the great society of nature, of angels, and of God. He needed the mysterious power of social human influence, not merely for his comfort but for his worship, not merely as an aid to the attainment of spiritual truth and life, but as the very condition of enjoying them. The apostle Paul, speaking of all past believers, says, "that they without us should not be made perfect." This is the voice of the Church to all the past, and to all the far off and the future. Believers have a sense of loneliness and imperfection without the society of others likeminded with themselves, and hence in their own conversion they have received a call to convert others. We see in the triune God, when He said, "Let us make man in our image after our likeness," the desire to extend and propagate His own likeness; and one great feature of our resemblance to Him, one striking proof that we are indeed made in His image, is the instinctive desire that we have to enlarge the field of our sympathies by moulding others into conformity with our own ideas and experience, to propagate ourselves in them. The more branches he forms, the larger and more perfect branch is the Christian himself.

Thus we see that the vine is not more necessary to the branches than the branches are to the vine. If the vine imparts support, vitality, nourishment, and a corporate unity to the branches, the branches are the true sources whence is derived the elaborate formative material used in the construction of the vine. It is the branches that bear the leaves; and by the leaves all the solid and enduring parts of the tree are produced. They are the wonderfully simple and effective contrivances by which the green absorbent surface of the vine is increased. In their tissue the sap is aerated, and by exposure to the chemical influence of the sunshine rendered nutritious. By means of their net-work of capillary vessels, in which the woody system of the vine terminates, the sap is conveyed in this highly organized state to all parts of the plant. Every leaf on every branch, during summer, is actively engaged in taking in nutritious gases from the atmosphere; absorbing the dew, rain, and sunshine, decomposing them, as in a laboratory, in order to add new shoots to the extremities and sides of the twigs, and to form an annual deposit of growth around the main branches and trunk, and the entire surface of the tree. The roots, indeed, eliminate nourishment from the soil, and contribute their part to the general structure, but the most efficient and useful agents are the leaves; and the growth of the tree depends upon the amount of leaf surface which it spreads abroad upon the atmosphere. With every increase in the number of its leaves, a young tree or branch must necessarily grow more rapidly. How strange to think that the huge boles of trees that have braved the storms of a thousand years have been produced by the labour of many generations of fragile and perishing leaves; that the enduring timber employed in constructing our shipping, our furniture, and our dwellings, has been formed by the dead leaves of autumn which we tread beneath our feet; that the vast fields of coal throughout the world, upon which the grandest triumphs of our modern civilization depend, have been deposited by the green delicate leaf! * And thus is it in the economy of the spiritual Vine. It is by the leaves and branches that the enduring parts of it are formed. The glory of Christ is the result of the believer's toil as well as of His own. He works by means; and it is by His people that He chiefly carries on His cause in the world. Frail and perishing in themselves, fading like the leaves, they build up the enduring struc-

* The useful and the beautiful are separated by man, but always joined together by God. We get useful things only through beautiful things—timber through the foliage, and fruit through the blossom. Our furniture was once covered with leaves, and formed the lovely furniture of the woodland. The cotton that we weave in our looms into articles of dress, was previously woven for us in the beautiful loom of the mallow-like blossom; the petals fell off that this soft down might be formed. Through the bright blue flower of the flax have come to us the fibres of our household linen. God's beautiful things not made with hands, prepare for our useful things made with hands, and sacrifice their natural beauty for our profit. They lay aside their heavenly garments, and gird themselves with the homely towel in our service, in imitation of their Creator.

ture of the Church, organize schemes of Christian usefulness, and produce Christian results which will long survive them. Every Christian contributes something to the general stock. Every Christian is the heir of all the ages—inherits the accumulated labours of previous generations—grows in the Vine on the deposits of work done by the godly men of old who preceded him. This is a most interesting and solemn thought, that just as every leaf, however fragile and transient, helps to form the solid and enduring tree, so every Christian, however weak and ignorant, helps to form the lasting Vine which covers the hills with its shadow, and whose boughs are like the goodly cedars. What an importance does this thought lend to the efforts of the most humble and obscure believer; what a dignity does it give to the smallest act done for Christ! The stability, grandeur, and usefulness of the whole vine depend upon the labours of its most transient and apparently unimportant parts. The noble Christian literature, the wealth of Christian experience, the rich products of Christian enterprise and zeal throughout the world, have been left behind as enduring monuments by those who faded like the leaves of autumn, and whose dust has been scattered to the four winds of heaven.

But not only do the branches of the vine build up its own economy; they also benefit the world outside. It is by the leaves which the branches bear that God purifies the world and neutralises the evil that is in it. The leaves of natural trees are sanitary agents in the household of nature. They absorb the carbonic gas, with which the breath of animals and the various processes of decay and combustion, are constantly contaminating the atmosphere, convert this noxious waste into wood and other vegetable substances, and thus preserve the air in a fit condition for human breathing. The fresh air which we quaff from the hills has been purified and made healthy for us by the foliage of the trees, not merely those of our own country, but even the pines of Norway and the palms of India. In the light of this idea we see a new significance in the incident of the dove bringing back the olive leaf in its bill to the ark. The green leaf indicated not merely that the flood was over, that the former condition of things was brought back, but also that the polluted earth was purified; freed from all its moral taint, as the air is freed from its physical impurity by the action of the green leaf. The new earth, of which this was the first product, was to be first pure, then peaceable. And are not the leaf-bearing branches of the True Vine the purifiers of the world? "Ye are the salt of the earth," said Jesus to His disciples. It is by the lives of God's people that the world is preserved from total corruption and decay. They influence public opinion for good; they act as restraints upon the conduct of the wicked; they lead others to admire and imitate them; they counteract, by their example and deeds, the evils and impurities which would otherwise accumulate until the moral atmosphere became utterly vitiated. Like the aromatic breath of pines, their pure healthy presence breathes through the taint of the world's wickedness, purity and health.   They are in closest sympathy with the spirit of their Master, who came into this world that He might purify and heal.   Branches also are harmless conductors of electricity.   Every twig is far more efficient than the metallic point of the best constructed rod.   It helps to disarm the storm of its terrors, by drawing down the destructive lightning and passing it gently to the earth.   How greatly, then, do we depend for our safety in thunderstorms upon the branches of the forest!   In this respect, what a beautiful type do they afford of the righteous, who are the safeguards of the human world—of the Noahs and Lots, who draw away God's wrath, and preserve the wicked in the midst of whom they dwell.

Between the vine and the branches the closest resemblance may be seen.   Each branch is a perfect representative of the whole tree; every vine leaf is a vine in little—the vine, in its turn, being a vine leaf enlarged.   There is a Greek word for branch which expresses this idea—viz., *oinareon*, derived from *oine*, the vine, indicating that a branch is a diminutive vine. In the natural world, a oneness exists between all the parts of a tree.   The root, stem, bud, flower, fruit, and seed, are constructed on precisely the same type.   However widely diversified they may seem in form, colour, or function, their essential nature is the same.   The leaf is the basis of the whole—the essential and prototypical plant.   It is from it that all the floral organs are developed, and to it that all parts are reducible by homology.   Hence every leaf is a miniature of the tree from which it falls; the outline of its shape is like the outline of the tree; the foot stalk and centre vein represent the trunk and main axis, and the side veins the lateral branches and twigs; while the green cellular matter which fills up the spaces between the ramifications of the veins on the same plane, represents the foliage. The veins of the leaves ramify from the midrib at angles which coincide with those formed by the branches and the trunk. Similarly, the branches are miniatures of the whole tree; each is capable of becoming itself a separate individual, as is found by cutting, budding, grafting, and other horticultural operations. The smallest twig is a type of the branch on which it grows, and the branch a type of the trunk from which it springs. The whole tree, with its branches, is of the same general form as every individual branch with its twigs; and every branch, with its twigs, is a type of the whole plant in its skeleton and outline. The tree by developing branches merely repeats itself. And while the leaf is a typical plant or branch, the tree or branch is a typical leaf. From all these considerations, it will be seen that the vine presents a repetition both of homotypal parts and of homotypal arrangement of parts or forms; or, in other words, that all its parts are similar to one another, and in nice accordance with the whole. And is it not so with the True Vine? The Son of God stood among His creatures as one of themselves—assumed our nature, with all its necessary limitations. "In all things it behoved Him to be made like unto His brethren." His humanity was sanctified by the same Spirit that sanctifies us, and developed by the same conditions which develop us. "He that sanctifieth, and they that are sanctified are all of one." He is a partaker of our nature, and we are partakers of His. We have the same mind which was in Christ Jesus; we are conformed to His image. We not only receive His doctrines, but imbibe His Spirit, live as He lived, think as He thought, and feel as He felt. The eye of man sees Christ's image upon our character and conduct, and the eye of God sees the mind of Christ in our soul. We have the unity of the Spirit in the bond of peace—one body, one spirit, one hope, one faith, one baptism, one God and Father of all, who is above all, and through all, and in all. This unity in the living Church proves it to be indeed the new creation of God in Christ Jesus.

As an illustration of this typical resemblance between the True Vine and its branches, let us take the case of Moses. "A prophet shall the Lord your God raise up unto you from among your brethren, like unto me, Him shall ye hear," said the great Lawgiver of Israel to his people; and how marvellously do the incidents in the life of Moses correspond with those in the life of Christ! The destruction of the Hebrew children by Pharaoh, and the peril which Moses incurred as a child, are exactly like the massacre of the innocents by Herod, and the danger to the life of the infant Jesus. The sojourn of Moses in Egypt is like the sojourn of Jesus in Egypt with His parents. Moses visiting his brethren when he was of age, and his election to become the deliverer of Israel, are like Jesus beginning to preach the gospel of the kingdom to the Jews, and being baptised of John in the Jordan for His sacred ministry. The retirement of Moses into the wilderness for forty years is paralleled by Christ's temptation in the wilderness for forty days. The miraculous power with which Moses was endowed as the messenger of God, is similar to the signs and wonders which Christ performed as evidences of His Messiahship. The transfiguration of Moses on the mount, when the skin of his face so shone that those who talked with him could not gaze on the dazzling radiance, corresponds exactly with the transfiguration of Christ on the mount, when His face did shine as the sun, and His garments were whiter than any fuller on earth could white them. The very words which, on that occasion, God addressed from the cloud to the three disciples,—"This is My beloved Son, hear ye Him,"—were an echo of the words of Moses, "The Lord your God shall raise up a Prophet of your brethren like unto me, Him shall ye hear;" while the peculiar word *exodus* in the Greek text, translated "decease," used only by St. Luke and by St. Peter in a similar association, was suggested by the Exodus of Moses. Nay, the very scene which Moses found on his descent from Mount Sinai, was found by Christ on His descent from the mount of transfiguration. Satan had taken advantage of the absence of Moses to tempt the Israelites to idolatry and riot; Satan had taken advantage of the absence of Christ to prevail against the disciples, for they could not cast out the evil spirit in the lunatic child, and the Scribes and Pharisees were pressing to the uttermost the advantage which they had gained by this miscarriage of the disciples. St. Mark records that when Christ came down to the multitude, "straightway all the people, when they beheld Him, were greatly amazed, and, running to Him, saluted Him,"—which indicates that His face still shone with the reflection of the transfiguration, like the face of Moses when he went down to the camp of Israel. The character of the miracles which Moses performed closely resembled the character of Christ's miracles. Moses changed water into blood; Christ changed water into wine. Moses led the Israelites through the Red Sea; Christ walked on the water. Under the guidance of Moses the Israelites were fed with heavenly manna; by the power of Christ the multitudes that followed Him into the wilderness were fed by the multiplication of a few loaves and fishes. Moses proclaimed the law from Mount Sinai; Christ preached the sermon of the Beatitudes on a mountain in Galilee. Moses instituted the Passover, and appointed the same as an ordinance in Israel for ever; Christ instituted the Lord's Supper, and said, " As oft as ye eat this bread and drink this cup ye do show the Lord's death till He come." Moses made a brazen serpent, and erected it on a cross, that the serpent-bitten Israelites might look on it and be healed; Christ said of this type, " As Moses lifted up the serpent in the wilderness, even so must the Son of Man be lifted up, that whosoever believeth in Him should not perish, but have eternal life." The farewell discourses of Moses to the Israelites, which are recorded in the last chapter of Deuteronomy, are like the last touching discourses of our Lord to His disciples, as recorded in the last chapters of the Gospel of St. John. The death of Moses on Mount Nebo was like the death of Christ on Mount Calvary; and as Moses, with dying eyes, beheld from that lonely summit the goodly land flowing with milk and honey, which was to be the future possession of his people, so Christ beheld, with dying eyes, a glorious prospect of the salvation of the true Israel of God, and the inheritance of the saints in light on Mount Calvary, when He uttered the significant words, "It is finished!" A profound mystery and uncertainty overhang the burial-place of Moses,—"No man knoweth of his sepulchre to this day;" and so darkness closes upon the grave in Golgotha, and no one knoweth of the sepulchre of Jesus unto this day. Our Saviour appeared to His disciples, after His death, on a mountain in Galilee: and Moses, after his death, appeared with Elijah, on the mount of transfiguration, to Christ and His disciples. Or, if we accept the Jewish tradition, that Moses was translated to heaven from Mount Nebo, we can only see in it a further resemblance to the ascension of Christ from the Mount of Olives. A multitude of other features of resemblance between Moses, in his character and public functions, and Christ, might be mentioned, but those given are sufficient to show the homology.*

* Delitzsch, in a small pamphlet, entitled "Neue Untersuchungen über Entstehung und Anlage der Karonischen Evangelien I

Another very striking illustration of this conformity of believers to the image of Jesus, not only in character, but in outward circumstances, is seen in the case of the first martyr, Stephen.   He is as true a type looking back to Jesus as Moses is looking forward.   The one was in the dawn, the other in the sunset; the one pre-figured, the other reflected, the glory of the same Sun of Righteousness.   Stephen was apprehended, like his Lord, with sudden violence, brought before the San-hedrim, and accused by false witnesses of saying that the temple was to be destroyed, and that the Jews were to be deprived of their exclusive privileges as God's peculiar people.   Though his meek and daunt-less demeanour was a copy of his Lord's, yet he too broke out in righteous indignation against the Jews: " Ye stiff-necked and uncircumcised in heart and ears, ye do always resist the Holy Ghost; as your fathers did, so do ye."   Like Jesus, he saw the heavens opened, and the glory of God, and the Son of man standing at the right hand of God.   Like Jesus, he was cast out of the city and suffered there, and called upon God, saying, " Lord Jesus, receive my spirit," and forgave his murderers, crying with a loud voice,

Das Matthäus Evangelium," admirably demonstrates the marvel-lous correspondence which exists between the acts and teachings of Christ, and the acts and teachings of the Law as recorded in the Pentateuch.   Indeed, the whole chronological arrangement, literary plan, and general scope of the Gospel of Matthew is evidently a reproduction and fulfilment of the Old Testament Thora, or Five Books of the Law, and may, therefore, well be called the " Evan-gelical Pentateuch."

"Lord, lay not this sin to their charge." We can easily conceive that this remarkable conformity to his Master's image and circumstances must have deeply impressed the mind of Stephen himself, and imparted strength and encouragement to him to be faithful unto death.

And as it was with Stephen, so was it in the case of St. Paul. In many things we can trace a remarkable resemblance between the circumstances of the great apostle of the Gentiles and those of Christ. He talked like a man who would seem to have, in some measure, lost his old personal identity. After his conversion, he was no longer Saul of Tarsus, but a man in Christ Jesus. He could say of himself, "I live; yet not I, but Christ liveth in me." He bore about with him the marks of the Lord Jesus; he was always carrying about in the body the dying of the Lord Jesus—in perils by land, in perils by water, in stripes, in imprisonment, in tumults, in fastings—troubled on every side, yet not distressed—a man of sorrows, and yet experiencing the joy of the Lord as the strength of his heart. Very specially is it to be noticed, that in the closing years of his life, he trod very closely in the steps of his Master, both in the circumstances in which he was placed and in the character and conduct which he displayed. He was brought before Nero as Christ was brought before Pilate; and all St. Paul's companions and friends forsook him and fled, as did the disciples of Jesus in His hour of need. St. Paul said, "At my first answer no man stood with me, but all men forsook me; I pray God it may not be laid to their charge. Nevertheless, the Lord stood by me, and strengthened me." Christ said, "All ye shall be scattered every man to his own, and shall leave me alone, and yet I am not alone, because the Father is with me." St. Paul and Stephen, and all Christ's early followers, were baptised with His baptism, and drank of His cup. Even in their outward circumstances they literally knew the fellowship of His sufferings, and were made conformable unto His death. What befell the Master was what befell the Apostles over again, in fulfilment of His own words, "The disciple is not greater than his Lord; if they have persecuted me, they will also persecute you." The spiritual conformity was based upon the physical. And so is it with every Christian still. He is a homologue of the Great Archetype. His circumstances repeat those of his Lord. Such, then, is the mutual resemblance in character and circumstances between the True Vine and its branches. They are predestinated to be conformed to His image. That image is partially developed in them already, but it will become more perfect through the discipline of life. The Godhead says once more of every believer, "Let us make man in our image;" and, in the performance of this great work of grace, every believer is crucified together with Christ, dead with Him, buried with Him; and as he dies with Him, so he rises with Him and reigns with Him; and in the end shall be wholly like Him, for he shall see Him as He is.

But while there is thus a general resemblance between all the branches of the vine, while they are each modelled on the type of the whole tree, there are also characteristic differences between them. Variety, which is the law of nature, is displayed in their unity also. The infinite depth and richness of the new life which Christ hath brought into the world manifests itself in the rich variety of forms in which it embodies itself in the lives of men. The very excrescences and malformations witness in their own way, for the fulness of this life. We see in the extravagances and excesses of pillar saints and early Christian ascetics, the intoxication of the new wine of the heavenly kingdom, the joyous sense of a new life, which, like children, they knew not how to express. It is the law of nature that the elevation of the type is accompanied by an increased variety in the specific organs; witness a mushroom and a vine, the extremes of the vegetable kingdom. Through differentiation of its parts, the plant advances to a higher unity and simplicity. No two leaves, or blossoms, or fruits, or seeds, are precisely alike. Each branch has its own peculiar history of growth; and separate trees differ not more widely in this respect than two branches in the same tree. The formation of crystals, of the lead tree, or of imitations of ferns and foliage on frozen windows, or in moss-agates, or in what are called dendritic pebbles, is always the same, because the matter operated upon is mineral and inert; but in the tree where the matter is organized and living, and therefore easily impressible, the growth of each branch fluctuates, and its appearance varies with the favourable or unfavourable state of the weather from year to year. Numerous examples of heterophyllous

and dimorphic plants, in which there is a very considerable difference in form in the same organs, not only at
different times, but even simultaneously, might be advanced.   The common honeysuckle has often two kinds
of leaves on the same stalk, one entire and the other
more or less divided.   The ivy also varies widely in
the shape of its leaves; while, in the yellow jessamine,
almost every intermediate stage may be traced, from an
ovate entire leaf to one very deeply and irregularly
divided.   A variety of the potato produces first double
and sterile flowers, and subsequently single fertile ones.
In one kind of grape, black and amber-coloured berries
are produced in the same cluster; another variety often
bears on the same stalk small round and large oblong
berries.   Similar differences exist among Christians
under the cultivation of Christ.   The Christian being
the highest type of man, exhibits, therefore, a greater
variety of character—develops more fully the " tendency
to individuation," which Coleridge calls the true idea of
human life.   Christians in the Church are not zoophites
in a coral cluster, but branches in a vine, in which the
specific parts are more complicated, and yet are all
embraced under a greater unity and simplicity of plan.
There are diversities of gifts and diversities of operations, but the same Spirit.   Every individual case is an
individual variety.   In one, reverence predominates; in
another, faith, or hope, or love, or joy.   The religion of
one is retiring, objective, and self-distrusing; that
of another is active and aggressive.   St. Paul exhibited
the strength of faith; St. Peter the power of zeal; and

St. John the force of love. Each believer has what the others have, but each blends the gifts of the Spirit in different proportions, and forms a distinct compound of them according to his own natural temperament and his peculiar experience of the grace of God. As the honey in Madeira tastes of violets, and in the Highlands of Scotland of the heather; as the wines of different countries taste differently, so the products of the Spirit take their taste and colour from the individual experiences through which they are formed. And this polymorphism of the Christian character, not only secures the charm and the contrast of an endless variety, but also leads believers to the exercise of an enlarged charity, to esteem others better than themselves, to prefer one another in honour on account of the graces which in themselves are wanting, to provoke one another to good works. If, as Dr. Westcott truly observes, we were all alike in our attributes—if religion were in all the same exercise of the same gifts,—then the defection of one would make little difference to the general result ; but if, as we see it must be, the faithlessness of one subtracts from the whole that which no other can supply, all is changed. We feel at once the overwhelming majesty of the Christian life, even in its ultimate details. We feel that we can never be alone, and confine to ourselves the issues of our actions : we feel that, in each of us, and in our own duties, the highest well-being of the whole Church is at stake.

The word in the original for branch is *klema* and means a *little branch*. It is a term of endearment, indi-

cating the preciousness of those who are united to
Christ.   St. John saw in the midst of the throne not a
lamb merely, as it is in our version, but, "a *little* lamb
as it had been slain," as it should be translated; and
the diminutive form in the original greatly enhances the
pathos and tenderness of the image.   As Jesus is the
"little lamb," so His disciples are the "little branches."
He becomes as a child to His children, condescends to
their humbleness and weakness, adapts Himself to their
state, measures His step by their step, shortens His
octave to the stretch of their fingers.   "Fear not, *little*
flock," He says, "it is your Father's good pleasure to
give you the kingdom."

In the mystical Vine there are no branches of natural
spontaneous growth; there are none who are born in
Christ, and, without change, grow up in Christ as
naturally as its own branches are produced and grow up
in the physical vine.   Believers are *added* to the Church
—*added* to the Lord.   Some Christians, indeed, may
not be able to remember when their spiritual life
began, any more than when their natural life began,
though they may be as sure of the one as of the other.
They cannot point to any great change or crisis of
their life, and say, "it was then I began for the first
time to know the Lord."   Children of godly parents,
reared in pious households, their love to Christ and
life in Him grew with their growth; and dedicated
to the Lord from their infancy, early taught of the
Lord, and planted in His house, they flourish in the
courts of our Lord, and bring forth fruit in old age,

when others fade. Such cases present the nearest likeness that can be found to natural branches in the vine. They seem as if they were never separated from Christ, but were produced by Him, and formed in Him from the very beginning. But it is not really so. Even these were born in sin and conceived in iniquity, and needed a saving change. They too were children of wrath, even as others, and needed to be born again, to be brought from without and grafted upon the True Vine, although the process took place by the Spirit's agency so silently and gently that it left no consciousness or memory of its operation. It is a truth admitting of no exception, that it is by grafting alone that the True Vine becomes furnished with branches. All have sinned and come short of the glory of God; all have been originally dead in trespasses and sins; and every branch in Christ has been taken from the natural corrupt stock, and united to Him in newness of life.

Very marvellous, when we fully consider it, is this process of grafting. Although a few instances of contiguous branches, and the roots of neighbouring trees—principally pines—uniting by a natural process of grafting, have occurred; the process, nevertheless, is not natural. Grafting requires the intervention of human skill; and in this way it admirably symbolises the mode in which believers are united to Christ. This mode is not natural and spontaneous; it requires, on the contrary, the intervention of the Spirit, the operation of the means of grace; it is the work of Divine skill and power.   Self-salvation is impossible.   No Christian ever converted himself.   He uniformly ascribes the very commencement of the saving work to the Spirit.   It is God's work in the beginning and continuance of it.   In every garden this important parable is taught.   In the world of natural things may be seen, as plainly as in the Word of God, the refutation of that false doctrine which would make the poor, finite, feeble effort of depraved man the efficient cause of his own salvation.   In the garden, too, we find that if from the artificial graft seed be taken and caused to germinate, the plants so arising no longer present the special and valued peculiarity, but revert to the original or wild stock. The children of godly parents do not inherit grace ; they have each to be engrafted personally in Christ. The seed of believers has the same atavism, the same tendency to go back to the original depraved nature, as the seed of the unconverted ; and hence the Vine is furnished with branches, not by hereditary descent, but by a continual and ever-renewed process of grafting.

All this teaches us that it is the Spirit that unites us to Christ—the Husbandman who grafts us in the True Vine.   And He does this for the very same purpose spiritually for which the gardener grafts his plants naturally.   It is well known that the period of blossoming and fruiting is accelerated, and the quality of the fruit improved by grafting.   The young scion or graft that is united to a vigorous stock, is enabled to obtain a larger supply of nutritive matter from the accumulated store in that stock than it could obtain from its own parent stem; while the process of separation from its old situation to a new checks its vegetative powers,—that is, its tendency to produce barren shoots and leaves,—and causes it to develop instead blossoms and fruit. By this method all our good varieties of cultivated fruits are produced from the original wild ones, which are sour, small, and worthless. By the same means, also, the life of slips may be prolonged much beyond the usual limit of the life of the parent stock. Vines have been transmitted by perpetual division from the time of the Romans; and a slip taken from a tree dying of old age, by being grafted upon a fresh stock, will live for many years in undecaying vigour; whereas, if left on its parent tree, it would have perished with it. And does not a similar process of *ennobling* take place when a branch of the wild vine is united to the True Vine. Formerly the believer, like Onesimus, was unprofitable. He produced only the selfish fruits of a corrupt nature. But now he is profitable to God and man. His selfish tendencies are checked; he no longer makes provision for the flesh to fulfil the lusts thereof. He uses the things that he possesses, as in the nature of a trust, for the good of others; feels that in the bestowment upon him of worldly advantages God looked beyond himself, and designed to make him not only the subject of His goodness, but the instrument; not only the recipient, but the diffuser. By union with Christ, the source of all life, he also prolongs his days. His soul is satisfied with long life. Partaking of the fulness of comfort that is in Christ, casting all his cares on Him who careth for him, having the peace ·of God, which passeth all understanding, he enjoys the blessing of a long and useful life; while the wicked do not live half their days.

And may not the various methods adopted in grafting indicate the different stages of life at which believers are joined to the Lord? The process of budding, whereby a mere unexpanded bud, with a portion of the bark and new wood, is removed from one plant and added to another, symbolises the union of youthful believers with the Lord—of those who offer themselves to Him before life has unfolded its powers and beauties. The method of grafting by scions, slips, or cuttings, whereby a portion of the stem and foliage is cut off from one plant and applied to another, is an emblem of those who are converted at a later period, and who have devoted more of their life to the service of the flesh; while the method of grafting by *enarching*, whereby two growing plants are united together, and after adhesion, one is severed from its own stock, and left to grow on the other, points to those who, in mature life, with powers fully developed, have given up seeking their portion in this world, and made the Lord their portion. And the season in which grafting is most successful, viz., the spring-time, just previous to the rising of the sap, indicates that no period is so suitable for the operations of grace as the spring-time of life, when the heart is fresh and tender, and the mind easily impressed by divine things.

Beautifully does the susceptibility of the vine to the process of grafting correspond with the facility with which the union between Christ and His people may be effected. It is not every plant that possesses the peculiar power of being engrafted; that power is confined to a few plants, chiefly cultivated fruit-bearing trees. It is difficult to engraft a branch upon a pine or an oak. These plants are too self-sufficient to impart their own life and growth to members artificially added to them. But the vine is one of those plants that admit of endless grafting, and in which the process is easiest performed. Its nature is so plastic and susceptible, that it at once communicates its own sap and powers of growth to the branch of the same species which man by his skill unites to it. And in this respect, how admirably does it symbolise the suitableness and all-sufficiency of Christ —His ability and willingness to save to the uttermost all who come unto God by Him! " Him that cometh unto Me," He says, "I will in no wise cast out." Through the cultivation of the Father, He was made perfect, and *became* the Author of eternal salvation to all them that obey Him. Just as, in order that grafting may be successfully performed, there must be an affinity between the scion and the stock, as regards species, sap, &c.—for if species of different natural orders be grafted, they will not take—so, in order to become our salvation, He became partaker of our nature—our brother born— connected with us by a relationship which rests on a participation of our flesh and blood, and a sharing of our infirmities, and which therefore renders possible a nearer and more blessed communion with Him than even His angels or archangels can ever know. And in grafting He makes us partakers of His nature; we become His congeners—specifically identical with Him. He was called on earth the Friend of publicans and sinners; but He abode with these, He ministered to them, in order that His purity might remove their impurity, His saving health might overcome their moral disease. He changed their hearts when He chose them for His friends, and made them holy when He received them into His fellowship. They became, by His influence, like-minded with Himself. "He that is joined to the Lord is one spirit."

And here, we are brought to the most interesting point of all—viz., the way in which the union between the vine and the branches is formed. In order that the stock may be prepared for receiving the scion, its bark is pierced, and portions of it removed. Into this wound is inserted the graft. And was not the True Vine wounded for our transgressions, and bruised for our iniquities, in order that we might be united to Him by a living faith. It is through the sufferings of His human nature that we enter into fellowship with Him. It is by the prints of the nails, and the mark of the spear in His side, that we become one with Him. The Messiah from heaven manifested His Divine nature to us by suffering, and not by enjoyment. He could only be known to us in His highest glory through a fellowship with our miseries. "It behoved the Christ to suffer." It is in the Man Christ Jesus—in the incarnate, suffering, bleeding, and dying Son of God, that we are hid. Our salvation is, in Scripture, more frequently ascribed to His degradation and sufferings than to His power and greatness. It is by His stripes that we are healed; it is His blood that cleanseth us from all sin. We are made rich, not by His riches, but by His poverty. It is through the clefts of the stricken Rock that we seek for refuge from the storms of conscience and of heaven—through the sufferings of Christ that we are joined to the Lord. We feel that there can be no other point of contact between us than this—no other way to the Father than through the rent veil of Christ's flesh. It is the suffering form of the Son of God which is most welcome and precious to us perishing sinners; for in that form, bruised and pierced, we read God's answer to our deepest sense of need; we understand as we adore, that "we are justified freely by God's grace, through the redemption that is in Christ Jesus." And in heaven the glorified Church will still preserve the grateful memory of the cross and the grave :—"Thou wast slain and hast redeemed us to God by Thy blood."

And just as He prepared Himself by suffering to unite with us, so we must be prepared by suffering to unite with Him. The scion is cut off from its parent stem, its wood is shaped so as to form a sloping surface, and its bark is partially removed, in order that it may be inserted in the wound of the stock. There must be the application of wound to wound, of bleeding surface to bleeding surface. The scion must suffer as well as the stock. The inner heart of the one must be united to the inner heart of the other. It is no mere surface-application of unbroken bark to unbroken bark. The branch, in its most vital part, must come into closest contact with the vine in its most vital part, if there is to be an incorporate union; the two alburnums and the two libers. There must be a perfect anastomosis of juices, a complete harmony of life and oneness of growth. And does not this fact in nature point out to us how we are to be joined to Christ? It is not by an outward profession and following, costing us nothing; it is, on the contrary, by the deepest and most vital experiences of the soul. It is by penitence and faith, by self-denial and self-sacrifice,—not merely in the outer regions of our being, but in its innermost sanctuaries,— not the mere denial of lust and vice,—not the mere reformation of the outward conduct; but the denial of *self*—all self-denial in detail, springing from denial of self in the heart and in the soul. "If any man will come after Me, let him deny *himself*, take up his cross, and follow Me." It is the cross that unites God to man, and it is the cross that unites man to God. It is by His self-sacrifice that Jesus meets us, and it is by our self-sacrifice that we meet Him. Jesus did not die upon the cross that we might lead a self-seeking life. " He died for all, that they who live should not henceforth live unto themselves, but unto Him who died for them, and rose again." Self-renouncement is the temper of which His death was the highest expression; and only when we renounce ourselves, do we enter into the practical spirit of that death—do we have any part or lot in the blessed results of it.

In grafting, we see the violent shock that is given to the scion when cut off from its old situation and placed in a new, in the arrest of its vegetative growth and its hastening to produce blossoms and fruit, which is the sure sign that it is hurt; for nature, "so careful of the type and so careless of the single life," expedites the process of flowering and seeding, when the plant is in danger of perishing. But we see the sorrows of conviction and conversion more clearly typified in the growth of the corn of wheat. At first, when the wheat sprouts, the blade which it sends up to the surface is green and beautiful. But after a while the field of emerald loveliness looks suddenly sere and yellow; the blades seem to droop and languish, as if a worm were at the root. This remarkable change is caused by what the farmers call the "*speanin brash.*" The corn is weaned from its mother's milk, as it were; for the supply of food that was stored up for it in the seed is now exhausted, and it has to seek food for itself in the soil and air. It has not yet strength to do so, and therefore fades and becomes sickly. It falls off, just as a human child falls off when weaned. "The fruit of last year's harvest is becoming the root of this year's; but the agony of dying must be gone through." So is it in conversion: so long as we are satisfied with the traditional faith which we inherited from our fathers—so long as the mere form of godliness, without any experience of its power, suffices us, we are serene and undisturbed—life is fair and pleasant. But when the Spirit convinces us of sin and righteousness, and we begin to inquire and take root for ourselves—when we are weaned from our former carnal associations, and made to thrust out the radicles of our being into new and untried soil—then we sicken for a while. We are like the disciples during the transition period between the Ascension and Pentecost,—we mourn that we shall know Christ after the flesh no more, that the mere outward Christ, found in ordinances and in a decent profession of religion, is gone from us, and cannot yet rejoice in the possession of a Saviour formed in us by the Spirit the hope of glory.

But it is only thus that we can come into real vital union with Him who gave Himself for us, and enter into the fellowship of His sufferings. We are companions, thus, like St. John, in tribulation and in the kingdom and patience of Jesus Christ; and there is no companionship like that.   It is not in hours of prosperity and ease that we know what is best and truest in our friends, that their love comes out in all its warmth and devotion. The light summer breeze of joy ruffles the surface of the stream, but stirs not the still depths and silent currents below. But the volcano of suffering agitates the whole mass from the bottom to the surface. Those who have listened together to the beating of their own hearts in the awful hush and loneliness of bereavement; those who have been baptized in the same cloud and sea, who have done stern battle side by side with the same foes, and received the same wounds, they unveil what is truest and deepest in each other's nature. And a companionship founded upon or strengthened by this discovery and experience, can always enter into finer feelings and withstand ruder shocks than any other. And this is the union, this is the fellowship into which we enter with Jesus, when through our own sorrow for sin, and our own suffering through self-sacrifice, His nature and His work are unveiled to us, and we know the secret of His heart of love. Our pain brings us into conformity with His likeness. Our sorrow illuminates with a more vivid light the characters of His ineffable love traced upon our souls. And the union thus formed and welded through a fellowship of Christ's self-sacrifice,—which is an unknown experience to the mere professor who lightly names the name of Jesus, who has never sorrowed for sin, who indulges self and conforms to the world in all things,—is as lasting as it is vital. Out of it is nurtured a deep tender love and confidence, such as grow not on any other soil. And the last page of the Book of Life reveals to us this picture of it in its fullest consummation,—" These are they which came out of great tribulation, and have washed their robes and made them white in the blood of the Lamb. *Therefore* are they before the throne of God, and serve Him day and night in His temple; and He that sitteth upon the throne shall dwell among them. They shall hunger no more, neither thirst any more, neither shall the sun light on them nor any heat. For the Lamb which is in the midst of the throne shall feed them and lead them unto living fountains of waters ; and God shall wipe away all tears from their eyes."

And finally, may not the mode in which the stock and graft, when mutually united, are retained in their position by means of bandages, and protected from the air and rain by means of clay or wax, until an incorporating union has taken place, represent the ministration of human ordinances, by which believers are added to the Lord, confirmed in the faith and rooted in the love of Jesus. Weak, and apparently inadequate, like the clay with which Jesus opened the eyes of the man born blind, as these means of grace may be, the Holy Spirit blesses and uses them to enlighten the understandings of God's people, to confirm their good resolutions, and to preserve them from temptation. They never in this world outgrow their need of them. It is in waiting upon the Lord, in the use of His ordinances, that they renew their strength. Not till the cloudless sunshine of the everlasting spring shines upon them, shall these ligatures of ordinances and that clay of human ministrations be removed, and the growth of paradise shall be as the growth of Eden,—free, spontaneous, natural and altogether perfect.

CHAPTER IV.

THE FRUIT.

"Ye have not chosen me, but I have chosen you, and ordained you, that ye should go and bring forth fruit, and that your fruit should remain."—JOHN xv. 16.

SINCE Newton analysed the solar beam, we have made marvellous progress in our knowledge of the nature of physical light. We know of no less than four additional colours in the spectrum which were unknown to him; we produce photographs by a power in the sunbeam called the chemical or actinic power, of which he was ignorant; we investigate the nature of the substances which compose the remotest stars, by means of dark lines—the *runes* of the stars—crossing even the most brilliant parts of the spectrum, whose existence was hid from him; and we penetrate into the secret, inner structure of transparent bodies, by the aid of that peculiar condition of light called polarization, of which he had not the most remote idea. Has not our knowledge of that Divine light which streams to us from the sun of God's Word—of

the spectrum which the True Light, white and undivided, forms when refracted through the prism of a
written revelation—advanced in an equally surprising
degree during the same period? The wonderful
discovery of Tischendorf's manuscripts—the New
Testament, in its completest and most accurate form,
coming to us, strange to say, from Mount Sinai—is
like the addition of several luminous hues to the
spectrum of the sacred text; the refinements of
modern Biblical criticism are like polarized rays, that
show us meanings and applications in the most transparent truths, formerly unsuspected; while the various
sciences, though they seem like dark lines crossing
and intercepting the light of Scripture, have, nevertheless, revealed to us something of the nature of its
profoundest and farthest-reaching thoughts. The
darkness of many of the old prophecies has been
dispelled by the explorations of Nineveh, Egypt, and
Palestine; and the immensely-magnifying lens of
human history has every year been bringing out into
larger and clearer outline the records in the sacred
narrative of the common experiences of mankind.
Along with these aids and improved methods of study,
are there not greater Christian earnestness, more
candour and freedom from prejudice, and more spiritual
insight and subjectivity of mind, at the present day
than at any former period; all combining to make the
letter and the spirit of God's Word more thoroughly
understood.

On the other hand, it is objected by some that the

tendency of bringing the resources of human knowledge to a focus in the interpretation of Scripture, even when it is done in a reverent way, is to force more gospel upon the gospel than its Divine Author has placed there; and to make the truth, as it were, truer than itself.   Like the Egyptian boy, gazing into the ink enclosed within his palm, the mind itself is apt to turn painter, and dream that the secret lies in the passage it broods over.   Such a tendency, no doubt, does exist, and it has to be guarded against.   But we must ever remember that Scripture is the Word of Him who is *The Truth*, in whom are hid all the treasures of wisdom and knowledge, and that therefore it is justifiable to bring out of it, by all the helps of modern research, harmonious meanings, which, though they do not lie on the surface, are yet consistent with the analogy of faith, and are the vivid outgrowth of true, Biblical ideas. For instance, in explaining the allegory of the Vine, modern science enables us to trace analogies between the plant and Christian life which were altogether unknown in less scientific times, and can only be eliminated by those who have made a special study of this department of knowledge.   These analogies give a deeper and wider meaning to our Lord's words; and who shall say that He, "without whom was not anything made that was made," did not intend that they should be suggested to our minds by His figurative language?   Are we not at liberty to regard His allegory as a generalization of many latent spiritual ideas connected with the vine, which He left ourselves to find out. When He said, "Consider the lilies how they grow, they toil not, neither do they spin; and yet I say unto you that Solomon in all his glory was not arrayed like one of these;" the ordinary reader, who knows nothing of science, sees in the words only an allusion to the brilliant beauty and elegance of the whole flower. But the botanist sees a deeper meaning in the image. He knows that the calyx or outer clothing of the corolla, which in other plants is green, leaf-shaped, and inconspicuous behind the blossom, is in the lily tribe as brightly coloured, and of the same shape and texture as the petals themselves. Flowers with such petaloid calices are technically called "naked;" but in reality, so far from being left naked, the lily is arrayed in an external robe which rivals in beauty of tint and texture the inner floral organs. And may we not believe that He who made the lily had this peculiar feature of its structure before His eye, when he said—" If God *so clothe* the grass of the field," and meant the student of nature to find it out; while at the same time the general allusion is sufficiently obvious and expressive to the simple reader, who is ignorant of the particular fact.

Being the expression of the Divine mind, Scripture truth must have in it a depth and fulness of meaning which the human intellect can never exhaust. We cannot expect too much from it, or take too much out of it, in the line of its own laws of spiritual interpretation. Our Saviour Himself found rich meanings lying under words and figures, in which the Scribes, who made a special study of the Old Testament, saw nothing. He showed that the doctrine of the resurrection was contained in the formula, "I am the God of Abraham, and the God of Isaac, and the God of Jacob." St. Matthew and St. Paul had a key to the interpretation of the older Scriptures, which seems mystical even to us. St. Paul, for instance, reveals to us the spiritual significance hid in incidents so purely domestic and biographical as the relations of Hagar to Sarah. He says of these incidents, "which things are an allegory"—Hagar is Sinai, and represents the covenant of works; Sarah is Jerusalem, and represents the covenant of grace. And if we have some of their spirit, we too shall discover in Scripture treasures new and rich, previously unsuspected. Star-rays from the central truth of the heavens, travelling to men's sight in various epochs, will for the first time break upon our astonished eye. Vast truths lying faint and nebulous on the confines of human vision, will be resolved and realised. In the parables of Christ we shall find concentrated the wisdom of the earth and the sky, and the mysteries hid in rocks, woods, and seas,—all the ultimate results of science and philosophy. The truth that, like the sun, is seen even by a child in its own light, will to us, like the sunbeam to the philosopher, be full of new and strange wonders. God's Word will be, not like mere human knowledge that lies only in the sense and memory, but like a seed growing in the soil of our hearts, the *emphutos logos*, the *ingrowing word*, entering into the very essence of our spiritual constitution, and growing in expansiveness and richness of significance with our own growth in wisdom and knowledge.

These remarks ought, I think, to be sufficient to justify a method of interpreting our Lord's allegory which has been regarded with suspicion by some, because it has often been disfigured by unlicensed fancies. In this chapter I shall apply it, in the endeavour to get at the interior spiritual thoughts, of which the figure of the text is the outward vehicle. Having already considered the vital relation that exists between Christ and His disciples under the symbol of the branches in the vine, I shall now proceed to consider the purpose or object of this union. "I have chosen and ordained you that ye should go and *bring forth fruit.*" Fruitfulness is the great end of God's ordinances in the vegetable kingdom. The whole mass of the earth, from pole to pole, and from centre to circumference, has been weighed in the balance and exquisitely adjusted to enable the snowdrop to hang its head, and allow the pollen of the shorter stamens to fall upon the longer stigma. In order to produce fruitfulness, the dimensions of the solar system, the axial rotation of the earth, and the changes of the seasons have all been adapted. For this, the laws of the inorganic world have been made to agree in every point with those of the organic world. For this, storm and calm, sunshine and cloud, dew and rain, day and night, seed · time and harvest, cold and heat, summer and winter, succeed each other. For this, all the processes of vegetable life are busy from the sprouting germ of spring to the sere and yellow leaf of autumn. Fruitfulness is the focus into which all the various secondary purposes of nature are concentrated, the *end* towards which all her energies are bent. We see the force of this tendency strikingly displayed in the case of plants that are placed in unfavourable circumstances. The weed growing by the dry, hot wayside, often trampled under foot of man, as if conscious of impending danger, will begin to put forth blossom and fruit when scarcely an inch high, although in other circumstances it will grow to a considerable height before doing so. The fruit tree that is injured, or that is about to die of old age, hastens to develop a richer show of blossom and fruit than usual, so that while the individual perishes, the type may be preserved. On the summits of lofty mountains, exposed to the scorching sun by day and to blighting frost by night, and having only two or three months of growing weather in the year, alpine plants concentrate their entire vital energy in the production of flower and fruit. They cease to put forth leaves, which are therefore small and stunted, in remarkable contrast to the large size and brilliant hue of blossoms; and until they have accomplished their purpose of producing fruit, they will keep their hold on life with a tenacity almost invincible, growing and propagating themselves year by year by means of annual shoots. We thus see how essential in the economy of vegetation is the development of fruitfulness; plants preparing for it from the first moment of existence, and all things in nature working together to bring it about.   And is it not so in the kingdom of grace?   For the fruitfulness of those who love God, and are the called according to His purpose, the whole material system of the earth is upheld; for we are told that when the spiritual harvest is ready, the earth and all the works that are therein shall be burned up.   Fruitfulness is the consummation of all that God has done in creation, in human history, and in the work of redemption.   All sacraments and ordinances, all providences and dispensations of goodness or of severity, are working together, like the seasons of the year and the influences of nature in ripening the natural harvest, in promoting the one great end of general and individual fruitfulness.   In short, the whole spiritual world exists and revolves on its axis, that the harvest of spiritual life may be produced in the Church and in the believer.

But while fruitfulness is thus the great end of vegetable life, there are some plants in which this quality is of more importance than in others.   It is necessary that every plant should bring forth fruit in order to propagate itself; but besides their own specific propagation, some plants have been singled out to confer benefits upon the rest of creation by means of their fruit.   The vine is one of the most conspicuous of the plants so honoured. Like the cow in the animal world, which produces more milk than its progeny needs, and the bee which stores a larger quantity of honey than it requires for its own consumption, the vine produces a fruit whose exceptional excess of nourishment is intended for the use of man;

so that a land flowing with wine, milk and honey, is a striking example of the wise forethought of Divine benevolence, accomplishing a particular and a general purpose by the same simple agency. Fruit is not so important to the vine itself as it is to man. The vine could be propagated artificially, in the same way in which some other plants propagate themselves naturally, independently of flowers and seeds. The lily of the valley, and the strawberry, can propagate themselves by means of runners, so that flowering is quite of secondary importance, so far as their own economy is concerned. And, therefore, when the one produces its fragrant snow-white blossom, and the other its delicious crimson fruit, we see in the superfluous growth of a seed-producing apparatus, a beautiful proof that God has other purposes to serve than those which concern the plants themselves—that He has a regard to the wants of man. In the same way, the vine could be propagated by slips or cuttings, without any need for it to produce grapes. Its fruit is thus not for its own diffusion, but for human necessities. For the sake of that fruit alone it is cultivated. We grow some plants in order to produce seed by means of which their own individual beauties may be perpetuated; but we can perpetuate the vine in other ways, and, therefore, we grow it solely for the sake of the fruit, that is not needed in the economy of the plant itself, but is needed to supply man's wants.

Apart from its fruit, the vine is, indeed, a beautiful plant; its foliage is luxuriant, its tendrils graceful; it diffuses an agreeable perfume, it adorns the landscape, and affords a tender green shade from the heat of the sun. But all these uses are subordinate to the one great purpose of producing grapes. Other plants have these qualities, and are cultivated for the sake of them. But the vine is cultivated exclusively for the sake of its fruit; and did it cease to produce fruit, no other quality, however excellent, would compensate for the loss. It would be condemned as a failure. The worthlessness of the tree apart from its fruit, is graphically indicated in these words of Ezekiel,—"Son of man, what is the vine tree more than any tree, or than a branch which is among the trees of the forest? Shall wood be taken thereof to do any work? or will men take a pin of it to hang any vessel thereon? Is it meet for any work?" Now so is it with the True Vine. It was for the sake of the fruit of salvation—the redemption of a fallen world—that God cultivated His own Son by the sufferings which He endured; and the rich produce formed an ample recompense for the toil and sorrow. And as with the Vine Himself, so with the branches. The Husbandman of souls grafts these branches in the Vine for the special purpose of producing spiritual fruit; and if this result does not follow, no mere natural beauty or grace will compensate. What does it matter that the branches put forth the clustering leaves and fair blossoms of mere social virtue, if, year after year, as the vintage season returns, the Lord of the vineyard comes, and finds upon it no fruit? Surely no surface excellences, no polished amiabilities or refinements, will save it from condemnation as a failure.

"I have chosen you, and ordained you, that ye should go and bring forth fruit." Jesus does not say, that He simply wishes His disciples to bring forth fruit—that this is one among the many purposes which He cherishes for them; but He speaks as if in the bringing forth of fruit was summed up all that He desired of them—all possible duty and privilege—was realised the highest ideal of the Christian life. God's glory is the chief end of man; but, says Jesus, "Herein is my Father glorified that ye bear much fruit." God requires of us to believe in Christ; but faith is the root of fruitfulness, the beginning of that Divine life of which fruitfulness is the end. Faith and fruit are not two things, distinct from each other, and capable of being set over against each other; but, on the contrary, the same thing at different periods of its existence; just as the fruit of autumn is the seed of spring, and *vice versa.* God's will is our sanctification; but the fruit of the Christian is unto holiness. He desires our highest happiness; but our highest happiness is indissolubly linked together with our fruitfulness. No man can have a continual feast of gladness who is barren and unfruitful; nor can he be a stranger to true happiness who is fulfilling the great end of his existence, and bringing forth the fruit of a holy and useful life. The fruitfulness of His people is thus the universal and all-inclusive desire of God. He has chosen us from the wild waste of nature, ordained us in the cultivated vineyard, and suited the communications of His grace, and the dispensations of His providence, to our individual necessities, in order that we might bring forth fruit.

And here we come to the great outstanding question, What is the real significance of fruit? Every physiologist knows that the fruit of a plant is simply an arrested and metamorphosed branch. This is proved by the fact that all the parts of the flower—viz., the calyx, the corolla, and the pistil, will readily change into normal leaves, and the peduncle into a normal branch; and also by the gradual transition of leaves proper into floral parts. In very wet or warm springs some of the flower-buds of the pear and apple are occasionally forced into active vegetative growth, so as to completely break up the flower, and change it into an ordinary leafy branch. It is also by no means uncommon to see a green branch, covered with leaves, growing out of the heart of a fully-expanded crimson rose, or from the summit of a large and perfectly-formed pear, or from a ripe strawberry, or from the apex of the cone of the larch. And what is an occasional phenomenon, and therefore called a monstrosity, in these plants, is the normal mode of growth in other plants, as, for instance, in the pine apple, from whose golden fruit springs up a beautiful tufted crown of green leaves; and in several of the Australian myrtles, which exhibit this striking onward growth. All those cases in which the terminal bud goes on to grow, even through the flower and fruit, clearly prove that the flower or fruit which, according to the normal method, arrests all further development of the axis that bears it, is a mere metamorphosed branch.

The bud of a plant which, under the ordinary laws of vegetation, would have elongated into a leafy branch, remains, in a special case, shortened, and develops finally, according to some regular law, blossom and fruit instead. Its further growth is thus stayed; it has attained the end of its existence; its life terminates with the ripe fruit that drops off to the ground. Whereas the bud that does not produce a flower or fruit grows into a branch, lives for years, and may ultimately attain almost the dimensions of the main trunk itself, clothed with half the foliage of the tree. In producing blossom and fruit, therefore, a branch sacrifices itself, yields up its own individual vegetative life for the sake of another life that is to spring from it, and to perpetuate the species. Every annual plant dies when it has produced blossom and fruit; every individual branch in a tree which corresponds with an annual plant also dies when it has blossomed and fruited.*

* This law applies not only to the individual part, but also to the whole tree. Fruit trees are the most short-lived of all trees ; and cultivated fruit trees are less vigorous in growth, and do not last so long as the wild varieties. Producing larger and more abundant fruit, than is natural, they necessarily so much the more exhaust their vital energies, so that their bark and wood will be less perfectly developed, and less thoroughly matured than is requisite for their full vigour and permanency as trees. In proportion to the largeness, the juiciness, the abundance, and the usefulness to man of the fruit which they yield, so in proportion is the term of life of trees abbreviated. All the plants which minister to man's food or luxury in a civilized state, from the corn to the apple and plum tree, are exceedingly short-lived ; and thus the natural law which ordains that rapid or excessive reproductive expenditure shortens life, is correlated with the spiritual

Delay in flowering prolongs life. By nipping off the flowers as soon as they appear, the duration of some plants may be greatly extended; by converting single blossoms into double, and thus preventing their seeding, annuals may even become perennials; and the great American aloe, which on the table-lands of Mexico comes into bloom and dies in five years, in this country, owing to unfavourable climatic conditions, lingers so long in a barren state that it is proverbially said to blossom once in a hundred years. It is interesting to notice the strange effect of this mighty effort to flower in the aloe. It appears to exhaust all its energies, so that the huge fleshy leaves, which before stood firm and erect, gradually shrink, shrivel, and droop, as the process of inflorescence advances, and the plant becomes a mere ghost of its former self. So, too, the Talipot Palm, which lives to a great age, and attains a lofty stature, flowers only once, but it bears an enormous quantity of blossoms, succeeded by a crop of nuts sufficient to supply a large district with seed, while the tree immediately perishes from the exhaustion of over-production. On these grounds, then, we may regard the flower and fruit of a plant as the most striking and beautiful natural illustration of the law of self-sacrifice.

When the Spaniards first landed in America, they

law of man's economy, which ordains that in the sweat of his brow he shall eat bread—that he shall always have to expend care and labour upon the growth of his food—and by the operation of which he rises in intelligence and morality.

were greatly astonished at the strange new aspects which nature presented. Among the constellations of the nocturnal sky they noticed a group of stars conspicuous above all the rest by its brilliancy, to which, from its cruciform arrangement, they gave the name of the "Southern Cross." Among the plants of the woods was a kind of calabash tree called the Jicara, worshipped by the Indians, whose leaves grew in fours, forming always a perfect cross. And more wonderful still, they observed a kind of vine climbing up the trees and adorning them with its luxuriant foliage. Its flower was a beautiful coronal of brilliant rays, bearing in the centre organs shaped like a cross. To this plant they gave the name of the Passion flower. Everywhere their superstitious eyes detected the sign of the cross; the whole continent seemed to be marked with it: and they called one part of the land, where all these types of nature reminded them of their religion, Vera Cruz, the True Cross. Every spot of earth whose wonders are first discovered by the eye that Jesus has opened and endowed with heavenly vision, and by the heart that Jesus has touched and gifted with spiritual insight, is a Vera Cruz. Every blossom is a Passion flower. The sign of the cross, which superstitious eyes saw in one mystical flower, the enlightened eye sees in every blossom that opens to the summer sun. One large order of plants is called Cruciferæ, from the cruciform arrangement of the corolla; but all plants, whatever may be the number and shape of their petals, are Cruciferæ. The great spiritual principle which every blossom shadows forth is—self-sacrifice.   The plant produces a flower, and consequently a fruit, for the purpose of imparting life—yea, more abundant life—and in the production of the flower and fruit it dies.   It gives its own life for another's—one life for the sake of countless lives that are to spring from it in long succession, generation after generation.   And is it not most instructive to notice that it is in this self-sacrifice of the plant that all its beauty comes out and culminates? The blossom and the fruit in which it gives its own life for another, are the loveliest of all its parts.   God has crowned this self-denial and blessing of others with all the glory of colour and the grace of form, the sweetness of perfume, and the richness of flavour.

And is it not so in the kingdom of grace? Christian fruit is an arrestment and transformation of the branch in the True Vine.   Instead of growing for its own ends, it produces the blossoms of holiness and the fruits of righteousness for the glory of God and the good of men.   The life of selfishness, self-righteousness, and self-seeking, is cut short and changed into the life of self-denial.   The believer who is united to Christ considers the time past of his life sufficient to have wrought the will of the flesh, and henceforth lives no more unto himself, but unto Him that died for him and that rose again.   The Christian life begins in self-sacrifice : " If any man will come after me, let him deny himself."   We can bring forth no fruit that is pleasing to God until, besought by His mercies, we yield ourselves a living sacrifice to Him.   We are barren and unprofitable so long as we live for ourselves. Just as there could be no fruit on the tree, if each branch were to develop its own vegetative life to the fullest extent—to run to selfish wood and luxuriant foliage; so there can be no spiritual fruit if self-love be our highest affection, and self-seeking our loftiest aim. Fruit, in the natural and spiritual worlds, originates from self-sacrifice. This is the arrestment of the natural bud, the metamorphosis of the self-pleasing branch—the passage, as in the case of St. Paul, through an ideal death, through the martyr-dom of will and deed, to nobler action, to a heavenly life even on earth. And in this self-sacrifice all the beauty of the Christian life comes out and culminates. The life that lives for another, in so doing bursts into flower, and shows its brightest hues, and yields its sweetest fragrance. As the common coarse green leaf changes into the delicately formed and brilliantly coloured petal in the conversion of leaf buds into flower buds; * so in

---

* This exaltation of the leaf in the process of producing seed, is very remarkably seen in a species of Dalechampia growing in Brazil. The blossom of this plant is formed of two leaves placed base to base, differing in no respect from the ordinary green leaves, except that they are smaller in size, and of a bright rose-colour. The shape and venation are precisely the same in both. When the fruit is formed the rose-colour vanishes, and the two leaves become green like the common ones. The same thing takes place in one of our own Alpine plants, the *Cornus Suecica;* the calyx, which is of a brilliant white colour, more beautiful than the corolla, in the early stage of the blossom, changing to a green hue when the fruit is formed. In these plants, brilliantly coloured to serve a temporary purpose, we have beautiful natural analogies—of those who are lifted above themselves, and transformed by some noble purpose or action; of prophets inspired by the Holy Ghost; of

the conversion of lovers of pleasure into lovers of God —the common things of life, the gifts and attainments of the natural man, are taken up into a higher experience, and beautified and ennobled. Nothing is lost in the transference, but all is changed and enriched. All is given to Christ, and all is received back an hundredfold. Solomon in all his glory is not arrayed like one of those human blossoms on the tree of life, that can say, "I am not my own, but bought with a price, and therefore bound to glorify God in my body and my spirit, which are His." Every spot on which the disciple talks with Jesus of His decease, and is bound by the cords of love to the same altar, is verily a mount of transfiguration. There the glory of the inner life bursts through, and irradiates even the outer garment. The face of Moses, when he descended from the mount, shone with a supernatural splendour, because he yielded himself up for the good of Israel. The face of Stephen became like an angel's when he gave up his life, a witness for Christ, and, in imitation of his Master's wondrous self-forgetfulness, prayed for his murderers : "Lord, lay not this sin to their charge." And have not many an unknown man and woman been similarly transfigured when becoming one with Christ's Spirit, in sublime self-abnegation? Have we not seen the glory of self-sacrifice ennobling even the aspect of the countenance, the expression of the eye, the carriage of

apostles endowed with miraculous powers; of saints sacrificing themselves for principle; of common men and women devoting themselves on the altar of duty or affection.

the form, making the plainest and homeliest face beautiful and heroic? Who has not beheld, with a feeling almost of awe, some lowly root out of a dry ground suddenly blossoming into a miracle of beauty, as he entered into the cloud with his Lord, and was baptised with His baptism. The pains of martyrs, the losses of self-sacrificing devotion, are indeed the blossoms of life—"the culminating points at which humanity has displayed its true glory, and reached its highest level." In the sacrifice of self-will in its bud and root to God, a glory and a bliss are opened up of which the selfish worldling is utterly ignorant and destitute. We "prove what is that good, and acceptable, and perfect will of God."

> " For who gives, giving, doth win back his gift ;
>   And knowledge, by division, grows to more ;
>   Who hides the Master's talent shall die poor,
> And starve at last of his own thankless thrift.
>
> I did this for another; and, behold,
>   My work hath blood in it ! but thine hath none ;
>   Done for thyself, it dies in being done ;
> To what thou buyest thou thyself art sold.
>
> Give thyself utterly away.   Be lost.
>   Choose some one—something ; not thyself, thine own ;
>   Thou can'st not perish, but, thrice greater grown,—
> Thy gain the greatest where thy loss was most.
>
> Thou in another shalt thyself new-find.
>   The single globule, lost in the wide sea,
>   Becomes an ocean.   Each identity
> Is greatest in the greatness of its kind.

> Who serves for gain, a slave, by thankless pelf
> Is paid ; who gives himself, is priceless, free.
> I give myself, a man, to God : lo, He
> Renders me back a saint unto myself."

It is worthy of remark that it is *fruit* and not *works* that the believer produces by his crucifixion with Christ. *Work* and *fruit* are contrasted in a very striking manner at the close of the fifth chapter of Galatians. "Now, the *works* of the flesh are manifest, which are these,—adultery, fornication, idolatry, hatred, and such like." "But the *fruit* of the spirit is love, joy, peace," &c. This contrast is very instructive. Works bear upon them the curse of Adam. They are the produce of a blighted and ruined world, filled with thorns and thistles ; the result of toil, and pain, and sorrow. They are wrought in the sweat of the brow and in the sweat of the soul. They give evidence of the grievous bondage under which man has come by reason of sin. There is no spontaneity, no free, glad effusion of the heart in them. Those who do the works of the flesh have no real pleasure in them. They are driven to do them by lust, by the force of circumstances, by the temptation of the devil. All that a natural man does comes under the category of *works*. And even in the case of believers, some things which they do are works, because they are the result of a legal and servile spirit. They are done perfunctorily, in obedience to rules and laws, from selfish and unworthy motives, through fear, or in order to satisfy a self-righteous and complacent conscience. Such works are only parts of one's nature. The works of a manufacturer, for instance, display his skill and power, but they do not reveal anything of his character. You cannot tell what kind of a man he is who makes your furniture or your clothing from his productions alone. You may be able to say that he is a clever workman, but not that he is a wise, a good, or an upright man. The man and his works are separate and distinct. He throws into them only a part of himself. They have no necessary relation to his highest and deepest life. But *fruit*, on the other hand, is the spontaneous natural manifestation of the life within. The soul that has the life and the love of Christ in it cannot help producing fruit. It does so, not by an outward arbitrary law, but by the inward necessary law of life and growth. Fruit is the free unrestrained outpouring of a heart at peace with God, filled with the love of Christ, and stimulated by the presence and power of the Holy Spirit. The curse is removed from it. It brings back the pure and innocent conditions of Eden. The whole man is displayed in it, as the whole life of the tree is gathered into and manifested in its fruit. By their fruit we know believers as well as trees. Our fellow-creatures can only judge what we *are* by what we *do;* but in the eye of our Master what we *do* is of no importance except as it flows from what we *are.* "Not because I desire a gift, but I desire fruit that may abound to your account."

It is fruit that Christ wants, not works. It is the free-will offering of a heart of love, not the constrained service of fear or of law. The whole relation of Christ's disciples to Him is one of perfect liberty. No one does his duty because he must, but because his heart is in it. The service of Christ may seem to some who look on as strangers very hard and uninteresting. But to those who are not strangers to the love of Christ, whose heart is in the service which He requires, it has endless attractions. They feel quickened by His sap, constrained by His love ; His life is in them, and therefore fruit is produced, and not works done.

It is fruit, too, that Jesus wants, and not works, because He studies the individual character, and regulates His discipline according to individual requirements. If works were what He desired, He could order Christians in the mass to do them, caring nothing for any one of them in particular. It would be enough for Him if certain duties were performed, a certain amount of work done, no matter what might be the effect upon the doers. But, in order to produce fruit, His sap must flow to, His personal influence must reach, the smallest twig, the humblest individual that yields it. He must study each believer separately, work upon his inclinations, draw him by His personal favour, know him by name, and lead him out. If a gardener wants to cultivate fruit, he must study the nature of each tree, each branch, and adapt to it the most suitable kind of treatment. If a shepherd wants his sheep to *follow* him, he must know them individually.

On the other hand, if he wants to *drive* them before him, there is no need to know them particularly; there is no need of getting any of them under a power of confidence and attraction. Works can be done by bodies of believers, by churches, in obedience to general laws, and without any regard to individual peculiarities and necessities; fruit can only be produced by individual believers under the special treatment of the great Husbandman of souls, and by the quickening influences of personal communion and fellowship with the life of Christ.

How significant in the light of this idea is the reward promised to the Church of Smyrna, "Be thou faithful unto death, and I will give thee *a crown of life.*" It is not an arbitrary reward from without that God gives to His people, but the fruit of their own efforts, a living crown, the crown of their own life. The athlete in the Grecian games was crowned with the laurel chaplet which had no relation to the nature of the struggle in which he had been engaged. The workman is paid wages which have no correspondence with the labour which he has expended—the waste of tissue and the consumption of life; but God's wages and rewards are the fruits of what we ourselves have sown, and cultivated, and tended. We have the richness of our own experience, the strength of our own convictions, the blessedness of our own purity, spirituality, and elevation —we emphatically live. It is with us, to change the metaphor, as it is with some mountains whose deepest or primary formations appear on the summit—which are not mere masses laid in dead weight upon the surface of the earth, but the protrusion of their own energies—organized parts of themselves. For instance, the summit of Goatfell, the highest peak in the island of Arran, is composed of the same granite which forms its base, and which has been erupted through intermediate rocks of a different kind. So we are crowned with the deepest and most essential part of our own life. Our highest summit is our deepest foundation. Our crown of life is that which we ourselves have formed, and which passes through our whole being. How different is this from the notion of those who *exteriorate* religion, who care only for the loaves and fishes of the gospel here, and only for what they believe to be the external arbitrary rewards of the paradise above! Heaven is the fruit of what we have sown, the living crown of the life that we have lived, the summit of the mountain whose base and whose whole inner nature are formed of the same material. " Blessed is the man that endureth temptation : for when he is tried he shall receive the crown of life, which the Lord hath promised to them that love Him."

Further, it is *fruit*, and not fruits, which the branch in the True Vine produces. " The *fruit* of the Spirit, is love, joy, peace, long-suffering, gentleness, goodness, faith, meekness, temperance." The original Greek word is singular, not plural. The fruit of the Spirit is not so many apples or pomegranates, growing on separate twigs, and having no organic connection with each other, except as produced by the same tree. It is a cluster of dates* or a bunch of grapes, all growing from one stalk and united to each other in the closest manner. The fruit repeats in miniature the plan of the whole structure of the plant. Just as the vine and the branches constitute a corporate unity, made up of many individuals—so each cluster of grapes which the branches bear, constitutes a corporate unity of fruits made up of many individuals. Each grace is, as it were, a separate berry, connected with the others by organic ties, and forming together one most lovely and complete cluster. There is a perfect correlation between them—if one is present all are there; for the believer receives out of Christ's fulness, and grace corresponding to grace in Him—a picture or reflection in us of each grace in Him. It should be the Christian's endeavour, therefore, that the whole cluster should appear—each grape full formed and in due proportion to the rest. The Father is the Husbandman, and He is glorified if we bear *much* fruit; if we produce the whole cluster of righteousness. There is not a lovelier sight in nature than a full and perfectly-formed bunch of grapes. The

---

* The tendency to branch which is suppressed in the trunk of the palm, breaks out in the blossom and fruit ; for the dates are borne on structures as richly ramified as those on which grapes are produced. In its inflorescence, the palm would seem to make an effort to become assimilated to the higher exogenous structure ; and, as if the whole plant were elevated in the process, the very trunk itself sends out subterranean branches from the root when the fruit becomes mature. It would thus appear to be true, that there does not exist, perhaps, one plant which, throughout the whole course of its development, is but a single, simple individual, uncomplicated by subordinate branches.

light and shade, the form and colour, the symmetry and harmony of the whole, afford matter for unwearied admiration. And so, there is not a lovelier sight in the spiritual world than a well-developed cluster of the fruit of the Spirit, in which each berry is present, and each reflects harmony and beauty upon all the rest.

Further still, it is *heavenly*, and ·not *earthly* fruit that the Husbandman demands. The fruits of Egypt were melons and cucumbers, grown close to the earth, over a heap of decomposing substances; while the most characteristic of its edible vegetables were leeks, onions, and garlic, which are not fruits at all, but roots. For these fruits and roots of the earth the Israelites longed in the wilderness, when their hearts turned back to the house of bondage. It is such low earth-born fruits that the natural man produces, and for which alone he has a relish; fruit that grows upon this earth, and has respect only to this earth. All his tendencies and labours are earthward; all his affections, hopes, and aims, twine round the earth and the decaying things thereof. The cucumber and the melon are climbing plants by nature; they have tendrils to raise them up among the trees, but they are cultivated on the ground, and, therefore, their tendrils run along the soil wasted and useless. So, every man has tendrils of hopes and aspirations that were meant to raise him above the world, but he perverts them from their proper purpose, and they run among earthly things utterly wasted. He loses all hold of the heavenly, unearthly side of religion. He is content with the world as he finds it. He has no longings to be purer, truer, more spiritual. The outer life is more to him than the inner. Satan has bound him with a spirit of infirmity. The Greek name for man is *anthropos*, the upward-looking; his erect countenance being the sign impressed upon his outward frame of his noble destiny, of a heavenly hope. What uprightness of purpose, then, does his upright carriage imply in the inner life of which it is the support and stay! But Satan deprives man of this attribute; and, by a heart and soul turned earthwards, wholly forgetful of his true home, and of his true good, which is not below him, but above him, assimilates him to the bent, downward aspect of the beasts that perish. Every downward course into mere animal pleasure is a reversal of the order of his nature.

In marked contrast with the earth-borne fruits of Egypt were the fruits of the Holy Land, called distinctively a land of vines and fig-trees and pomegranates —a land of olive oil and honey. It is not a level, but a mountainous country, a lofty plateau, on which everything is lifted above the world. The people went literally, as well as spiritually, *up* from Egypt to Palestine, *up* to God's house. Its fruits were grown on trees, raised up from the ground and ripening in the pure air and bright sunshine of heaven. The fruit of the natural vine, as I have elsewhere said, is produced on the same tendril which raises the plant above the earth, and assists it in its rapid and extensive climbing among the trees. The tendril divides into two parts. One part produces a bunch of grapes, and the other part, instead of developing inflorescence, becomes abortive, and is metamorphosed into a slender curling stem.*   And so it is in the

* The tendril of a plant is spiritually as significant as we have seen the branch to be. It is simply a prolongation of the stem beyond the last leaf, or a development of a leafless stem-summit. Now, the stem is an original independent structure, forming the axis upon which the leaves are arranged in ranks—the bridge from step to step of the graduated progress of the plant from seed to flower. It is the connecting organ by which all the processes of development in the plant are carried on from stage to stage, and have a vital continuity. The plant has a tendency to halt at each stage—to bring each story or formation of leaves to its own permanent and strictly-limited development. But the stem counteracts this tendency, pushes beyond this halting-point, secures a future development, and exhausts all the capabilities of the plant. Usually it terminates with the formation of flower and fruit—the aim and concluding structure of all the previous growth. But in the case of the tendril, it is continued beyond this stage ; it bears no leaf, or flower, or fruit ; even in the case of the vine, while one-half of it bears grapes, the other half is leafless and fruitless. It carries the ascending growth of the plant—its elevation above dead, inert matter, its internal impulse towards an increasingly purer, and more victorious representation of its true nature—to the highest possible point. And in all these respects, is it not an admirable natural symbol of that immortal hope which is the stem that runs through our whole being, as it were—which maintains the identity and spiritual vitality of all the stages of our life—which makes us restless and dissatisfied with every point of advancement, and pushes us forward to higher and fuller growth? In the case of some, indeed, it terminates with the flowers and fruit of this world's enjoyments and possessions. The immortal longing is quenched and ended in the riches, pleasures and honours of the life that now is. But in the case of the heavenly-minded Christian it becomes a tendril, rising above all the possessions and pleasures of life, failing to find its full fruition here, content to be poor and destitute of this world's good things, if only it can rise

spiritual Vine. The fruit of the Christian life is borne on the same tendril of faith that overcometh the world, and rises superior to all its circumstances. Believers are loosed from their infirmity; they are made straight, and glorify God; they are *risen* with Christ. The resurrection of Christ is a germinant principle out of which they derive a new and higher life. They are not merely elevated a little, shifted from a lower to a higher position in the same sphere; they are raised from the darkness of the tomb to the sunshine of the upper air; from being roots in the earth to being fruits in the sky. The fruit of righteousness is supernatural; is produced by the continuous exercise of the same power which raised up Jesus from the dead. The Christian seeks the things that are above, covets earnestly the best gifts. He is like one of those strange orchids or air-plants, which grow upon the boughs of

to heaven and lay hold of the things that are unseen and eternal there!

> "Gives the poor present, gains the boundless scope,
> And keeps him virgin for the further hope."

And there is this further analogy between the stem of the plant and the hope of the Christian, that just as the stem participates in the exaltation of the plant, its lower part being like the root-leaves, colourless and without breathing pores, its middle part being green and furnished with breathing pores, like the middle leaves, and its higher part that bears the blossom and fruit, coloured and refined like them, changed even into a fruit-like structure as in the strawberry; so the higher and more spiritual the life, the purer and more elevated does the hope become. It grows in beauty and grandeur as the Christian grows in grace, and when near the fruition of heaven, assumes the heavenly hue and form, and becomes transfigured into the likeness of its glorious object.

tropical trees, with their roots exposed to the warm, reeking air, and drawing their nourishment solely from it. With affections weaned from the earth, he grows freely in the air of heaven. He is quickened, raised up, and made to sit in heavenly places in Christ Jesus. The "things" above are not precisely the things of another world, but those of another sphere than the habitual order of our natural thoughts and affections. They are not the things above our heads, but those which are above our carnal instincts. They may be here below; and just as over every scene of earth, however homely and commonplace, bends down the ideal sky, so every deed of men should be idealized by having the beauty of heaven over it. We must remember that the earth itself is even now *among the stars*. Everything about us should partake of this upward tendency. Our conversation should be in heaven; it should keep a high tone, never degenerate into idle gossip or frivolous talk. Our friendships should be those that raise and refine the nature; the books that we read should be those which instruct rather than stimulate, edify rather than amuse; the Bible should be studied, not for the sake of its literary interest, but for the sake of the wisdom that maketh the soul wise unto salvation; the business of life should be chosen and pursued, not because of the wealth that it brings, but on account of higher considerations of usefulness and moral discipline; solitary thought instead of gravitating to the earth, and lying among the pots of its sordid passions and paltry ambitions, should soar aloft into the purer regions of faith and love, with wings covered with silver and feathers with yellow gold. The heart, it has been well said, determines the gravitation of moral beings; and He who possesses for the Christian heart a supreme and irresistible attraction is in heaven. And, therefore, an active personal love for our Lord Jesus Christ makes seeking the things that are above a constant reality in the life of the soul; makes the production of heavenly fruit a natural and spontaneous growth.*

* We long to get rid of the attraction of the earth—the burden of this carnal body which weighs us down—this law in our members warring against the law of our minds, and bringing us into captivity to the law of sin and death. But the gravity of sin while we are in the body is universal, and will continue to the end to modify the forms of our Christian life in spite of all our resistance. We cannot do in the spiritual world what can be done in the natural. We can withdraw a liquid from the action of gravitation, that most universal of all powers, and leave it free to be acted upon by other forces which might tend to modify its form. Fat oils are less dense than water, and more dense than alcohol. We may make a mixture of water and alcohol having a density precisely equal to that of a given oil—say olive oil. "Now, if a certain quantity of this oil be introduced into the mixture thus formed, it is evident that the action of gravity upon the mass of oil will be completely annihilated, for in virtue of the equality of density, the oil will only hold the place of an equal mass of the ambient liquid. On the other hand, the fat oils do not mix with a liquid composed of alcohol and water; consequently the mass of oil must remain suspended and isolated in the midst of the surrounding liquid, and it will be perfectly free to take the exterior form which the forces that may act upon it will give it." In the spiritual world the conditions cannot be so balanced, as that we shall be withdrawn from the attraction of in-dwelling and all-prevailing sin, and left free to take the beautiful shape which the

The fruit of the Christian life is *permanent*—"that your fruit should remain." You have often noticed in the orchard in spring, when the blossoms have withered and fallen off, that a large proportion of these blossoms have left behind young fruits that have actually set. These fruits grow for a few weeks; they acquire shape; they become tinted with colour; they cheat the eye with the hope of a rich harvest of ripe and full-formed fruit in autumn. But, alas! ere long, they wither and fall off the parent twig; and only one here and there of the dozen, it may be, that once loaded each bough, remains to grow to maturity. Sometimes, the young fruit of the plum forms after the blossom falls off—continues to increase in size—until, at the end of a fortnight, it is as large as a full-formed walnut. Its colour is of a rich, ruddy yellow, so that it looks like a ripe apricot; but, like the fabled Dead Sea fruit, though tempting to the eye, when examined it is found to be hollow, containing air, and consisting only of a distended skin, insipid and tasteless. After a while a greenish mould is developed on the surface of the blighted fruit, then it becomes black and shrivelled, and at the end of a month the whole is rotten and decomposed. The flower appears about the beginning of June, and before the middle of July not a plum is to be seen on the tree. And is it not so with most—nay, with all the fruits which unsanctified man pro-

powers of the world to come are striving to give us. Only in heaven shall each human life be freely suspended in the midst of its circumstances, and take as it were the form of a perfect sphere.

duces? They are beautiful in blossom; they minister to his self-glorification and enjoyment; they delude him with fair promises; but they never come to maturity and abide. They are fleeting as they are fair; they are perishing as they are promising. There is ever a worm at the root of the fairest and strongest gourd that shelters mankind; so that it comes up in a night and perishes in a night. You laboriously rear some structure of happiness, and as you are putting upon it the cope-stone, it all at once collapses and falls to the ground, a melancholy ruin. You fill your cup at some slow-trickling rill of created good, drop by drop, and just as it is almost full, and you are about to raise it to your eager, parched lips, it is dashed from your hands, and its precious contents spilled hopelessly in the sand. You rear up a family; your wife is as a fruitful vine by the sides of your house, your children like olive plants round about your table; you go through all the trials and self-sacrifices connected with the up-bringing of children, and one after another dies or leaves you, as your cares are about over, and the period of fruition is nigh. You educate a son or a daughter; you spare no expense, you give up many comforts in order that the education may be perfect; and just as your hopes are about to be crowned, and you expect to reap the fruits of what you have sown, some fell disease comes and takes away the beautiful and costly life. You strive for years to make a business that shall yield you a competence, and make your closing days comfortable, and suddenly and unexpectedly some adverse stroke of fortune comes and sweeps away the savings of years. Alas ! it is so with all earthly hopes and expectations. They are fruits that *set*, but do not ripen. On every brow we see care planting his wrinkles—bare wintry branches whose stem is rooted in the heart, from which have fallen, one after another, the fairest fruits of life, and which, through future springs and summers, will bear no more leaves or fruit. " Then I looked," says the most prosperous man that ever lived, "on all the works that my hands had wrought, and on the labour that I laboured to do, and, behold, all was vanity and vexation of spirit, and there was no profit under the sun."

> " I stand amid the roar
> Of a surf-tormented shore ;
> And I hold within my hand
> Grains of the golden sand :
> How few ! yet how they creep
> Through my fingers to the deep,
> While I weep ! while I weep !
>
> Oh, God, can I not grasp
> Them with a tighter clasp ?
> Oh, God, can I not save
> One from the pitiless wave ?
> Is all that we see or seem
> But a dream within a dream ?"

But in contrast with all the passing and perishing fruits of earth—the result of that fatal act of eating the fruit of the forbidden tree, which has set the teeth of the human race on edge, and filled the world with lamentation, and mourning, and woe—we have the abiding fruits of righteousness. It is the glorious distinction of the fruit which Christ enables us to produce, that it endures : " I have chosen you, and ordained you, that ye should go and bring forth fruit, and that your fruit should *remain.*" How wonderfully, in the most literal manner, were these words fulfilled in the case of the disciples themselves ! Of all the works of all the men who were living eighteen hundred years ago, what is remaining now ? Here and there a name, and here and there a ruin. But twelve poor uneducated peasants went forth — north, south, east, and west — from the smallest country in the world, from the most despised nation—in the face of every opposition and persecution —preaching to every creature that Gospel of a crucified Saviour, which to the Jews was a stumbling-block, and to the Greeks foolishness : and where is the fruit of their labours ? Look around ! In every Christian con-gregation, in every Christian society, in every Christian kingdom, we see the abiding fruit of those whom Christ chose, and ordained, and sent forth. " The voice of these humble Galilean fishermen sounds this day in all parts of the earth. High and low hear it ; kings on their thrones bow down to it ; senates acknowledge it as their law ; the poor and afflicted rejoice in it ; and as their works have triumphed over all those powers which destroy the works of man—as, instead of falling before them, they have gone on, age after age, in-creasing in glory and power — so are they the only works which can triumph over death, and turn the king of terrors himself into an angel of light."

And what is thus true of the glorious fruit of the disciples, is also true of the humblest fruit of the humblest Christian. Nothing of vanity cleaves to any work that is done in Christ and for God; no worm gnaws at the root of it; no tempest will overthrow it; it stands and will stand for ever. "When Mary anointed our Lord's feet," as Archdeacon Hare says, "the act was a transient one: it was done by an obscure woman in an obscure place, and for a burial. The fragrance of the ointment soon vanished; the holy feet which it refreshed soon ceased to walk on earth. And yet Christ declared that wheresoever His Gospel was preached in the whole world, that act should be told as a memorial of her." It is recorded that so strong and persistent was the odour of the ointment in many of the alabaster boxes of antiquity, that they retained their scent for hundreds of years. But far more powerful and persistent has been the odour of Mary's alabaster box. It has perfumed all the Christian ages; and we this day feel its spiritual sweetness as powerfully as the company felt its material sweetness in Simon's house at Bethany. While nations have gone down into indistinguishable dust; while names which cast a potent spell upon the world have been forgotten; while works, which seemed in their own day as if wrought for eternity, have perished without leaving a vestige behind,—this humble deed of a humble woman in a humble village has been handed down to us with sacred reverence. And so it will be always. What has been done for God cannot be lost or forgotten. "However blindly and erringly," as it

L

has been well said, "the gift that is laid upon God's altar will endure when all other things perish. So inherent is permanence in religion, so akin is it to eternity, that the monuments even of a false and corrupt religion will outlast every other memorial of its age and people." The pillars of some temple dedicated to the worship of a false god, remain standing to this day on the deserted plains, as the sole surviving relics of the ancient greatness of Egypt and Greece. Time dare not lay his sacrilegious hand upon anything connected with the kingdom that cannot be moved.

As the Tree upon which the Christian is grafted as a branch is the Tree of Life, so the fruit that he brings forth when nourished by its sap, is "fruit unto holiness, and the end everlasting life." That fruit is never abortive, and never fades prematurely. It is fully formed and fully ripened. The fruits of many plants are dehiscent—they open to scatter the seed, and are thus resolved into the original carpels, and come back to the condition of leaves, from which they were metamorphosed. Their purpose as fruit is served when the seed is ripe, and they become afterwards mere withered leaves. But the fruit of the vine is indehiscent—it does not open to scatter its seed, but retains its seed enclosed in its delicious pulp, and remains to the last in the condition of a juicy edible fruit. The cluster of grapes continues a cluster of grapes till it has decayed on the tree or on the ground. And Christian fruit is like this cluster of grapes—it is indehiscent; it abides as a sweet and palatable fruit continually. The things that are done from love to Christ, and in the strength which He imparts, always remain as rich and satisfying fruits. The just shall be in everlasting remembrance. The memory of the good shall blossom, and smell sweet even from the dust. Generation after generation will arise, and call those who have diffused blessings in their day blessed. How different from the works of selfishness and worldliness—from the things that are done for human glory, and pleasure, and profit! The property we spend upon ourselves perishes in the using; the property we spend upon Christ becomes a part of the inheritance, incorruptible, undefiled, and that fadeth not away. The wealth that we lay out in the selfish and needless indulgences of life dies with us, and obtains no resurrection, for it has no principle of immortality in it; it contains no seed that bears fruit in eternity. We shall see it under no form in the other world. But the wealth which, under the influence of pure motives, we devote to the cause of Christ will be perpetuated into heaven, in the new and more delightful form of those spirits of just men made perfect, which it had been employed to convert. The friends we have made of the mammon of unrighteousness shall receive us into everlasting habitations. Our alms and prayers will go up for a memorial before God. They will be registered in the archives of heaven, and when the books are opened, and Christ shall give to every man according to the deeds done in the body, we shall find, to our astonishment, the wonderful interest that has accumulated upon what we have lent to the Lord.

The cup of cold water given to a disciple will flow back to us a fountain of living water, springing up into everlasting life; the mite given to the Lord's treasury will become a rich and inexhaustible treasure; the barrel of meal and the cruse of oil, with which we sustained the perishing, will become the unwasting resources of eternity. The alabaster box of precious ointment with which we have anointed Christ's head and feet, will become the vials full of odours sweet with which the worship of eternity will be perfumed.

Yes! the fruit of the Christian remains in himself and in the world. It remains in himself; for never does he lose what he has won. The permanency of his spiritual acquirements and possessions adds bliss to bliss. His pleasures are pleasures for evermore. The life that he has gained is eternal life. The salvation that is wrought out for him is everlasting salvation. The kingdom of heaven that is within him is a kingdom that cannot be moved. The crown that awaits him is a crown of glory that fadeth not away.* And the fruit of the Christian

---

* "An inheritance incorruptible, undefiled, and that fadeth not away." How beautiful is the Greek word (*amaranton*) thus translated, "*fadeth not away!*" It brings before our imagination the asphodels and amaranthine bowers of the Elysian fields, celebrated by the classic poets. In this world we get the fruit only through the falling of the blossom and the fading of the leaf. Sometimes, indeed, a large portion of the blossom is metamorphosed into the fruit—the flower itself becomes the fruit. Usually, however, the ovary alone, or a portion of the perianth with it, is incorporated in the fruit—as in the case of the apple, pear, and rose. The succulent portion of the apple is a transformed calyx. But in the heavenly inheritance the foliage is unfading and the blossoms *im-*

remains in the world. Amid all the shattered and dissolving pageants of time his fruit is abiding. It is abiding in the world, because it has within it a living germinating principle that is capable of perpetuating it for ever—a power of indefinite rejuvenescence, of reproduction and self-renewal.

In the grape there are two parts, that serve two purposes; there is a fleshy, or succulent part, and there are the seeds imbedded in the core, or interior. The fleshy, or succulent part, endowed with nutritive properties, is for nourishment to man or beast; the seeds are intended to perpetuate the plant. And so every fruit of the Spirit contains these two parts—holiness and usefulness. Personal holiness is the succulent nourishing portion, delighting God and man; and imbedded in it is the seed of usefulness. The fruit is to be *sown* as well as eaten : it is to do good as well as to be enjoyed. In the economy of nature, why does God make fruit so beautiful and luscious, but just that the seed contained in it may be sown by birds or beasts, or by man himself, and thus the plant that produced it be perpetuated in a surer way than if left to fall upon the ground. And why does God's Spirit produce the beauties and the fruits of holiness in the Christian? Not that they may be selfishly enjoyed, but that they may be the means of attraction to others, and recom-

mortelles. The flower and the fruit both remain. There is no loss for gain. Every growth is persistent; and in the going on from glory to glory, there will be no forgetting the things that are behind in order to press forward to the things that are before.

mending the Christian life, so that it may be diffused and perpetuated. "The *fruit* of righteousness," says the apostle James, "is *sown* in peace of them that make peace," not the seed merely, but the whole fruit—the entire *indehiscent* grape, with all its beautiful bloom and rich nutritiousness. This, too, is signified in our Saviour's words, "Except a corn of wheat fall into the ground and die, it abideth alone; but if it die, it bringeth forth much fruit." The original word translated *corn* of wheat is not *sperma*, a seed, but *kokkos*, a berry, a fruit. It shows the extreme, even scientific, accuracy of our Saviour's language; for the corn of wheat, and other cereal grains, consist of seeds incorporated with seed-vessels, and are in reality *fruits*, although they appear like seeds. It is not the bare seed that falls into the ground, and, by dying, yields much fruit; but the corn of wheat—the whole fruit with its husk-like coverings. An earnest desire to extend the blessings of the Gospel is an invariable result of their true enjoyment. What the soul has received, it would communicate. Having been enlightened, it would shine. Bringing forth fruit itself, it would seek to enable others to bring forth fruit. "Restore unto me," says David, "the joy of Thy salvation, and uphold me with Thy free Spirit. Then will I teach transgressors Thy ways, and sinners shall be converted unto Thee." And thus the fruit of the Christian sows itself, and rears other fruit, that in its turn will germinate and fructify, and a ceaseless growth of fruitfulness will be kept up till the end of time. Well did the ancient

Egyptians and early Christians understand this spiritual symbolism of the fruit, as shown by the beautiful custom of placing seeds in the hands of the dead, in the tombs and sarcophagi. The unchanged renewal of a plant, by means of its seed, year after year, and age after age, is a miniature of immortality—a pre-figurement of eternity—an emblem of the Divine life itself. The fruit of the Christian is thus, indeed, unto holiness, and *the end everlasting life.* "Therefore, my beloved brethren, be ye steadfast and unmoveable, always abounding in the work of the Lord; forasmuch as ye know that your labour is not in vain in the Lord."

There are cases in nature in which the fruit swells, and becomes, to all appearance, perfect, while no seeds are produced. Seedless oranges and seedless grapes are often met with. High cultivation has a tendency to induce this .state; and it has been observed, as in the case of bananas, plantains, and bread-fruit, that the non-development of seeds seems to lead to a larger growth, and a greater succulence of the fruit. The neuter flowers of the Guelder-rose have the lobes of the corolla enlarged; while the neuter flowers of the Hydrangea have the lobes of the calyx enlarged. What is taken from the reproductive is given to the vegetative system. By preventing plants from repro-ducing, leaves and wood are produced instead of generative products. And is there not good cause to fear that too much of what is called Christian fruit contains no seed with the embryo spark of life in it, although it may seem fair and perfectly-formed? What should go to develop the seed of righteousness for others, is diverted to the production of greater self-righteousness and self-indulgence. Many Christians are satisfied with enjoying themselves spiritual blessings which they ought to communicate to others. They are pampered in the selfish use of privileges and means of grace. They are dissatisfied if they are not getting good in the sanctuary, although others may be edified. They imagine that the Church exists for the sole purpose of ministering to their necessities. It need not be wondered at that such fruits as these individuals produce fail in fulfilling the object for which they were intended. In ceasing to do good and communicate to others, the finest fruits they bring forth are seedless grapes, which have no perpetuating principle, and therefore necessarily perish. It is only the fruit that has seed in itself that God pronounces to be very good—that remains, and whose end is everlasting life. Moreover, it is necessary that the fruit should have pulp as well as seed—that the perpetuating principle of righteousness should be imbedded in all that is lovely, and amiable, and of good report. The fruits of some Christians are harsh and hard as the wild hips on the hedges—all seed and no luscious pulp. They are zealous in recommending religion to others, while they do not exhibit the amenities of it themselves. With harsh dispositions, and uncharitable judgments, and sectarian bitternesses, and hard views of life, they seek to do good to others—to spread the Gospel, to perpetuate the Christian life—and fail miserably, as was to be expected, and as they deserved. Nobody would be attracted by such fruit to make it the seed of the Church. The fruit of such Christians is not the type upon which Christ desires the fruit of His people to be formed. The fruit of the True Vine is the grape with its life-giving seed and its rich nutritious pulp. His plants are an orchard of pomegranates, with *pleasant* fruits. The pomegranate is the *grained apple*—all seed and all sweetness; each pearly seed resting in its crimson bed of luscious pulp. Such should be the Christian fruit—not all sweetness without seed; not all seed without sweetness; but sweetness and seed—fruit unto holiness; not meaning thereby Pharisaic righteousness and sanctimoniousness, but tender, loving, Christ-like spirituality; and the end, the seed-principle, everlasting life.

It is by this indehiscent fruit, this sowing of the whole luscious, seed-containing grapes of righteousness, that all the permanent good in the world is done. The palingenesis of creation is accomplished, not by the rooting-up of evil, but by the sowing of good. This is a truth which needs to be constantly held up to view, for it is constantly forgotten. The instinct of destruction seems to be so strong within us, that we need ever and anon to be reminded that our task as Christ's disciples is mainly to contend against evil, not by directly destroying it, but by sowing the seeds of good, to be ministers of salvation, not of destruction. The whole experience of life teaches us this. We find in our nurseries how impotent is the negative, and how powerful is the positive command. Tell the child *not* to do a thing, and it refrains with reluctance, if it refrain at all; but tell it to do something, and it obeys with pleasure. Take it away from one kind of mischief, and it goes to another; but give it something to do, and it is satisfied in doing it. We learn in our dealings with men how much more convincing is the constructive than the destructive argument—the development of the measure of truth that is in every error, than the extirpation of both by unmitigated abuse. And so in every work ordained for man, it is not by laying the axe at the root of the tree, but by sowing the good seed of eternal life, that evils and abuses are effectually remedied. The roots of evil that are cut down will grow up again as luxuriantly as before, for they are native to the soil and the heart cherishes them in its depths; but the seed of righteousness sown in the midst of evil, will, by its inherent life and power of growth, choke the evil out, exhaust the ingredients upon which it fattened, and so change the heart that it will be rendered incapable henceforth of bearing any other crop than that of righteousness. The growth of the fresh leaves of spring will push off the old dead leaves that cling to the hedge, more effectually than the storm can tear them off. This was the way our Saviour acted; He came not to destroy but to save, not to cause death, but to give eternal life. "If any man hear my words, and believe not, I judge him not; for I came not to judge the world, but to save the world." His great pattern, fundamental, parable of the kingdom of heaven was the sower going forth to sow; sowing seed, not uprooting plants. And His apostles after Him were sent forth, not to denounce woes against the superstitions and profligacies of the world, but to preach the Gospel of salvation to every creature, and in so doing the whole powers of paganism fell before them; the truth in Jesus which they proclaimed set the people free from everything that enslaved them. The apostle Paul and his companions lived for two years in the midst of all the splendid vice and idolatry of Ephesus; and yet the town-clerk appeased the tumult of the people, raised by Demetrius on account of the preaching of the Gospel, by saying " Ye have brought hither these men, which are neither robbers of churches, nor *yet blasphemers of your goddess."* These true missionaries wasted no strength in attacking by scorn and vitupera- tion the idolatrous customs of the city, confident that the magnificent temple of the great goddess Diana would fall to the ground, like the walls of Jericho, before the sounding of the Gospel trumpet of glory to God in the highest, peace on earth and *goodwill* to all mankind. And so every Christian is chosen and ordained of Christ, that he should go and bring forth fruit and that his fruit should remain; is sent to help in making the wilderness and the solitary place to be glad, and the desert to rejoice and blossom as the rose, not by uprooting the noxious growths of evil—that method is left to the wicked, "which is His sword,"—but by sowing the *peaceable* fruits of righteousness.

The high priest of the Jews, when he appeared

before the Lord in the Holy Place, wore a robe whose hem all round was adorned alternately with golden bells and with pomegranates of blue, and purple, and scarlet. The only ornaments of his heavenly robe were fruits gathered from the earth, the fruits especially mentioned as peculiar to the Holy Land. He brought into the presence of God not only the profession but the fruit of religion. Every Christian is a priest unto God, yielding himself a living sacrifice, holy and acceptable, which is his reasonable service. The priestly garment which he wears in ministering before the Lord daily, should have also a bell and a pomegranate, a bell and a pomegranate all round his skirts. The bell sounds out the intelligence that he is serving the Lord; it is his profession of religion before men. The pomegranate indicates that he is bringing forth the fruit of heaven, fruit unto holiness. The bell and the pomegranate should be inseparable. There should be no profession of religion without the fruit of it; and no fruit of religion without the profession. " Herein is My Father glorified that ye bear much fruit; so shall ye be My disciples."

CHAPTER V.

THE MEANS OF FRUITFULNESS.

"Every branch that beareth fruit, He purgeth it, that it may bring forth more fruit."—JOHN xv. 2.

" Herein is my Father glorified, that ye bear much fruit ; so shall ye be my disciples."—JOHN xv. 8.

EVERY · whole repeats itself in every part. The great is represented in the little; the particular is a miniature of the universal. Every object is an *imperium in imperio,*—a kingdom within a kingdom,—exhibiting, in a manner appropriate to the sphere of its own utility, all the facts, principles, and phenomena of the magnificent totality of nature. The earth is like two great snow-covered mountains joined together at the equator, the summit of the one being the north pole, and the summit of the other the south pole. Consequently, every equatorial mountain that rises above the snow-line, is an epitome of a whole hemisphere ; the ascent, from its base to its summit, being like a journey from the equator to the pole. The traveller passes successively, in the course of a single day, through all the climates of the earth, through all the seasons of the year, through all the zones of vegetable and animal life.

Altitude corresponds with latitude. He can see, when he has reached the top, what is elsewhere spread horizontally over the earth's surface and over the whole year, vertically represented along the side of the mountain below him. So, too, the successive appearances of vegetation on the earth in geological history, and the intervals between them, are like the growth of an individual plant, and its internodes, or intervals between its leaves. As the earth brought forth, epoch after epoch, plants that produced no bright-coloured blossom or nutritious fruit—a constant repetition of ferns, pines, and other flowerless plants—and at last, in the tertiary epoch, the roses and apples appeared; so the individual plant produces series after series of green leaves, and at last, in the fair summer-time, it bursts into flower, and ripens into fruit. The same law that produced the one produces the other. He, to whom a thousand years are but as one day, makes the individual plant to pass, in one summer, through the same changes, and reach the same results which it took the geological plant untold ages to accomplish.

Further, the leaves of a plant are spirally arranged around the stem in the same way that the planets of the solar system revolve around the sun. Agassiz has clearly shown that the same numerical relation holds good in phyllotaxis as in astronomy. The number of turns made on the stem, and the number of leaves passed before reaching the leaf directly above the one from which we started, form a regularly ascending series, 1, 2, 3, 5, 8, 13, etc., of which any two added together will make the third. So likewise the planets, from Neptune to Vulcan, revolve around the sun, and complete their orbit in periods which exhibit precisely the same succession of numbers, a series of threes. This wonderful similarity and simplicity of arrangement surely proves, that the same Hand adjusted the leaves of the herb of the field, which set in motion the stars of heaven; that the order of the whole system is repeated in the smallest of its contents. Indeed, we may regard a plant with its leaves, from this point of view, as a miniature solar system, and the solar system as a gigantic plant. The leaves of the one answer to the planets of the other; and as the leaves of a plant come closer and closer together, until at last they culminate in the radiance of the flower, so the planets of the solar system come closer and closer together, until at last they blossom, as it were, in the splendour of the sun. The ocean, like the land, has its mountains and valleys in its waves, rivers in its currents, forests and meadows in its sea-weeds, and varieties of climate and zones of animal and vegetable life corresponding in altitude and latitude. The deepest abyss of the ocean is an inverted mountain top; the shoaling of the water forms the mountain slope, and the mountain base is the shoreline. And just as the mountain exhibits, from its base to its summit, a regular succession of climates, from the tropics to the arctic regions, and a regular succession of belts of life, from the palm of the equator to the lichen of the pole; so we can trace downwards in the ocean a regular succession of belts of temperature and zones of organized life, from the huge palm-like Macrosystis of the shore to the minute lichen-like Conferva of the profounder depths; and as we find on the mountain summits an arctic flora, so we find in the ocean depths an arctic fauna. The delta of a river is a horizontal cone; the denudation of a mountain is a vertical cone. All the great continents terminate in wedge-shaped extremities. Thus, the abrading action of water produces the same pyramidal form in continents and in their mountains and rivers—in altitude and latitude. The earth has its secular seasons as well as its annual. The carboniferous epoch represents the geological summer; the glacial period, the geological winter; the tertiary epoch, the geological spring. Every primitive cell of which a plant is composed is a miniature plant, representing in itself the whole vegetable kingdom, performing within itself the whole series of vital functions. Every leaf on a tree is a miniature tree, and every tree is a gigantic modified leaf. The animal kingdom is also a grand whole, of which the smallest cellular polyp is a perfect representation. Every vertebra is an epitome of the animal frame; and the whole animal skeleton is an enlarged and modified vertebra. The whole mineral kingdom is seen in every grain of dust or particle of sand. The universe is but a vast expansion of the atom. In short, the whole is contained in every individual thing. "*Omne minus continet in se majus.*" Every larger whole is a microscope, magnifying and showing more clearly every smaller whole of which it is composed. "There is something that resembles the ebb and flow of the sea—day and night, man and woman, in a single needle of the pine, in a kernel of corn." Because of this unity of nature, there is but one science, and that science is Theology, understood in its true sense, as the highest generalization, connecting all the details and classifications of science with the one great law —the unity of nature with the unity of the Supreme Mind which pervades and rules over nature. Theology is the bond of union between all the departments of human knowledge—the synthesis which shows the re-semblances between their differences. And from the loftiest summit of human research, it beholds all things gathered together in one, and reconciled in Christ, even in Him; and acknowledges that the vegetable and animal, the living and lifeless, the earth and the stars, and the numberless worlds that are beyond our vision— are all the offspring of one primitive idea, and the con-sequences of one primordial law—that " of Him, and through Him, and to Him, are all things: to whom be glory for ever and ever.   Amen."

I have thus illustrated at some length the plan of God's working, every member of whose universe is at once a part and a whole, because this plan is as applicable to the spiritual as to the natural world. As the great sky is mirrored in the roadside pool as well as in the ocean, and imparts to that shallow pool something of its own depth and extent, so the infinite life of Christ is represented in the finite life of every one who bears His name, and dignifies and ennobles it.   The Christian is Christ in little. "Ye are my witnesses," says Jesus to His disciples— witnesses to men not only of His doctrine, but of His life.   They are the golden clouds that indicate the sunset, reflections by a vapour-life of the unseen Sun of Righteousness.   The Saviour Himself departed from Gadara, but He left behind Him a witness of His love in the restored demoniac, whose presence was less insupportable, because not associated like His own with sacrifice and loss.   Those who could not bear as yet the immediate teaching of Christ, the bright rays of the Sun of Glory Himself, might willingly listen to the testimony given by another of His deeds of mercy and love, might endure the soft reflection of the sun upon the cloud.   And this was the actual result, for we are told that, when the restored demoniac began to publish in Decapolis, how great things Jesus had done for him, *all men did marvel.*   Jesus has departed from our world, for His presence prolonged into history would have been overpowering to us, would have so completely riveted the gaze of men as to allow no time or strength for reflection and inference; but He has left behind men of like passions with ourselves, whom He has transformed into His own image; and who, there- fore, represent Him on a level that is not too far above us for imitation.   They are parts of the Great Whole; branches of the True Vine; rays of the True Light; repeating within their own narrower sphere, and in their own limited way, the glories of Him whose they are, and whom they serve.

In a previous chapter it was shown that every branch of the vine is a miniature vine. It follows from this that the treatment of the whole tree must necessarily be extended to every branch. We cannot cultivate the vine without cultivating every part of it. The Father is not the Husbandman to Christ alone, but also to all His disciples. The True Vine was cultivated by the Father, that every branch in Him might share in the cultivation. By virtue of the relation in which the believer stands to God through Christ, his whole life is a discipline of His Father the Husbandman. Every branch can say, in some measure, "I am the true vine, and my Father is the Husbandman."

The purging of every Christian is the purging of a branch *in* Christ—*the fellowship of Christ's sufferings.* So close is the union between Christ and His people that what is done to them is done to Him, what is suffered by them is suffered by Him. In all their afflictions He is afflicted. The culture of the whole Vine is not completed until the cultivation of each branch is finished. And hence the Apostle Paul says, "Who now rejoice in my sufferings for you, and fill up that which is behind of the afflictions of Christ in my flesh, for His body's sake, which is the Church." There is, indeed, no deficiency in the expiatory sufferings of Christ; but such is His affinity and oneness with His people, that He considers their sufferings as His own; those of His body, the Church, as of Himself their Head; so that His sufferings will be incomplete until the last tear of His afflicted people has been wiped away by His own hand. We see this very strikingly illustrated in our Lord's tender rebuke to the Apostle himself on the Damascus road,—" Saul, Saul, why persecutest thou *Me ?*" and also in our Lord's account of the awards of the judgment-day,—" I was an hungered, and ye gave me meat; I was thirsty and ye gave me drink; I was a stranger and ye took me in ; naked and ye clothed me; I was sick and ye visited me ; I was in prison and ye came unto me. Inasmuch as ye have done it unto one of the least of these my brethren, ye have done it unto me." Beautifully is the idea of the whole passage expressed in the single word in the original for "took me in;" *sunegagate*—a collective verb, from which the word *synagogue* comes, signifying literally *an assembling together*. With every stranger to whom in the true spirit we show hospitality, we take in Christ Himself; an idea upon which the monks of La Trappe act literally at the present day; for the door-keeper of the monastery, whenever he admits a stranger, kneels down reverently before him on the floor in homage to the invisible Christ, who in his belief has come in along with him.

Every branch is purged *in Christ*, in communion and fellowship with Him, drinking of His cup and baptized with His baptism. There are several plants which superstition connects with our Saviour's death upon the cross. The common bistort of our corn fields is supposed to have bloomed on Calvary, and to have been sprinkled with the drops of blood that fell from Christ's side. Hence the pink stains on its white flower-heads, and the strange dark blotches on its green leaves. On the Mount of Olives, and on every prominent spot about Jerusalem, rich clusters of red anemones grow among the green patches of grass, and are called by the Christian residents "blood-drops of Christ." In a truer way every believer grows in grace under the cross of Christ, and therefore bears "the marks of the Lord Jesus," the blessed *stigmata* of the cross, not in fleshly wounds like those which have been fabled of visionaries of the cloister, but in chastened affections and a crucified temper. And what a blessed thought is this! Though the sufferings of Christ do not secure us from suffering, but rather cause our sufferings, because through this stern experience alone can we be made conformable to His image; still His sufferings change the nature and design of our sufferings. They are no longer the punishments of wrath, but the corrections of love. The pangs of our purging are the wounds of a friend, whose arms are outstretched to clasp and guard us. In them God gives us the privilege which He gave His own Son—to be used and sacrificed for the best and greatest end. Through them He enables us to understand in some measure what Jesus suffered for us. Through them we enter into fellowship with His life, and sympathy with His work. In our Gethsemane, though withdrawn about a stone's cast from our fellow-creatures—isolated by our sorrow—we are brought into closer and tenderer relations with Jesus : we feel, indeed, that in our affliction He is afflicted, and that the angel of His presence is strengthening and saving us. Like the banished Apostle in Patmos, we see, through eyes full of tears, in the innermost core of Heaven's glory—" a Lamb as it had been slain," opening for us, as for the whole suffering Church, the seven-sealed book, revealing the mystery of redemption,

> "And in the midmost heart of grief,
> Our passion clasps a secret joy."

Yet more, we have not only fellowship with Christ in our sufferings, but also with all Christ's people. Carlo Matteucci, by his curious experiments, proved that the influences which pervade the whole plant, making up the sum of vital force, are disturbed by every movement throughout the system : an incision across a leaf, the fracture of a branch, or the mere bruising of any part, is known to disturb the whole plant, and interfere with the functions of every individual leaf. In like manner, so sensitive is the corporate life of believers in Christ, that an injury done to one is felt as if done to all; if one member suffer, all the members suffer with it ; if one rejoice, all feel a thrill of sympathetic gladness. The welfare of each is the welfare of the whole. When we are afflicted, we are apt to think that there is no sorrow like unto our sorrow. A strange feeling of loneliness comes over us, isolating us from our fellow-creatures. When stricken of the Lord, we seem to ourselves to retire into a spiritual solitude, as the whale when struck by the harpoon dives from the midst of its fellows, into the lowest depths of the ocean ; or as the wounded deer retreats from the herd, into the loneliest recesses of the forest. But the constant lesson of Scripture is, that sorrow is the one touch of nature that makes the whole world kin—that so far from isolating, it is the closest bond of union and sympathy between man and man. It tells us, on almost every page, that our afflictions are not peculiar—that the same afflictions are accomplished in our brethren who are in the world. "Whom the Lord loveth He chasteneth, and scourgeth *every* son whom He receiveth." We imagine that we see around us many Christians who are not afflicted. But we do not know whether such persons are true Christians; we do not know whether they have been, or may not even now be afflicted. The Christian is not *always* suffering, and his sufferings are not always visible. The trial is not always, or in every person, of the same kind. Sometimes it is in our circumstances, sometimes in our friends, our minds, our hearts, our souls. The kind of trial is peculiar to each afflicted person; but trial itself is peculiar to no Christian. As no branch develops naturally and spontaneously its full fruitfulness, but requires to be pruned, so no believer grows in grace naturally and harmoniously, but requires to be chastened. Chastisement is the special privilege of God's people. It is a proof that the branch is a living and fruitful one. The Husbandman *takes away* the branch that has only a name to live—that has only the form of godliness; while He *purges* the branch that beareth fruit. He dismisses the erring servant, but He chastens the erring child. "We are chastened of the Lord that we should not be condemned with the world."

The starting-point as well as the end of all God's discipline of the branch is *fruitfulness*. This is the cause of His special interest in it—the reason why He becomes the Husbandman to it. " For the earth which drinketh in the rain that cometh oft upon it, and bringeth forth herbs meet for them by whom it is dressed, receiveth blessing from God; but that which beareth thorns and briers is rejected, and is nigh unto cursing; whose end is to be burned." Most labour is bestowed upon that which rewards it most. The poor, unproductive field is abandoned to sterility, while the rich soil is carefully cultivated. The barren tree is left in its barrenness, while the fruit-bearing tree is stimulated to produce more fruit. The marsh that is full of water gets more rain, while the drained glebe suffers from drought. The branch that has life is helped by all the influences of nature to more abundant life, while the dead branch is blanched and crumbled into rottenness by every raindrop and sunbeam. The busy man gets more business, while the idle man has nothing to do; the apt scholar becomes the favourite of the teacher, while the dunce is neglected. The destruction of the poor is their poverty, while the rich are made richer. This principle, which runs throughout life, also obtains in the kingdom of heaven. " For to him that hath shall be given, and he shall have more abundantly; while from him that hath not shall be taken away even that which he seemeth to have." God acts upon this principle. He gives more abundant life where He sees life. He purges the branch that bringeth forth fruit, that it may bring forth more fruit. He labours most for that which will reward Him best.

Besides, fruitfulness is the convincing proof that complete incorporation has taken place between the branch and the vine, that the very same sap which pervades the one flows into the other, and sustains and fertilizes it. Fruitfulness necessarily follows from a vital union of the branch with Christ. There is no such thing as an unfruitful Christian. The duties of believers follow necessarily and inevitably from their relations to Christ. We can trace the increasingly higher character of these duties in the increasingly closer relations which Christ revealed as subsisting between Himself and His disciples. At first, as Mr. Bernard says, He charged them as their Master and counselled them as their Friend. He then went on to use the power of His example, "I have given you an example, that ye should do as I have done to you;" and afterwards appealed to the claims of His love, "As I have loved you, that ye love one another." And finally He opened up that spiritual bond of personal union, from which both the motives of duty and the power for its fulfilment, must be derived. It is upon the consciousness of being *in* Christ, redeemed with His precious blood, risen with Him, and having His spirit dwelling in us, that all the practical instructions of the Gospel are founded. Having had unfolded to us the fulness of grace that is in Christ, we are besought by the mercies of God to yield ourselves a living sacrifice, holy and acceptable unto God, which is our reasonable service. We live in the Spirit, therefore we are to walk in the Spirit. All goodness, righteousness, and truth, are the fruit of the spirit of Christ dwelling in us.

But while fruitfulness is thus the test of a living union of the branch with the True Vine, it is possessed by different branches in different measure. The Husbandman is not satisfied with the lowest degree of fruitfulness that indicates life at all. Many persons are content with a mere hope of their safety, while they are careless of religious advancement. Thus, it is said, Cromwell having asked a minister, "What is the *lowest* evidence of regeneration?" said on receiving an answer, "Then I am safe!" But, however such a condition may please men who value deliverance from wrath more than likeness to Christ, it does not please God. He is not satisfied with the lowest degree of grace in His people. He is not contented if the smallest indication of fruit appears on the branch that is in Christ. "Herein is my Father glorified that ye bear *much* fruit," said Jesus to His disciples. To glorify God, we must not only bear fruit, even though it be good, but much fruit. The farmer is not satisfied with his crop, if there be only a few ears of corn here and there, and these almost choked with weeds; or if the ears be small and lean and only half filled with grains; he wishes his whole field to be covered with the finest produce, tall in stem, full-formed in ear, bending under the weight of the golden grains, waving from end to end in rich billows of light and shade. He wishes a return of not thirty or sixty merely, but an hundred-fold. This only will adequately reward the heavy toil and patient waiting of the sowing, and tilling and reaping. This only will maintain his reputation as a skilful cultivator of the ground in the eyes of his neighbours. The true farmer, whose heart is in his work, takes pride in his fruitful harvest fields. They are his glory, as the spoils and results of victory are the glory of the warrior.

It is a remarkable fact that God has connected the tilling of the ground more closely with man's moral character than any other species of work. It was upon the culture of the ground that the curse first fell when Adam sinned; it was to be an outward symbol in its scanty produce, struggling to grow amid thorns and thistles, of the inward tangled wilderness into which sin had changed the fair garden of his soul. The culture of the earth was the special witness of the earliest wrong committed between man and his brother man. God said to Cain, "The voice of thy brother's blood crieth unto Me from the ground. And now art thou cursed from the earth, which hath opened her mouth to receive thy brother's blood from thy hand; *when thou tillest the ground*, it shall not henceforth yield unto thee her strength." And from that time till this, in every age and country, the earth has been the first witness of a breach of the personal and relative duties which God devolves on those who cultivate or inherit her gifts. "There is a *still life* in the soil," says Talpa, "a rebounding vitality, as it were, for good or evil, a moral reaction upon man's character, as man's moral character has a physical reaction upon it. It is the destined mirror of the mind and heart of man. Every variety and sub-variety of character is self-drawn and pictured on the soil, a photographic *portrait* of the cultivator." Its varied produce, culture and condition, tell to an expert eye, in the plainest manner, its separate tale of the character of the cultivator, or the proprietor, or both. The industry of one is reflected in the rich and abundant fruitfulness of his farm; while the idleness of another is seen in the meagre, weed-choked produce of his neglected fields. Well then may it be said, that the farmer is glorified by an abundant harvest. He is identified with the fruit of his fields. He feels as if it were a personal matter. And may we not believe that God, the Great Husbandman, has this feeling too; that our experience in this is but a shadowy reflection of His own. For His pleasure all things are and were created. He rejoices in His works. Herein, therefore, is He glorified that His people bear much fruit, that they respond in the fullest manner to the fulness of His care and tillage of them. How lavish is His goodness to us! The superfluous wealth of blossoms on the apple-tree in spring, is an emblem of His large-heartedness and open-handedness. He provides more than is needed, so that after every feast twelve baskets full of fragments have to be gathered up; so that looking round on creation, we have often to ask in wonder, to what purpose is all this waste of precious beauty and unutilized abundance, this surplusage of goodness and power? The rivers of His pleasures are ever overflowing their banks. And can we suppose that He has no delight in seeing this feature of His own image reflected in us? If it be His glory to give richly, as the Husbandman, all the needed means of fertility, is it not His glory to receive from us bountifully, as husbandmen under Him, the teeming fruit of the vineyard?

" So shall ye be My disciples." Christ was a fruitful bough hanging over the wall. His whole life was filled with the fruits of love to God and man. He went about continually doing good. The cultivation of the Father met in Him with the richest return. He glorified the Father by the much fruit which He bore. " In His work of expiation He did not tender a bare equivalent for a debt incurred, or undergo only that precise amount of shame and pain needed for our redemption. One drop of His precious blood, one pang of suffering endured by Him, might have satisfied the Father's justice, merited His grace, and redeemed our world, representing, as it did, the perfect offering of His will, and penetrated by the informing presence and boundless merits of His Divine love." His redemption is a *plenteous* redemption. He is not merely a river, but *rivers of water* in a dry place. He says to His disciples, upbraidingly, " Hitherto ye have asked nothing, ask, and ye shall receive, that your joy may be full." As The True Vine thus exhibited the profusion and generosity of self-sacrifice and benevolent activity, so every branch in Him must bear the utmost possible amount of fruit. It is only a prodigality of fruitfulness that can reward this prodigality of sacrifice. The motive that constrained the one must constrain the other. By bringing forth much fruit we prove ourselves to be Christ's disciples. Others seeing our good works will glorify our Father in heaven, and take knowledge of us that we have been with Jesus. Every branch that bears "much fruit" shows by the best and surest of all evidence that it is a miniature of the True Vine.

There are three kinds of fruit trees, viz., the vine, the olive, and the fig, employed in Scripture more frequently than any others to denote abundant fruitfulness. The vines of Palestine were celebrated for the immense clusters of grapes which they produced. The spies sent forth to view the Promised Land brought back from the valley of Eshcol a branch with one cluster of grapes so large and heavy that two men had to carry it between them on a staff. And, in our own country, the celebrated vine of Hampton Court is a most productive bearer, having seldom fewer than two thousand clusters upon it every season. There is no more appropriate natural image of plenty than a vineyard or a vine. No plant more richly rewards the toil of the husbandman, bearing fruit at a very early stage of growth, and continuing fertile to the utmost limits of old age. The olive is, if possible, still more productive, being seldom barren. It clothes with shade and beauty the arid slopes where almost no other vegetation would grow; it extracts nourishment and fatness from the driest air and the barest rocks; and repeats in its lavish abundance of oil-producing berries, grown in such unfavourable circumstances, year after year, a natural imitation of the old miracle of the multiplication of the widow's cruse of oil. The gleanings of the olive harvest are more abundant and valuable than the whole crop of other fruits. While the fig-tree is almost always loaded with fruit, yielding three different crops in the course of the year. These three kinds of fruit-trees, so common in Palestine, and so valuable for their commercial and domestic uses, represent, according to Mr. Grindon, the rich development of human qualities and activities. The vine has been regarded in all ages as the natural emblem of wisdom; *sophia*, the Greek word for wisdom, meaning, originally, the juice of the grape; hence, the fruit of the vine represents intellectual fruit—the practical results of the understanding. The olive has been identified from time immemorial with peace, mercy, and charity; its Greek name, *elaia*, being continually employed to denote forgiveness and mercy—the precept of the sermon on the mount, "Blessed are the merciful, for they shall obtain mercy," being literally, "Blessed are the *olive givers*, for *olives* shall be given to them." Hence the fruit of the olive represents moral fruit—the products of the emotional life. The fig tree has always been associated with the bodily part of our nature; its peculiar fruit being borne in idolatrous processions as the symbol of the productive powers of nature; and its leaves being the earliest covering of man. Hence the fruit of the fig may be regarded as representing the activities of the body. By the combination of the fruit of these three trees, the most characteristic and abundant in the Holy Land, we may express symbolically the santification of the body, soul, and spirit of man; the full development, by the grace of God, of his mental, moral and bodily powers—of his whole nature. Man is God's "holy land," set apart from the rest of creation, and peculiarly adapted to show forth His glory; and Christianity is the bringing forth of the fruit of this land in fullest measure and most perfect manner, the fruit of the olive, the vine and the fig, of the threefold constitution of his nature.

The fruit-bearing of the genuine branches, we have seen, is subject to the law of gradual progression. Their being *in Christ*, or, in other words, their justification or acceptance in Him, does not admit of degrees. It can never be greater or less. Perfect at its beginning, it can never make any advancement. The believer can never be more in Christ at one time than at another: the aged saint, ready to be offered up, is not more in Christ than the believer born again only yesterday. The most tender shoot is not less in the vine than the largest and oldest branch; and that branch is not more in the vine at one stage of growth than at another. But this is not the case with the fruit-bearing of the branch in Christ, or, in other words, the sanctification of the believer; *that* admits of all degrees. Our sanctification is progressive; it is a work, and not an act. The branch that is in Christ is to bring forth more fruit; so that every spiritual vineyard may be a valley of Eshcol, and every branch in the True Vine may be laden with the rich clusters of that valley. This advancement in fruitfulness presupposes the fostering care of the Husbandman. The productive branch is in Christ, and therefore it has the privilege of being cultivated in Christ and with Christ by the Father, the Husbandman. The word " purge," by which this spiritual cultivation is denoted in our text, is generally supposed to mean the process of pruning, the severer operations of God's providence. But this is an unwarrantable restriction of its significance. The specific words in Greek which indicate the pruning of trees are *oinarizo* the pruning of the vine, *kladeuo*, *klonizo*, *apokopto*, the pruning of any kind of tree, or of any branch. But the word translated in our text " purgeth " is none of these; it is *kathairo*, which is a generic expression. Pruning is not the only process by which fruitfulness is produced; and, therefore, a more comprehensive term must be employed. The word *kathairo* includes all the varied operations of husbandry, positive and privative; the means that are necessary to develop the fruitfulness of the plant, and the removal of all the hindrances that would prevent or diminish this fruitfulness. It means to purify the ground and prepare it for sowing, by removing weeds and rubbish—to winnow the corn, to separate the chaff from the wheat. Its root-idea is purity, freedom from all that is foul, false, useless, or noxious—from everything, whether in the way of deficiency or excess, that would hinder the tree from carrying out its natural tendency, and attaining its true ideal, which is the utmost possible fruitfulness. It is interesting to notice the close resemblance that exists between the word *kathairo*, to purge, and *kathaireo*, to destroy. The addition of one letter makes the one word to mean a very different thing from the other. And so there is a superficial, or temporary resemblance between the purging of the fruitful branches in the vine and the destroying or taking away of the unfruitful ones. In the garden during spring, the process of digging the ground, and throwing it into disagreeable confusion, cutting the roots of the trees, and mercilessly lopping off their branches and disfiguring them, seems purely a process of destruction and ruin; but in the added beauty of summer and the richer fruitfulness of autumn, it is seen to be a remedial and constructive process. And so the means which God employs to promote the fertility of His own people seem. so like those which He employs to punish the wicked, that the righteous are not seldom perplexed at the strangeness of His providence, and their feet well nigh slip. The very same events that are evils to the wicked are blessings to the righteous. But one thing distinguishes between what is sent to purge and what is sent to scourge; viz., the love of the Father. Where that exists, the nature and design of the dispensation are changed,—the curse becomes a cross, and the judgment a chastisement. It is *kathairo*, and not *kathaireo*.

1. In considering the means of fruitfulness, let us look first at the nature of the soil in which believers are planted. It is a well-known fact that some of the finest grapes are produced on volcanic soil. From the rich red mould into which lava is disintegrated when long ex-

posed to the weather, the vine draws the juices that form the largest and most generous clusters of fruit. The passion of the soil, as it were, passes into the produce. In Madeira, in Greece, in Lebanon, this is very strikingly the case. Palestine, the native country of the vine, exhibits, for its size, more than any other country, evidences of extraordinary geological convulsions. Everywhere the table-lands are roughened by rocks of volcanic origin; and the valleys give evidence of vast denudation. These geological features of the country, which were so eminently favourable for the growth of the physical vine, were paralleled by the historical revolutions—the wars and social convulsions which were intended to make Israel the true vine of the Lord. While Moab was at ease from his youth—was allowed to rest on his lees, and therefore his natural scent remained in him, Israel was emptied from vessel to vessel, and was therefore clarified. And so it is in the experience of every nation that is intended to produce much fruit. Africa, with its uniform geology and its monotonous history, has done little for mankind compared with Europe, whose geology and history are exceedingly varied and complicated. Britain is like Palestine—a perfect geological diagram, and a miniature of universal history; and therefore it occupies a somewhat similar position among the nations. Having passed through many revolutions in its physical features and its social and political economy, it is fitted to lead the van of human progress, and bear much fruit for all the world. Compare the rich variety of its physical and social history with the vast monotonous steppes and the unvarying barbarism of Russia, and you cannot fail to see what a. powerful effect geological convulsions and historical revolutions have in developing a country's greatness and usefulness. It is as true of individuals as of nations, that because they have no changes, they do not fear God or prosper. The Husbandman of souls places the vines which He means to be most fruitful and useful in volcanic soil, amid changeful circumstances. They are planted amid fiery trials, where they are exposed to constant temptations, outbursts of violence from the world beneath, lava-floods of the wrath and malice of the Adversary and of wicked men. So was it with Moses in Pharaoh's court, with Joseph in Egypt, with Daniel in Babylon, with the " saints in Cæsar's household." Their fiery trials made them " strong in faith, giving glory to God "—helped to develop graces which, in other circumstances, would have remained latent, and to call forth into greater strength and beauty their spiritual life. So is it with many believers still. Since the ground beneath them is insecure, and liable to constant convulsive shocks, they are thereby induced to set their affections more firmly on things above, and to walk as pilgrims and strangers on earth. The lava-floods that seem to make their home and their heart desolate, disintegrate when cool into the most fertile soil; and they *afterwards* derive greater spiritual vigour from that which for a while seemed to have weakened and impoverished them. They grow best in the soil formed by the failure of their hôpes, and the disappointment of their wishes, and the passing away of what was dearest and most essential ; just as the tree grows best in the soil formed by the decay of the leaves that have dropped from its own boughs. "Therefore, behold, I will allure her, and bring her into the wilderness, and speak comfortably unto her, and I will give her her vineyards from *thence*, and the valley of Achor for a door of hope."

The influence of external circumstances upon objects so plastic as plants is confessedly very powerful, leading often to great modifications of form, structure, and substance. Darwin mentions several very striking in-stances. The English Ribston Pippin assumes, in the hotter parts of India, a fastigiate or pyramidal aspect, which is the natural habit of a Chinese tropical species of apple. In Ceylon the apple-tree sends out numerous runners under ground, which continually rise into small stems, and form a thick forest-growth around the parent tree. The oak is worthless when grown at the Cape of Good Hope. Hemp and flax flourish, and yield plenty of seed, on the plains of India, but their fibres are brittle and useless for manufacturing purposes; while, on the other hand, hemp fails to produce, in England, that resinous matter called haschish, which is so largely used in India as an intoxicating drug. The Rhubarb does not produce in England the medicinal substance which it yields in Chinese Tartary. The Pistacia grows abundantly in the south of France, but it yields no mastic. The Sassafras loses in Europe the odour peculiar to it in North America. Add to these examples, given by Mr. Darwin, the fact, that species of mushroom, which in this country are poisonous, are eaten on the Continent with impunity; while the common edible mushroom of our country is carefully avoided on the Continent as unwholesome. The fruit of the pear will crack if the root of the tree gets no iron. The asparagus will wither and die of exhaustion unless its bed is supplied with salt. Cinnamon, cassia, and other spice-trees grown in our hot-houses, though supplied with all the conditions of soil, heat, moisture, and air of their native climates, so far as man can give them artificially, and though flowering and fruiting freely, nevertheless do not produce the aromatic secretions for which they are prized, but become insipid and tasteless. The nature of the produce and the quality of the wine yielded by the grape-vine, are often modified by changes which seem to us very slight. Hence the endless variety of grapes and wines of different countries. A similar modification in the character of the growth and fruit of the Christian, we may well believe, is caused by the circumstances in which God's providence places him. While he is lifted by the law of his spirit above the overbearing force of circumstances, he is not altogether independent of them. They constitute the means of his probation—the soil of his growth, and the climate of his ripening.* One thing, amid all the changes of his cir-

---

* The modifying power of circumstances is strikingly seen in the case of the silk worm. When about to undergo its transformation, each caterpillar is placed on a little twig fixed in a vertical position, when it produces a round cocoon, which serves its own purposes

cumstances, the Christian can command if he will,—
and that is, "the saving health," the sunlight of God's
countenance.   He does not, however, always avail
himself of it.   And hence, as the spice-trees in our
hot-houses are destitute of aromatic taste, because we
cannot supply them with the brilliant direct sunshine of
their native skies, so the Christian, amid all the privileges of the Church, is often destitute of the rich
aromatic fragrance of spiritual joy, because he seeks to
make up, by the heat of forced spiritual emotion
originating in himself, for the full, bright, joyous sunshine that beams from God's face.

Under this head may be noticed the discipline of
life's daily work as one of the means of developing
Christian fruitfulness.   Like the vine, the Christian
requires to be trained along the trellis of formal duties
and orderly habits.   He thrives best, and bears most
fruit, as a wall-tree.   If left to grow as a standard, much
of the force, which would have been expended in fruit,

and those of man perfectly.   But if allowed accidentally to remain
on a level horizontal surface, it produces a flat cocoon spread out
like a mat, which is useless to the insect itself, for it cannot wrap
round and protect its eggs, and worthless to the manufacturer, for
the threads cannot be separated or unravelled.   Numerous examples
of the result of external forces in modifying the forms of plants and
animals might be adduced.   Every leaf is modified by the conditions under which it is grown.   No part of a plant exhibits the
full symmetry and perfect growth natural to it.   The pressure or
shadow of other parts impedes its development and determines
its form, so that, in the whole plant, and in each part, we see only
the result of growth under limit; and it is just so with the Christian.
His spiritual development is also a growth under limit.   The circumstances of life modify his character and conduct.

is wasted in the maintenance of an independent position, in expanding his branches, and living according to
the wayward and capricious solicitations of the winds
and sunbeams of heaven. We need to have our work
prescribed to us, and each hour must have its allotted
employment, else we are apt to waste our time in idleness
and our energies in barren reverie. If left to measure
out our day's task for ourselves, the amount of time that
we shall devote to it, and the definite quantity of it
that we shall accomplish, we are in danger of unduly
sparing ourselves and achieving nothing. It is a principle in human nature, that the less we have to do the
less we will do. But if the outward limits of our work
are prescribed to us, this discipline wonderfully sharpens
our faculties, and stirs up all the latent powers of our
nature into full activity. The outward routine itself
will help to stimulate wonderfully the zeal and earnestness which we shall put into our tasks. Much of the
daily work that we do has no other value than that it
affords a moral discipline to our nature, a means of
support to our weakness, and a definite training to our
faculties. We become willing subjects in it to the
Divine law, that in the sweat of our face we shall eat
bread, and take up our toil into the region of spiritual
life, where the fulness of the promise, which that sentence unfolds, is enjoyed.

I may also notice under this head, the fact, that
God's tenderest vines are often placed in the most
trying circumstances. It seems a strange appointment
of nature, that the growing points of all trees should

be their weakest and most delicate parts. The first fragile leaves of spring are put forth into the chilly air, from which the winter hardness has not yet departed. The parts of the tree that are as sensitive to external impressions as the finger-tips are to the touch are those which have often to encounter the severest storms. When the new growth is fully-formed and becomes hard and strong, then only soft skies and warm sunbeams smile upon it. So is it, also, in the animal kingdom. The most slender and delicate corals— those with branching forms and a fine porous structure —form the outside of coral reefs, exposed to the enormous pressure and force of the ocean waves; while the roughest, most compact and massive kinds flourish within the quiet waters of the lagoon, under the lee of the reef. This seems a cruel, but it is in reality a wise arrangement of Providence. The delicate growths of spring submit to the chill winds of March, which pass harmlessly over them ; while the sturdier growths of summer would be broken off and destroyed in their resistance. The massive and compact corals opposing the force and pressure of the waves would be speedily ground to powder; but the slender, fragile, branched corals yield to the swirl of the surging sea, which passes harmlessly through and over them. And, as it is with these humble creatures of the sea and land, so it is with God's own people. Many of the most delicate and sensitive of them have to bear the full brunt of life's storms. Tender women have often to withstand the severest shocks of circumstances. The sorest trials often meet the Christian at the beginning of his course—the Red Sea—the bitter Marah—the lonely and pathless wilderness. He puts forth the tenderest growths of his nature often into the biting air, of doubt, and fear, and despondency. But it is good thus to bear the yoke in our youth. The elasticity and hopefulness of the young Christian can overcome trials which would crush the more aged and less buoyant. And the very patience and tenderness of those sensitive ones, who have to bear greater hardships and evils, disarm these evils of their bitterness, and turn them to profitable uses. If the weather in the early days of spring be more severe, there is more of that actinic power in the light by which seeds germinate and buds grow than at any other time; and the stormy winds cause the sap to rise and stimulate the dormant life of the trees, so that the tender leaves derive the richest pabulum from their cruel circumstances. Similarly—the waves breaking upon the coral reef furnish a large supply of aerated water, of carbonate of lime, and other salts held in solution with carbonic acid gas; consequently, the nutritive powers of the delicate branched corals which live in the surf are in constant activity, and they grow very rapidly. And are there not similar compensations to the delicate human natures, and fragile spiritual growths that flourish in the chill spring or in the raging surf of the world's circumstances? Do they not get from their very trials the means of greater nourishment and growth in grace?

2. Pruning is one of the most common methods by which increased fruitfulness is produced. Every one is familiar with this process. It is performed upon every fruit-tree in spring, when the sap is beginning to ascend; for even after trees have been grafted they are apt to run to wood and leaves, instead of flowering and fruiting. No plant requires more pruning than the vine. So bountiful is its sap, so vigorous its vital force, that we are amazed at the abundance of superfluous growth which it annually produces. If left to its freedom, it employs this superfluity of growth in climbing up, and mantling with its foliage, the loftiest trees; but, in order to adapt it to our conditions of cultivation, we must systematically cripple and restrict it in every part. The *geitzen*, as the German peasants call the head, or leading shoots, are carefully broken off; and the long luxuriant *lotten*, or lateral shoots, which grow all through the summer, and often until late on in autumn—forming a chain of many joints, endless in its nature, which is only forcibly terminated by the commencement of winter—are cut back to a few joints.

But besides the pruning of the *suckers on the branch*, for the sake of the fruit, the branch itself is sometimes pruned. This process is performed for two reasons; it removes superfluous, and stimulates latent growth—both processes being intimately related and interdependent. In almost every branch of a fruit-bearing tree, it happens that, owing to unfavourable circumstances, such as deficiency of light and heat, or overcrowding, many of the buds that are put forth every year become dormant.

They are produced in their proper place upon the branch, but they do not expand; their growth is arrested, and in the onward progress of the branch they are left behind, covered over with new tissue, and thus completely hid from view. Some of these· torpid buds retain a sufficient amount of vitality to carry them forward through the annually-deposited layers of wood and bark; so that they still continue to maintain their position visibly, year after year, on the outside of the bark. In most instances, however, they are too feeble to keep pace with the onward growth of the branch ; and, in that case, they fall behind, necessarily sink below the surface, and become buried beneath succeeding annual deposits of wood and bark. Like seeds lying dormant, deep in the ground, beyond the reach of influences that would cause them to germinate, these abortive buds remain for years below the bark in a state of passive vitality; and as the soil is full of seeds quick with life, so every tree always contains an immense number of these buried buds. The branch, instead of developing them, employs the sap which ought to have gone for that purpose, into growing fresh shoots. But the gardener comes, and with his sharp pruning-knife lops off these useless suckers; and the consequence is, that in a little while the sap that was wasted upon them goes back to the dormant buds, passed over and hid in the tissue of the branch, and stimulates their slumbering vitality so powerfully that they will force their way through the wood and bark to the surface, though that wood may be the growth of years. The bud which had slept in a condition of suspended vitality will break forth at last below the cut surface, and speedily conceal the injury by developing into blossom and fruit-bearing branches. Every one is familiar with pollard willows, and other trees whose branches have thus been cut off, and yet which are covered with young branches and shoots, the growth of buds which have been buried in the wood, and for years remained dormant below the surface. As the farmer digs up the soil, and thus exposes the dormant seeds in it to light, air, and moisture, when they immediately germinate; so the gardener, by pruning, brings these buried buds into contact with the quickening influences of the tree, and they are forthwith roused into full and productive activity.

Now, as the natural vine-dresser does in the natural vineyard, so does the Husbandman of souls in the spiritual vineyard. He prunes every branch in the True Vine for two reasons; first, in order to remove rank and useless qualities; and, secondly, to develop latent graces—the same chastisement of His providence producing both results. In no Christian is there an harmonious spiritual growth, a perfect expansion from a perfect germ in childhood. On the contrary, growth in grace in us is always unsymmetrical. Solid and valuable qualities are united with weak, worthless ones; graces that charm by their beauty lie side by side with defects that repel by their deformity. Some graces, also, are dormant in the soul, repressed by unfavourable circumstances of continued prosperity, or starved by the over-development of other graces. Some besetting sins, such as irritability, covetousness, worldliness, pride, impatience, are allowed to grow up and exhaust in their noxious growth the life of the soul. Now, to repress the evil and stimulate the good qualities of His people, God subjects them to the pruning of His providence. He sends personal, domestic, or relative affliction to cut off the rank growths of besetting sins, so that the bright blossoms and rich fruits of latent buds of righteousness may be developed in their place. Upon a bed of sickness, or when suffering from adversity or bereavement, besetting sins are often remembered, understood in all their sinfulness, lamented, confessed, and mortified. There can be no darker sign than when a professor's conscience is so dull and hard during a time of trial as to leave him unadmonished regarding these predominant sins; while, on the other hand, it is a blessed fruit of tribulation that they have been weakened, if not eradicated. Happy the Christian who comes out of trial with these noxious growths pruned away! No matter what he has lost, if he has gained freedom from these enemies of his spiritual welfare, it is ample compensation for any suffering.

But, the pruning of God's providence would be very unsatisfactory did it only lop off noxious qualities, mortify easily-besetting sins. Such injurious growths may be repressed by affliction, but unless the discipline develops the opposite good qualities, they will spring up anew, and make matters worse than before. Prohibition, so far from killing desire, has a tendency to increase it;

and, therefore, in order effectually to remove easily-besetting sins, spiritual graces must be developed in their room.   In order to get rid of worldly-mindedness, spirituality of mind must be cultivated in its place; covetousness, which is idolatry, will only yield to a larger experience of the Love that for our sakes became poor; anger will only be extirpated by meekness, and pride by humility.   The law of "natural selection," by which the weaker growth is rooted out and destroyed by the stronger, must prevail in the soul.   The grace that is richly endowed and admirably adapted to all conditions and circumstances, must crowd out of existence the natural quality that has only a limited power of adaptation.   The godliness that is profitable unto all things, having promise of the life that now is, as well as of that which is to come, must expel and extinguish the qualities that are suited only to a carnal life, and to success in this world.   The branch that has been broken off in its own selfish purposes and feelings, must start a new and better growth from the latent buds stimulated by this pruning.   How often do we see this two-fold result produced by God's chastisements!   The harshness, obtrusiveness, and loftiness of some Christians, which rendered them disagreeable in their intercourse with their fellow-Christians, are removed, and a sweet gentleness, humility, and mellow tenderness of spirit have come in their place.   Pride loses its offence, and becomes nothing more than simple dignity; acrimony is softened down to perception of character; and avarice melts like a bank of ice, and flows around in a hundred kindly channels of beneficence. One of the most beautiful and suggestive sights in nature is a tender green shoot, covered with the most delicate leaves, sprouting in spring from the rough, blackened, and time-scarred trunk of a tree growing in one of our city squares. The pinching grip of the hard pavement about its roots, and the dry, dusty, smoky atmosphere in which it struggles to live, have checked the further growth of its branches, and thus led to what powers of growth there are remaining in it going back, to stimulate a bud long hid and overpassed in its trunk, and restore in some measure the freshness and fairness of its youth. And so, one of the most beautiful moral sights is the appearance of some gentle Christian grace bursting, by reason of sorrow and disappointment, through the dark roughness of a time-scarred and world-hardened nature. What has checked its proud onward growth of success has brought back the humility and tender trustfulness of childhood. The teachings of life's early hours, long forgotten, are now remembered, and the grown-up man becomes once more a child, and as a little child he enters into the kingdom of heaven.*

* During the French war in Algeria the Arabs planted a hedge of agaves to obstruct the passage of the enemy's cavalry. The soldiers hacked these plants with their swords, and cut out the central tuft of leaves or the heart ; and yet strange to say, notwithstanding this barbarous treatment, and although the agave in ordinary circumstances does not flower except at long intervals of time, every one of the plants next season sent up the large handsome flower spikes.

But we must be guarded against the idea that affliction
of itself can develop the fruitfulness of the Christian life.
We find that in the fruit-tree the pruning is only of use
when there are latent or open buds to develop.   If
there are no dormant buds overpassed in the branch
the pruning of it will produce no new growth, develop
no blossom or fruit.   On the contrary, it will do injury
to the tree; it will arrest its growth, and after a while
the branch will wither and perish.   And so, unless we
have Christian life and Christian capabilities, affliction,
so far from doing us good, will only harden and injure
us.   Suffering is not holy in itself; it does not contain
any element of righteousness.   Many are under the impression that there is virtue in affliction to produce all
holiness; they have a leaning, though unavowed, to
substitute the purgatory of experience for the death of
Christ.   Scripture has been in many ways perverted on
this point.   The Roman Catholic subjects himself to
grievous penances in order to expiate his sins, or earn
rewards in heaven; while the Protestant imagines that
what he is made to suffer here is at least subtracted
from his punishment hereafter.   But God's Word tells
us that no sufferings are meritorious save those of
Christ; that our tears cannot wash out a single stain of
sin, or purchase for us a single blessing of heaven.
Our natural sorrows and sufferings are a part of the
original curse, and have nothing to do with the cross of
Christ, and the blessings connected with it, unless
suffered in living union with Him, and sanctified by
His Spirit.   We sorrow in our natural trials after the

similitude of Adam, with a sorrow that worketh death. But in Christ we sorrow after a godly sort, that worketh repentance unto life. Sorrow itself is thus the condition, not the cause of sanctification; man's redemption is accomplished through it, not in any way by virtue of it. It is only in the case of fruitful branches in Christ that it is efficacious. The only solicitude of a worldly man, and of a worldly-minded professor of religion, is to get rid of the trouble as fast as possible, and anyhow; but that of the spiritually-minded Christian is to get out of it only in God's good time, by righteous means, and with holy fruits. When there is a real inward desire that the trial may be sanctified, and that it may not be removed till this result is accomplished, then the soul is benefited. There are latent capacities which are being developed, as well as besetting sins extirpated; and such a branch in Christ will produce more and richer fruit from such gracious pruning.

But, while affliction cannot impart spiritual life, we must bear in mind that there are instances in which God uses it to quicken the soul dead in trespasses and sins. He employs it as a means of conversion, as well as of sanctification. And here, too, we find an analogy in nature. The buds of plants almost always grow in the axil—the vacant angle or interval between the leaf and the stem, where the hard, resisting bark which everywhere else invests the surface of the plant, is more easily penetrated, and allows the growing tissues to expand more easily. The axil is, so to speak, the joint in the armour of the stem. Now, "a wound is virtually

an axil, for the continuity of the surface is there broken,
and consequently, the resistance of the external investi-
ture diminished." It allows the pent-up formative
energies of the life within to expand in that direction
with new impulse. The process of budding, in which a
wound is made to enable a new root to grow, depends
upon this principle. Also, the leaves of many rapidly-
growing plants, such as the Hoya, Gesnera, and Gloxinia,
if cut across, or otherwise wounded, and planted, will
produce buds from the wound, which is just an artificial
axil; and gardeners often avail themselves of this
formation of buds from wounded leaves to propagate
plants. Now, this law of growth in the direction of
. least resistance, which prevails throughout the natural
world, is strikingly applicable in the spiritual. We all
invest ourselves with a strong, resisting envelope of
pride, worldliness and carelessness. Our property, our
friends, our reputation, our comfort, all form a kind of
outer crust of selfishness, which prevents our spiritual
growth. But God removes our property or our friends,
blights our reputation, destroys our carnal ease, and by
the wound thus made in our selfish life an axil is
formed, from whence springs up the bud of a new and
holier growth. Many are so armed at all points by their
prosperity, that no joint can be found in their armour
through which the arrow of conviction may reach
their consciences. The means of grace have no effect
upon them; seasons of revival come and go, but no
spiritual buds break forth from them. The harvest
is past, and the summer is ended, and they are not

saved. All goes well with them, and they are bound up in themselves. But God often chooses such in the furnace. He passes by them, and sees them in their blood, and says to them, " Live ; and the time is a time of love." He removes the resisting medium ; makes a rent through their affections, and thus calls forth, by His quickening Spirit, the dead soul to new life and spiritual fruitfulness. The time past is deemed sufficient to have wrought the will of the flesh ; the growth from the new axil is in a new direction—no longer towards self and the world, but towards God. Wonderful, indeed, is the result of *fracture* throughout the natural and spiritual worlds. It is everywhere the source of new life and beauty. The rays of light, when broken or refracted, reveal to us the lovely colours that are hid in them ; the sandal wood, when cut, yields its sweetest perfume ; the plant that is wounded puts forth a new bud. And so heart-break is the deepest and wisest teacher ; it refracts the life that surrounds us so naturally and simply that we know not its composition, into its true elements ; it brings forth the richest sympathies, and stimulates the unselfish growths of our nature.

" Knowledge by suffering entereth."

There is one process of unusual severity which the gardener has recourse to in cases of obstinate sterility. The barren branch is *girdled* or *ringed*—that is, a narrow strip of its bark is removed all round the branch. The juices elaborated by the leaves are arrested in their downward course, and accumulated in the part above the ring, which is thus enabled to produce fruit abundantly; while the shoots that appear below the ring, being fed only by the crude ascending sap, do not bear flowers, but push forth into leafy branches. The prophet Joel says, " He hath laid my vine waste, and *barked* my fig-tree." Many Christians are girdled or ringed in order to prevent the earthward tendencies of their souls, and enable them to accumulate and concentrate all the heavenly influences which they receive in bringing forth more fruit. Their present life is separated from their past by some terrible crisis of suffering, which has altered everything to their view, which has been in itself a transformation, and has accomplished in a day, in an hour, in a moment, what else is effected only by the gradual process of years. They feel as if they were divided from all their former happiness by their present misery. Between their former and their present selves a great gulf of desolation is fixed, which no earthly compensation can fill. The separation by death between husband and wife is one of the rings cut around the branch of life, and the most frequent and painful of them. When the marriage union is indeed what it should be in every case, "a two-celled heart, beating one stroke—life," then the taking away of "the desire of the eyes by a stroke," is indeed the quenching of half a being. But God barks our fig-tree in this terrible way, in order that what remains of our branch may be more productive than before. The lot that is thus halved may be more useful than in its full and joyful completeness. Ceasing to draw its nourishment from broken cisterns of earthly love, the lonely branch, separated from its happy past, depends more upon the unfailing dew and sunshine of heavenly love. Having once gone down the valley of the shadow of death with a beloved one, and come back alone, trim gardens and pleasant paths are never so sufficing again; and no life which has involved such a sorrow has ever the same capacity for mere worldly joy hereafter. The impress of that momentous hour is never lost.

As the painter rubs off half of his gold-leaf ere the letters which he is painting on the sign-board appear distinctly—so much of what is precious in life has to be taken away ere God's glory is fulfilled in us, and our title as Christ's disciples is made manifest. Every part of the vine requires to be pruned. We have seen that the suckers are removed from the branch that the fruit-bud may grow; that the branch itself is pruned in order that the latent buds may be stimulated to break through; that the bark is ringed in order that the elaborated juices may be concentrated in the fruit. But sometimes even the roots require to be dug about and cut short. There is a beautiful correspondence at all times between the horizontal extension of the branches in the air and the lateral spreading of the roots in the earth. As the one grows so does the other. For this reason the roots require pruning no less than the branches. If they are allowed to ramify too far, and develop too luxuriantly, the branches will keep pace with them, only they will be barren. But, on the other hand, if the roots are restricted, this will lead to the production of flowers and fruit on the branches above. Some of the richest shows of blossom and fruit I have ever seen were produced by wild apple and cherry trees, whose roots had been checked in their growth by masses of rock on the mountain side. One day, when passing through the Nærodal, one of the grandest gorges of Norway, I was struck with seeing a rich clump of wild violets growing on a heap of *debris* at the foot of a cliff nearly 6000 feet high. On every side were huge masses of rock that had fallen from the heights. The village of Gudvangen was near, and well deserved its poetical name of " God's field," for it was a little patch of fertility and human life miraculously, as it were, rescued from the awful ruins of nature strewn around. The roots of the violets were partially bare, and ever and anon some of the loose soil crumbled away about them, exposing them still more to the storm. But this severe treatment, instead of injuring, seemed, on the contrary, to stimulate them into greater beauty and luxuriance. Larger and lovelier blossoms than those which looked up at me so humanly with their meek faces, from the midst of their sorrowful circumstances, I have never seen, even in the most sheltered spot; and they seemed to have held possession of the place for several generations, judging from the size of the cluster. How forcibly they spoke to me of the promise, " For the mountains shall depart, and the hills be removed, but my kindness shall not depart from thee, neither shall the covenant of my peace be removed!" We are prone to root ourselves too firmly in the rich soil of our circumstances, to spread our roots far and wide in search of what shall minister to our love of ease and pleasure. But God digs about us—shows us that we are growing in a "God's field," existing by Divine appointment in the midst of the ruins of the most solid and enduring things, and that we have but the slightest hold of life. Our circumstances crumble away about our roots; the things and the persons in which we trusted prove as treacherous and unstable as a sand-heap on a slope. But, from roots bare and exposed, or cut off and circumscribed by uncongenial soil, we should seek to develop a higher beauty and richness of character. The little Litorella, or *shore weed*, which grows in the shallows of our lakes, never flowers under water, but maintains and increases itself by lateral runners year after year. When, however, the water retreats in the driest summers, and leaves it exposed to the air, it comes into flower. A change of elements puts a stop to the growth of its roots, and develops instead blossom and fruit; and, so, it often happens that a change of circumstances from prosperity to adversity, from health to sickness, from the joy of possession to the sorrow of bereavement, causes those who spread out their roots widely, and extended themselves on every side, to take in their roots, and produce in their place flowers and fruit of heavenward growth.

The leaves also need sometimes to be taken away, as super-abundant foliage would shade the fruit and

prevent the sunshine from getting access to it to ripen
it. We see the injurious effect of too much foliage in
the case of the common *woodruff.* When the shadow
of the wood is too dense it does not send up blossom
or fruit at all, but propagates itself many years without
flowering, by means of subterranean runners, waiting
from generation to generation the return of a favourable
period, when the over-arching foliage, thinned by the
cutting down of the trees, admits sunshine to stimulate
its powers of inflorescence. It is well to state, on the
other hand, that too free an opening of the wood also
interferes with its flourishing above ground, and causes
its development by lateral buds, and not by terminal
flowers. This will show us that the process of judging
what is superfluous foliage, and removing it, is a peculiarly delicate one. It needs to be done with great
care, for there is not only the difficulty of regulating
the proper degree of sunshine to admit or exclude, but
there is the further difficulty of determining how many
leaves should be removed, considering that the leaves
are the most essential parts of the plant, and upon their
offices depend the growth of wood, and the quality and
quantity of fruit. So, in like manner, is it in the spiritual
world. The fruit of the Christian is sometimes prevented from ripening or filling out properly by the
super-abundance of the leaves of profession. There
may be more profession than practice, more of the
rustling foliage than of the *silent fruit.* The fig-tree,
though not altogether barren, may have far more leaves
upon it than figs. We may hide ourselves from God

among our own leaves; they may screen heaven from our view. We may look more at their flickering shadows upon the earth, than through the branches to the blue heavens and the bright sun above. We may sit listless and discontented, like Jonah, under the shadow of our gourd, while God's command, "Son, go work to-day in My vineyard," is disregarded.

The most common fault of believers is letting their profession of the Christian life run ahead of their experience, exaggerating their emotions, expressing fervours that have little corresponding to them in their own souls, and thus making their religion an unreal and conventional thing. Young converts especially are apt to fall into this snare, tempted to publish prematurely what great things God hath done for them, until their religious life becomes a mere outward one, a thing of display, feeling, and excitement, and they value more the outward aspect of their saving change to others, than its inward relation to God and their own souls. It would be well for such persons to give more earnest heed to the deep significance of Christ's command to Jairus, when He raised his daughter from the dead, "See thou tell no man." In this case there was "danger of all deeper impressions being lost and scattered through a garrulous repetition of the outward circumstances of the healing, and therefore silence was enjoined that there might be an inward brooding over the gracious and mighty dealing of the Lord." To avoid a similar danger in the case of the professor of religion, the same injunction rests upon him, to hide for a while the things of his conversion in his heart, to meditate upon them in solitude and silence. The germinating grain is kept away from the light in the soil that covers it. We imitate this natural condition by keeping the hyacinth-bulbs which we have put in water in a dark place, until they have developed their roots in the glass. Thus should it be with the believer during the first season of conversion. While he is seeking to be rooted in the love of Christ,—established in faith—there should be no ostentation, no loud profession. The process should be in silence and secrecy. There would be no loss, but, on the contrary, great gain to the cause of Christ, if, in very many cases, young converts gave themselves more to meditation, self-examination and prayer, than to exhorting others on the strength of a very brief and imperfect experience. Where the profession is ostentatiously flaunted before the eyes of men, a grievous fall or back-sliding very frequently happens to correct the error. The rustling leaves of self-assertion in which they gloried are stripped off, that the sap wasted upon them may go to the formation and ripening of the silent and enduring fruit of Christian virtue. By their backsliding they are led to speak less and act more. This operation, however, is a very delicate one, considering how essential the profession of religion is in the formation of the Christian character, how powerful is the reaction of the outward profession upon the inward life. Not more necessary are the leaves of a natural tree to the production of the fruit, than the profession of a Christian is to the formation of the Christian character. But God, by some appropriate discipline, regulates what leaves of profession should be stripped off and what leaves should remain. He who said to the impulsive, social Jairus, "See thou tell no man," and to the morbid, brooding, solitary demoniac, "Go home to thy friends, and tell what great things God hath done for thee," will regulate His treatment according to the different moral condition of His people. He will allow the mouth of the proud self-satisfied, self-asserting David to be closed by reason of his grievous fall; and He will restore to the humbled, contrite David the joy of His salvation, that his lips may be opened, and his mouth may show forth the praises of the Lord. His people shall be taught to make their outward profession the genuine evidence and reflection of their inward growth in grace; the production and ripening of fruit co-extensive with the display of foliage.

Many of the tendrils of the vine require to be nipped off, in order that no sap may be wasted, or diverted from the fruit. If left to itself, the vine would put forth a tendril at every alternate joint; for it would seek to climb to the top of the highest tree. But this habit of profuse climbing must be restricted, in order that the energies of the plant may be concentrated in producing new and better fruit. In like manner, it is necessary that the excessive *upward tendency* of some Christians should be restricted, in order that the common duties, and the homely concerns of ordinary life—which in their own sphere are equally important—may not be

neglected. Some would like to be wholly spiritual—
wrapt up exclusively in the contemplation of heavenly
things—to develop an ascetic piety, that spends all its
force in meditation. Afar from the haunts of men,
like the monks of old, they would like to work out their
salvation in dreamy raptures and ecstatic musings. By
tendrils of soul-soaring aspirations, they would seek to
rise higher towards heaven, while of no use in the
world. Many deem themselves too heavenly-minded,
too spiritual, to care for the things that are pure, and
honest, and lovely, and of good report among men.
They are raised above all earthly considerations that
influence others by their piety, and exempted, they
think, by the law of Christ, from the rules and principles
of rectitude that are binding upon the people of the
world. Like tenants that are looking out for another
house, or servants who are about to change their situation, the formula much in use with them—that they are
preparing for another world—saves them much trouble
about the duties of the present world—the ordinary
courtesies and proprieties of life. But God cuts off the
superfluous tendrils of these persons by some humbling,
soul-searching dispensation of His providence, which
induces a soberer and juster habit of regarding things.
Gazing up into heaven after Christ in useless longings—
in yearning regrets, or in barren meditation, a cloud
hides Him from their sight; and they find the Christ
whom they have lost, as the disciples found Him, not on
the lonely heights of Bethany, but amid the busy haunts
of Jerusalem—not in idle reverie, but in active work in

the vineyard. Trial makes them more natural and more generally sympathetic. Their piety, while not less heavenly, becomes more human and congenial to all that is good and beautiful on earth; not less, but more spiritual, they attend diligently and faithfully to the business of life; and, amid scenes of common toil, and relations of social duty, they seek the things that are above. For useless tendrils of unpractical ascetic meditation, they produce richer and more abundant fruit of practical godliness.

Further still, the fruit itself must be thinned. The gardener prunes the cluster of grapes when young and tender, in order that the berries which are allowed to remain may be larger and finer. He does not wish the sap of the vine to be wasted in the production of a large quantity of small, crude, ill-developed fruit; but on the contrary, he is anxious that it should go to form compact bunches, composed of a smaller number of large, well-formed, and fully-ripened berries. And, therefore, he removes those that have the smallest promise in them. And so it is with the spiritual Husbandman. *Non multa, sed multum;* not many things, but much, is what He desires. Few are better than many. Gideon's picked three hundred were more effectual against the Midianites than the original twenty-and-two thousand who went up with him. The many pearls of our own are to be exchanged for the One Pearl of great price. In the Christian life there must be concentration of effort, conservation of force. Much moral energy is spent without effect on a multiplicity of objects, which, if husbanded and focussed on a few of the most important, would lead to far greater results. It is not the man who does a great many things ordinarily well who is the most useful, but the man who does a few things superlatively well. By essaying too much, and dissipating our powers we shall achieve little; our fruit may be abundant, but it will be small and comparatively worthless. The great fault of the Christian life of the present day is diffusion. It seeks to cover the widest surface at the expense of depth; and to perform every task at the risk of weakness. Euripides, the Greek poet, said, "The gods hate busy-bodies and those who do too much;" and there is a moral in the saying which was never more appropriate than now. Better far be content with faithfulness and thoroughness in the management of a few things, than in ruling carelessly and incompetently over many things. The cluster of righteousness composed of a smaller number of works of faith and labours of love, if only these be of the largest size and richest taste, is more precious in the sight of God than the cluster composed of innumerable petty efforts of zeal without wisdom or concentration.

It has been observed that the hues of the sunbeam which the growing plant does not reflect at one time are absorbed, like a stream running underground for a while, and re-appear in some after part. The whole spectrum appears separately or in combination, successively or contemporaneously, in the full growth of the plant during its life or death. The green foliage is followed by the crimson flower; the yellow corolla falls off and the purple pistil or the purple fruit appears. The branch begins in a pinkish hue, becomes a tender green, then advances to purple—at a further stage it is yellow, and finally it becomes russet in its decay. So is it with God's discipline of His people. Much of it may seem to be void and lost—to make no adequate return; but in some part or other of the life the effect of it is seen. If it fails to manifest itself in the leaf, it comes out in the blossom or fruit. The glory that is absent all its life from the common dull-green dock of the wayside, breaks out at last in the bright scarlet hue of its decay. The fragrance that is absent from the leaf and the blossom of the strawberry is apparent in the delicious fruit.

It may happen, however, that the purging, whose various forms and relations I have thus considered, may be here, and the fruition in eternity. The result of God's discipline is not always seen on earth; the *full* benefit of it is never enjoyed on earth. To the eye of sense the lives of many of God's people are failures, even when judged by their own Christian standard. They are placed in an unfavourable climate. Tropical by nature, they have been carried, like a wind-wafted seed, into a temperate zone, and have striven in vain to grow and flower among the hardy plants around them. They are incomplete. Their plans do not succeed. They seem to be useless; *infanti perduti*, perishing of the disease of life. Their branch is cut off in the midst of its promise. From the cradle to the grave they are sufferers. But it is a comforting thought, that what bears about it here the marks of incompleteness, and to our eyes the appearance of failure, belongs essentially to some vaster whole. The existence of so-called useless things is one of the grand proofs of another and a nobler state of being. We know not the use of such sparingly-distributed elements as the metals selenium, tellurium, vanadium; but they may bear the same relation to our globe that rudimentary organs do to the bodies of animals possessing them, which, though useless in the structure in which they occur, are typical of more highly-developed instruments or arrangements in other organisms. These rare and seemingly useless bodies on our earth, as Dr. George Wilson says, may be the prevailing or most important constituents of other worlds, and may perform functions there of which we have no conception. And so, apparently useless Christian lives here, that are tempted in the anguish of failure and suffering to exclaim with Elijah, under the bitter juniper-tree, "Take away my life, for I am not better than my fathers," may have in them the promise of rich heavenly fulfilment,—may be working out a far more exceeding and eternal weight of glory. The disk that the shadow of earth eclipses to the faintest crescent is full-orbed and flushed with light beyond that shadow. "The life that is here but a fallow field, bare and burning to the weary and assiduous toiler, amid the surrounding greenness and fruitfulness a converse oasis, a desert in a garden, is a fallow for the future garnering of the joyful crop that was sown in tears." Only that which is wholly of the earth can find its satisfaction on earth ; whereas that which is a failure here proves its heavenly character, becomes a sign of the fuller being into which all our efforts and achievements are destined to pass. Foxes have holes and the birds of the air have nests ; their desires and hopes are bounded by what they find on earth. They are at rest here; there is a complete correspondence between them and their circumstances. But the Christian who alone is truly man hath not where to lay his head. He is the pilgrim of eternity ; he cannot find amid all the fleeting show of this world a pillow for his head, a place of repose for his heart. For this reason all the Christian's sorrow should be, what the German poet calls it, *heimweh*, home-sickness, a heavenly hope that what he misses here he shall find hereafter, a heavenly belief that his ends are best subserved when most he feels them set at nought.*

---

* Every one is familiar with the peculiar vernation of the ferns, or in other words, the way in which they unfold their fronds in spring. When they emerge from the ground, they look like a bishop's crozier, their fronds being curled up on the stem. Gradually, as they feel the warm sunshine, they unroll themselves, until at last they are fully expanded in the summer air. It is a very remarkable fact, however, that there are certain ferns in which the points of the leaves are never totally unrolled. Several species of Jamesonia, growing on the Andes of Quito, retain to the very last the circinate vernation of their upper leaves. They are never seen fully expanded. So also, "there are many species of *Gleichenia* and *Mertensia*, in which the development of the leaf is arrested above the first pair of pinnules ; so that the point seeming to form a bud in the bifurcation either remains permanently undeveloped, or is only unfolded in the succeeding season. And then, again in

3. But I pass on to consider a third method of *purging* the branch in the True Vine, in order that it may bring forth more fruit—viz., *freeing it from its enemies.* The natural vine, owing to its rich productiveness, is peculiarly exposed to the attacks of numerous foes which prey upon it. A species of vegetable parasite not unfrequently assails it, called the *dodder.* This strange plant is a mere mass of elastic, pale-red, knotted threads, which shoot out in all directions over the vine. It springs originally from the ground, and if it finds no living plant near on which to graft itself, it withers and dies; but if there be a vine or any other useful plant within its reach, it surrounds the stem in a very little time, and henceforth lives on the fostering plant by its suckers only, the original root in the ground becoming dried up. A few minute brownish scales are all that it has instead of leaves, which are not required for the elaboration of sap, seeing that it feeds upon the prepared juices of other plants. One of the most remarkable peculiarities of this and other species of the same class, is the constant absence of all green colour,

like manner, only imperfectly." This sectional development of the leaf, which appears capable of lasting through many years, is a striking natural symbol of Christian lives that are imperfectly developed on earth. They partially unroll themselves—unfold some of their capabilities and beauties here, give promise of a brighter future; and yet through all their years that promise is not redeemed. Their highest powers are folded up in the bud; and their full unrolling and perfect expansion seem reserved for the congenial vernation of heaven's everlasting spring.

though exposed to the strongest sunlight. They
have also the curious property of resisting the attraction of light, towards which all the parts of other
plants irresistibly turn. The dodder is exceedingly
injurious to the plants it attacks, depriving them of
their nourishment, and strangling them in its folds.
Can we imagine a more striking natural emblem of
the law of sin and death with which the believer has
to contend, and from which he longs for deliverance?
The law in his members warring against the law of
his mind often produces a wretched discord and sense
of contradiction in his nature. He has a sense of
misery in which he does not acquiesce, of an alien
power, which often masters him and brings him into a
hated captivity to sense and sin. The evil that he
would not, that he does; and the good that he would,
that he does not. Maintaining this constant struggle,
hindered by this evil growth of former corruption
twining round his renewed nature, carried with him into
his highest aspirations and holiest services, and polluting
them, it is no wonder that he is not so fruitful in the
Master's vineyard as he might otherwise have been.
Of this body of sin and death it is impossible to get
wholly rid in this world. Like the dodder, whose
seeds begin to germinate before they leave the capsules,
and become immediately parasites, even before they
have quitted the parent plant, it has wonderful powers
of perpetuating itself. We can only hope to prevent the
dodder growing and spreading by perpetually breaking
and dividing its stalks before they have time to fruit, or

before the seed is mature; and we can only hope to keep down the remains of corruption within us by incessant effort, watchfulness, and prayer; not allowing them to develop into fruit and seed. How blessed will be the deliverance when this terrible despoiler of our peace and usefulness is finally and completely removed from us, when we are saved for ever from the power and presence of that sin from whose guilt the blood of Christ has freed us! Our Saviour said, that when the tares that obscured the beauty and hindered the development of the wheat should be gathered into bundles and burnt—that when all things that offended should be gathered out of His kingdom, then the righteous would shine forth as the sun in the kingdom of their Father. There would be no cloud of sin to hide their glory, no parasite of corruption to hinder their perfect development and detract from their bliss.

Other parasites of a vegetable nature attack the vine, and prove even more injurious than the dodder. Every one has heard of the terrible grape-mildew which, on its first appearance, utterly destroyed the vineyards in many parts of the world, and still annually re-appears to levy its tax upon the vine-grower. It consists of a fungus, whose growth spreads a white, downy mould over the surface of the grape, checking its development, and converting its pulp into a sour and watery mass of decay. Its seeds float in myriads in the atmosphere around, and lie on every inch of the vine's surface; but they do no harm unless the conditions of their germination exist—which are cold, wet seasons, with little sunshine—in which case they start into life, and grow with inconceivable rapidity, spreading ruin on every side. To a species of moral mildew the fruit of the Christian is also exposed—spoiling it, and making, as the prophet says, " his blossom go up as dust." In cold seasons, when clouds of unbelief rise up between the soul and the Sun of Righteousness, intercepting His light, this mildew is peculiarly destructive. It is a very solemn thought, that the spiritual atmosphere of the soul is full of the devices of the Prince of the power of the air— that the existence of another world of evil beyond our own world, makes all remissness on our part most dangerous. It is with us spiritually, as it is physically with the wanderer in the tropical forest, where life struggles with life so furiously, that, at the first sign of decay, a thousand pitiless enemies are crowding around. Woe to the sick, the wounded, the helpless, whose strength can no longer awe that creeping, leaping, hideous swarm ! So Satan and his powers of darkness are ever on the watch, waiting for the smallest opening of the door of our hearts, by unbelief or sin, to enter in and take possession. And whenever he has established his seat, we become more and more helpless in his hands, until at last a point may be reached when we become, like Judas Iscariot, identified with him in heart and mind. For, just as we become more and more identified by faith with Christ, until we can say, " I am crucified with Christ, nevertheless I live ; yet not I, but Christ liveth in me ;" so, on the other hand, by giving up ourselves to the will of the flesh, to do the work of the devil, we may become so identified with him, as that we shall think as he thinks, and act as he acts. How needful, then, to guard the heart against the first encroachments of evil; to walk in the light, so that the conditions in which the seeds of the kingdom of darkness can germinate, may not be found in us, and that, free from all spiritual blight and mildew, our abundant fruit may be all unto holiness !

It has long been held by farmers that the neighbourhood of barberry bushes produces rust in wheat, and science has recently established this opinion—has shown that the well-known orange-red spots so common on the leaves of the barberry, caused by a fungus, develop minute secondary seeds, which appear on the wheat in the shape of rust. A barberry hedge was recently planted on one of the railway embankments in the Côte-d'-Or, in France, when immediately the crops of wheat, rye, and barley in the neighbourhood became infested with rust—which was unknown before in the district. The railway company's own commissioners, after investigating the case, admitted that the account of the origin of the disease given by the farmers was correct, and considered them entitled to compensation. So, also, a species of blight on the pear-tree is closely connected with a glutinous parasite which grows on the juniper. Analogous to this natural fact is the spiritual one, that "evil communications corrupt good manners." We have a tendency to become like those with whom we associate; and if our friends are tainted with special evil practices, we lie very much at their mercy, if not to ruin us, yet to make us unhappy and sin-stained—to rob us of self-respect, and cloud us with perplexity. Christians are not altogether exempt from the common failing of falling into worldly, and not Scriptural estimates of men and things—of being misled by the customs of society, and adopting the peculiar conventional code of morality followed by the multitude among whom they live. Instead of giving examples of a higher standard of morality, they descend to the level of the average rate. The evils of the world cleave to them; their very Christianity is infected with worldliness, and thus becomes stunted, diseased, and uninfluential.

But the vine has also animal foes. In this country, the greatest pest of the vinery is the little red spider, whose movements over the leaves and fruit are exceedingly nimble, and which makes up by its vast numbers for its individual weakness. It punctures the fruit, sips its juice, and thus injures its appearance and quality. In the East, the land of the vine, the special foe of the vineyard is the fox. "Take us the foxes, the little foxes, that spoil the vines, for our vines have tender grapes"—or small grapes just out of blossom—says the beautiful Song of Solomon. The Eastern fox is a peculiarly attractive and graceful little creature. Its eyes are soft and bright, and ever on the watch; its motions agile and stealthy. Its cunning is concealed under a look of innocence and gentleness. No one would suspect it of doing so much damage in the vineyard. And, in this respect, it is a fitting symbol of some weakness or infirmity of believers—some sin of temper or tongue—which, although it may not endanger their safety, will, nevertheless, greatly mar their peace. Peevishness, irritability, obstinacy, uncourteousness, scandal-loving, unforgivingness of diposition, may seem so small and trifling as to be hardly entitled to be called sins at all. They may be extenuated and explained away, but they are in reality red spiders—little foxes, that spoil the tender grapes of the soul. They do not ravage the vineyard, like the boar of some fierce and gross transgression; but, like stealthy, cunning foxes, they spoil even more than they eat—they gnaw the bark which they do not devour, and thus cause the whole plant to wither and die—they brush off the delicate bloom, and mark with unsightly scars the sensitive purity of the various graces.

Ere I pass from this head, I may mention two other evils from which we must be purged. There is a disease called *rust*, which makes its appearance on the berries of the vine a few days after they are out. Every grape-grower is familiar with it. It is supposed to be caused by handling the berries while thinning them. Our vines have indeed tender grapes. The beauty of holiness is easily blurred: self-consciousness rusts it; affectation brushes off the fine edge—the delicate beauty of the various graces. From the Christian fruit that is handled in self-admiration, that is exhibited for the praise of others, that is paraded, an indefinable lustre has passed away. The crowning excellence of the fruit of holiness is its unconsciousness—the rich· bloom of self-forgetfulness and humility, on which the quivering dew-drop and sunshine of heaven may fall only to enhance its loveliness, but which the clumsy touch of man's self-consciousness blights and rusts.

Another disease known to gardeners is *shanking*, which makes its appearance just as the grapes are changing from the acid to the saccharine state, and arrests the transformation at once; the berry remaining perfectly acid, and at length becoming shrivelled up. It begins in the decay of the little stem or shank of the berry, and is supposed to be caused by the roots of the vine descending into a cold, wet subsoil. How often, alas, is it true of the believer, that his fruit is *shanked*, remaining sour when it should become sweet and palatable! Conversion in some seems to reverse the natural process, and change all the sugar of their nature into acid. Their fruit is bitter uncharitableness. The link of connection between their nature and their Christian profession seems to have decayed. The real sweetness of their natural disposition is not allowed to get access to and modify their forced and unnatural religiousness. Their roots go down into the cold, ungenial soil of Pharisaic strictness. The only cure for this spiritual disease is to seek more and more to be rooted in the love of Christ. The roots that go down into that heavenly substratum will draw up sufficient sap and force to make all the fruit on the branches sweet and natural as itself. Such are the diseases, parasites, and foes from which the vine-branch in Christ must be purged, if it is to bring forth much good fruit.

4. It remains to be stated, in conclusion, that God makes use of gentle influences to develop the fruitfulness of His people. The fruit requires to be gradually ripened by sun and rain and dew. At first it differs in no respect from a leaf. It is green in colour; it is furnished with stomates or breathing pores; its chemical constituents are the same; it acts upon the atmosphere as an ordinary leaf does. Nay, in some instances it produces adventitious buds from its summit, and if planted in the unripe state in the earth, it produces leafy shoots covered with flowers and fruit, like any ordinary seed or bud. Tasteless and bitter during its early growth, like a leaf, the fruit must be mellowed and sweetened by the heat-rays of the sun during the summer hours. As it ripens, it becomes more and more differentiated from the leaf, acts differently upon the atmosphere, absorbs oxygen, and thus becomes oxidized into luscious pulpiness and rosy or golden beauty.* Wonderful is the adaptation in the peculiar qualities of the sunshine at different seasons to the different stages of growth of the plant. In spring

---

* Blossoms and ripe fruits reverse the ordinary function of inhaling carbonic gas and exhaling oxygen, so characteristic of plants. They discharge the function of animals in taking oxygen from the air, and replacing it by carbonic acid. Hence the beauty and variety of their colouring. Leaves breathe after the manner of plants; blossoms and fruit after the manner of animals. In the flower and fruit—the most highly organized parts of vegetation—the plant thus aspires towards the animal. And it is interesting to notice that flowering plants and warm-blooded animals appeared at the same time on the earth, and for the same reason. In the highly carbonated atmosphere of the earliest geologic times,

there is more actinism or chemical power, so as to cause the seed to germinate, the bud to sprout, and the sap to flow. In summer there is more light, in order that carbon may be secreted, by which the plant may grow and elaborate its structure and elements; in autumn there is more heat, in order that the vegetative processes may be checked, the fruit and grain ripened, and the leaf browned before its fall. It has been observed that the plant bends *towards* the luminous and actinic rays of the spectrum, while it *bends away* from the heat-rays. Thus, we may argue, that the one class of rays stimulates and the other checks vegetation. The sap rises, and the seed germinates and grows in spring and summer under the excitement of light and actinism; the sap recedes, the processes of vegetation are checked, and fruit is formed and ripened under the influences of the heat-rays, from which the plant is found to bend. An adaptation no less wonderful to each growing stage of the believer may be seen in God's dealings with him. He suits the communications of His grace to our individual and special necessities. The Sun of Righteousness showers light and heat, and endows us with power from on high for our growth and ripening. His seasons of grace have their own special peculiarities,

flowerless plants, such as ferns and club mosses, alone could maintain themselves; while flowering plants could only appear when the air became purer and fitter for the respiration of the higher animals. This is another proof of the close correspondence between flowers and fruit and human life.

suited for the particular spiritual condition of His people. Sometimes they have more light and insight; sometimes more power of active effort; sometimes more warmth of feeling and passionateness of devotion. But all these varying influences and moods are correlated, and work together for the highest good. Through these seasons of grace, with their changes relatively to each other, the Christian advances to the joy of harvest.

We have considered the severer dealings of God's providence with His people—His pruning and afflictive dispensations. But we must remember that this is His exceptional treatment of us. Judgment is His strange work. Chastisement is occasional, while parental tenderness is uniform and continuous. Goodness and mercy follow us all the days of our life, though we may have wearisome days and months of vanity appointed to us. It is necessary that the general character of God's dealings with us should be gracious, and not grievous; otherwise, we could not sweeten and ripen. In the absence of sunshine, we should continue immature; our fruit would be like our leaf, sour and green. The plant needs occasional storm and cold to deepen its roots, harden its wood, and check its too luxuriant and flaccid growth. The frost that withers its blossom, its most frail and transient part, strengthens its root, its most enduring part. But it is the warm sunshine, shining day by day upon it, the soft dew refreshing it every night, the balmy breeze fanning its leaves, and setting its currents of sap in motion; it is these gentle, uniform, and long-continued influences, that cause it to bud, and blossom, and bring forth its fruit. And so, trials are occasionally needed to strengthen the believer's faith, deepen his hope, and purify his love; the chastisement that blights his beautiful, transient things, gives him a firmer hold of more precious and enduring things. But it is the continued light of God's countenance, the warmth of His love, the power of His Spirit, working mightily within him, both to will and to do of His good pleasure; it is the dew of God's grace upon him in the night watches, when he communes with his own heart and is still; it is these tranquil and uniform influences that transform him in the renewing of his mind, and make him a faithful and fruitful Christian. "The work of righteousness is peace, and the effect of righteousness quietness and assurance for ever." It is good to flourish in the calm, serene atmosphere of temporal prosperity, to be blessed in health, and friends, and success, in capacity, and scope for usefulness, if only these things are enjoyed in the Lord as covenant blessings; for, as it is the accumulated sum of light and heat that ripens the plant, so it is the accumulated sum of sanctified prosperity that ripens the Christian. Every cultivated plant requires a certain quantity of heat for its development; but it is the same thing whether this heat is distributed over a shorter or longer space of time, so that certain limits are not exceeded. If cold, stormy days intervene, it will get less heat, and therefore will take longer to ripen; if bright, warm days come, it will be sooner ready for the harvest. The varying date of our harvest

every season shows the operation of this law. Under
the influence of the midnight sun of the arctic regions,
the life of plants runs through the same cycle of change
in six weeks, which it takes four or five months to
accomplish in Italy. In like manner, some Christians
have long and uninterrupted enjoyment of favourable
circumstances of providence and grace, and therefore
ripen faster than others whose growth is often checked
by chill winds and stormy skies. But the life of the
latter is often more extensive than that of the former.
The Christian who has more trials is often allowed to
spread his process of ripening over a longer term.
Enoch, walking with God in uninterrupted prosperity,
ran, in three hundred and sixty-five years, through the
same cycle of life which it took the other partriarchs
upwards of nine hundred years to fulfil. Some require
to live to old age to ripen for heaven; others are ripe
in the prime and vigour of life.*

It is to one of these tranquil and continuous agencies
that our Lord refers in His conversation with His dis-

---

* It has been suggested—and the thought opens up a delightful
vista of meditation—that one of the sources of variety in heaven
will arise from the different ages at which the redeemed have been
called to their reward. Those who have died young will still
retain the freshness and fairness of youth ; those who have been
taken away in the prime and vigour of maturity will still exhibit
the dignity and vigour of that riper period ; while those who have
departed in the sunset of life will still show the mellowness,
tenderness, and serenity of a beautiful old age ; and this, notwithstanding the great change in the widening and transfiguration
of their being which eternity will have produced upon them.
Such a variety will give to the fields of heaven that interest and

ciples—"Now ye are clean," or *purged*, "through the word which I have spoken unto you." The disciples were already pure; ideally purified, through their union with Christ. They were separated by His Word from the superstition, and unbelief, and vain conversation of the world. His ministry in general had found out what was best and worthiest in them, and had elevated them morally above their countrymen. The peculiarity of His teaching was, that it not only imparted new ideas, but was accompanied by a spiritual power which penetrated their souls, and produced there new spiritual life and energy. It was a purifying element, seeking out every hidden sin, and concealed corruption and weakness; and removing the pollution, with the cause; healing sickness by its health, strengthening weakness by its might, and dissipating every form of darkness by its light. It was a spiritual ozone, purifying the spiritual atmosphere into which it was introduced, and making it healthy and invigorating. The word of Him who said to the leper, "I will, be thou clean," was in the disciples cleansing them. By the tribulation of His doctrine, the hard sayings which the carnally-minded could not bear, they were winnowed from the chaff of the multi-

beauty which the succession of the flowers imparts to the fields of earth. Who knows whether this may not be one of the reasons why death comes at every season of human life? At all events, a thought like this is fitted to cheer the hearts of those who yearn for their beloved lost ones, and who sorrow, most of all, that they shall see their familiar faces no more,—that those who will be restored to their arms in the glorified state will retain too little of what was so sweet and precious here.

tude who followed Jesus, and enabled to say, when others turned back and walked no more with Him, "To whom can we go but unto Thee, for Thou hast the words of eternal life."

But, though regarded by Jesus as ideally pure, the disciples were not so really, since even a Peter could fall, and all of them were capable of forsaking Him in His hour of need. After His resurrection, they were to be actually purified, by the Spirit bringing home to their memories and hearts the things which Jesus said and did; and how real and thorough was that purification we learn from the testimony borne to them by their enemies. "They took knowledge of them, that they had been with Jesus." And so it is with all Christ's disciples, in every age and country. St. Paul speaks frequently of this ideal purity through the word of Jesus. It is a great truth that underlies very much of his language. He contemplates the Christian as perfected *ideally*, and yet *practically* striving to realize this perfection. We have already put on the *new* man, but we are continually to *become new*. He who sees the end from the beginning, and all the processes of life at once, and as a whole, sees us complete in Christ, wanting nothing. But this completeness we are to work out in our own slow growth and experience. And the word of Christ, spoken to us, is the agency by which this process is to be carried on. We are to be sanctified by the truth as it is in Jesus. In proportion to our knowledge and improvement of the word will be our joy, our likeness to Christ, our growth in grace, our usefulness in the world, and our meetness for heaven. The word of truth will become in us the word of life. It will purge away and remove all the evils and hindrances to our fruitfulness within us and without us. If these things be in us and abound—if the word of God dwell *richly* in us—they make us that we shall neither be barren nor unfruitful in the knowledge of our Lord Jesus Christ.   Clean already, through the saving word which Christ has spoken to our souls in the hour of conversion, let us seek more and more to realize practically in our daily life this imputed purity.   "Not as though I had already attained, either were already perfect; but I follow after, if that I may apprehend that for which also I am apprehended of Christ Jesus.   This one thing I do; forgetting those things which are behind, and reaching forth unto those things which are before, I press toward the mark for the prize of the high calling of God in Christ Jesus.   Let us, therefore, as many as be *perfect* be thus minded."

CHAPTER VI.

ABIDING IN THE VINE.

"Abide in me, and I in you.　As the branch cannot bear fruit of itself, except it abide in the vine ; no more can ye, except ye abide in me."—JOHN xv. 4.

"He that abideth in me, and I in him, the same bringeth forth much fruit : for without me ye can do nothing."—JOHN xv. 5.

FRUITFULNESS in a natural tree is produced, as we have seen, by a combination of causes. The sunshine and the rain, the properties of the soil in which the tree is placed, and the surrounding circumstances of situation, climate, and exposure, are outward agencies by ·which the fulness of its growth and fertility is developed. To aid these natural means, the husbandman interposes with his artificial processes of cultivation, his digging, dressing, and pruning, repressing useless exuberant growth, and stimulating latent useful growth. But in order that all these natural and artificial agencies—which are entirely outward—may be effectual in accomplishing the desired end, it is necessary that the inward vital functions of the tree should be fully performed, that the vessels should be open, and the sap have free course through them, that there should be no obstruction anywhere to the carrying on of the various processes of life. The sunshine and the shower, instead of developing fruitfulness on a bough which, owing to some obstruction, does not participate in the general life of the tree—which does not get its proper share of sap and vital stimulus—will only help to wither and decompose it. The pruning of a branch that is imperfectly nourished, or that has no latent growth, will only hasten its decay. The outward means of growth, therefore, must be aided by the inward; the stimulating influences of light, heat, and moisture, and of purging and dressing, must be accompanied by the proper exercise of the vital force within.   And thus is it, too, in the spiritual vineyard.   Fruitfulness in the Christian is caused by the combination of outward and inward means; by the outward dealings of God's providence, and the inward dealings of God's grace.   He is pruned by chastisement, and he is stimulated by the indwelling Spirit. The afflictive dispensations of God's providence will have no beneficial influence, unless the spiritual life within be properly active.   The trials of life will only embitter and harden the nature, unless there be faith and love to use them as means of growth, as inverse aids to progress.   Affliction is not joyous, but grievous, nevertheless, afterward it yieldeth the peaceable fruits of righteousness, not in every one—not in those who are only anxious to get quit of it as speedily as possible, and who regard it as an unmitigated evil—no, but in *those who are exercised thereby.* Our light affliction, which is but for a moment, worketh for us a far more exceeding and eternal weight of glory, not necessarily—not in itself—but only *while we look not at the things which are seen, but at the things which are not seen.*

Affliction in itself is the curse of Adam that blights and destroys, the sorrow of the world that worketh death. If there is no spiritual life within to make use of it as a stimulus, it acts like a winter storm, increasing the dreariness and desolation of a nature that is already dead. But when faith is in lively exercise, when we look at the things which are unseen and eternal in the heavens, our affliction is like a summer storm, purifying the sultry air, restoring and renewing our jaded energies, and stimulating to greater loveliness and productiveness the life that is growing in our soul. Of course, this is equally true of the joys of life. Health, success, prosperity in the possessions of the heart and the hand, will also contract and harden the soul if there be no spiritual vitality to use them as its pabulum, to be led by the goodness of God to repentance and increased devotion. Our Saviour, in His allegory of the Vine, shows this necessary correlation between the outward and the inward means of growth. After mentioning the purging of the fruitful branch, He goes on to say to His disciples, "Abide in Me, and I in you. He that abideth in Me, and I in him, the same bringeth forth much fruit; for without Me ye can do nothing." The connection of thought here implied seems to be, that the purging of the branch by God's providence will be of no avail unless that branch abide in Christ. If there is no vital connection kept up all the time between the branch and the Vine, the purging will have no effect in developing fruit. While the Husbandman faithfully performs His part in cultivating the Vine and the branches, and the Vine fulfils its function in sending its sap into the branch, the branch must do its duty, must co-operate with them in abiding in the Vine. Thus, the fruitfulness of the branch is the result of the co-operation of three different powers—the will of God in our sanctification, the will of Christ in abiding in us, and our will in abiding in Christ. While the outward cultivation is going on, a living faith in Christ is inwardly in lively exercise. We have already considered the outward pruning of God's providence; let us now consider the inward abiding of the believer in Christ. We have seen what God's part in the work of grace is; let us see what the believer has to do.

That man has something to do in the development of his fruitfulness—that he is a fellow-worker with God in the matter of his growth in grace—is an idea which seems sufficiently obvious, and yet it is one that is constantly overlooked or misunderstood. While there are some who act upon the supposition that self-salvation is possible, that the first step in the conversion of the soul is taken by the sinner himself, there are others who go to the opposite extreme, and assert that man from first to last is passive in the work—that it is God's work entirely. Man is merely a vessel into which grace is poured, and by which it is contained. The operations of grace in us are like the functions of the physical powers in our bodies, carried on independently of our mind and will, like the process of digestion and the circulation of the blood, which go on as well when we are asleep as when we are awake. This popular notion is an utter perversion of Scripture language, which everywhere yields decisive testimony against that scheme of "irresistible grace" which would turn men into mere machines, and take away all moral value from the victories which Christ obtains over the obstinacy and pride of the creature's will. Lightning is the most striking natural symbol of God's power; it can cleave its way direct through every opposing obstacle, rend the rock and the tree to get to its end; nothing can resist it, and yet it uniformly chooses the path of least resistance. Its course down a tree is not in a straight line, but in a series of spirals or zig-zags, following the mode in which the tree develops its leaves, as if seeking the parts of the trunk that are softest and easiest to traverse. It prefers to pass through objects that are good conductors of electricity; and is carried harmlessly from the spire of the Church to the foundation by the lightning-rod. In the same way it may be said that God's power is irresistible. He could accomplish His will in us in spite of our utmost resistance; He could drag us captive at His chariot wheels. He could save the lost sinners of Jerusalem in this way instead of weeping over them and leaving them to perish; He could constrain the young man whom He loved to follow Him—instead of leaving him to go away grieved. But this would be contrary to the whole genius and design of the scheme of grace. God uniformly works only in those who are made willing in the day of His power. His grace chooses good conductors of its spiritual influence. He gives light according to the opening of the eyes; He makes as though He would pass by and needs to be besought. He knocks at the door and waits for its opening; He says "I am the door, by Me, *if* any man enter in, he shall be saved." All His offers of grace are conditional on our acceptance. He works in us mightily, but it is *to will and to do.* Faith and re-pentance are the gifts of God, yet we believe and repent, and not God. Christ abides in us, but we are to abide in Him.

In this respect the analogy between the branch of the vine and the believer fails. The union of the branch with the vine is not a voluntary, but a mechani-cal one. It is formed by the laws of growth; it is sub-ject solely to the irresistible law of vegetable life and the all-pervading law of gravitation. There is no choice or consciousness in the matter. The branch cannot but abide in the vine, so long as the conditions of nature are fulfilled. But the abiding of the disciple in Christ is a purely voluntary thing. He is not governed by an irresistible fate. God made the heavens to declare His glory and the firmament to show forth His handiwork by the operation of law. Gravitation prevails throughout the world of matter; instinct and vital force throughout the world of life. Every object in nature obeys the will of God mechanically; it has no consciousness, no choice; it acts of necessity; it is what it is, and does what it does in simple, perfect, unknowing dependence upon the will of God. But it is widely different with man. God created him a free agent, capable of free obedience or free transgression. This spirit which is in man is by far the most wonderful of God's creations. It can do what no mineral, or plant, or animal, however great its force or power of instinct, can do; it can disobey God's law, can rebel, can defy and resist God—in short, can *sin.* That little word *sin* expresses at once the height of man's glory and the depth of his degradation.

The first command addressed to Adam and Eve in Eden, " Of the tree of knowledge of good and evil, thou shalt *not* eat of it," implied the immense difference between man and the rest of creation. To all His other creatures God's command was positive, " *Thou shalt;* " indicating that they had no alternative but to obey. To man, on the contrary, His command was negative, " *Thou shalt not;* " implying that he had liberty of will—power of choice. And it is a most significant circumstance that all God's commandments to man are negative in form, each involving, of course, the positive equivalent; " Thou shalt not take the name of the Lord thy God in vain ;" " Thou shalt not kill," etc. This fact is made a strong objection to the morality of the Bible by Mr. Stuart Mill in his " Essay on Liberty," on the ground that it curbs man's freedom of will, and makes his religious character a mere negation—a low, abject, servile thing, which, submit itself as it may to what it deems the Supreme Will, is incapable of rising to, or sympathising with the Supreme Goodness. The God of the Christian, according to his showing, is a tyrant who rules by fear, who considers it no evil to crush out any of the human faculties and capacities, and whose laws, commanding obedience solely by authority, have a tame and dreary uniformity. But the above considerations show us how groundless is this objection; how thoroughly, on the contrary, the negative form of God's commandments establishes man's liberty, and makes his religious character an unconstrained and positive thing.   So far is Christianity from being an exclusively negative system of morality, that throughout it shows the relation of the negative to the positive, of prohibition to injunction, to be of the closest kind.   With all the necessarily negative admonition, is not the Christian always instructed to *abhor* that which is evil, and *cleave* to that which is good; to put *off* the old man and put *on* the new man?   " Putting away lying, speak every man truth with his neighbour."   "Let no corrupt communication proceed out of your mouth, but that which is good to the use of edifying."   " Thou shalt not commit adultery, thou shalt not kill, thou shalt not bear false witness, thou shalt not covet :" and if there be any other commandment, it is briefly comprehended in this saying, " Thou shalt love thy neighbour as thyself." The whole law hangs on two great commandments—love to God, and love to man; which are not negative, but positive. Nay, we have a still higher generalisation, by which one positive word, viz., *love*, is made to comprehend everything human. Love is the fulfilling of the law; and perfect love casteth out all fear. Instead, therefore, of there being no true liberty under Christianity, it is only those who are under law to Christ who walk at liberty. It is the truth of Christ that makes us free indeed. In proportion as a man becomes Christian, so in proportion is he set at liberty from the attraction of "the course of the world," from the brute laws of matter, from the magnetic currents of circumstances, from the law of averages, by which we can determine the moral disorders of men with as much certainty as we can predict an eclipse. He enters into a higher order than that of mere law; he is not under the law, but under grace. He is no longer a thing, but a person—separated from nature, made to recognise his personality, and called by God's name.

It is this unique immunity from passive and compulsory subjection—the profoundest mystery alike of philosophy and revelation—that renders man a fit companion for God. His first transgression of the law of God was, in one sense, a step in advance, inasmuch as it was a revelation to him of the dignity of his own nature, a development of the free power that was latent in him. His eyes were opened, and he saw himself invested as with a Divine sovereignty; he found himself capable of transgressing God's law. "And the Lord God said, *Behold, the man is become as one of us, to know good and evil.*" Had God brought into existence only creatures having no will or choice, then He would have been alone in the universe. He would have been—if we can make such a comparison—like Adam when the animals were brought before him, and he could find no partner among them. There would have been none among the creatures of His hand capable of knowing, loving, and worshipping Him. The animals, plants, and stones of the creation would have obeyed His will without knowing it to be His will; they would have fulfilled the ends of their existence without knowing what these ends were. They would have answered His purposes perfectly, but only as machines. They would have been incapable of transgression; and, therefore, of true obedience. They would have had no progress, no history; what they were thousands of ages ago, that exactly would they be thousands of ages hence. Such a mindless, will-less, impersonal solitude would have yielded, so far as we can see, no happiness or glory to God. He who said of man, "It is not good that the man should be alone; I will make him an help meet for him," must Himself have had the same feeling—wished not Himself to be alone, unrevealed and unloved. He desired, so to speak, to find an help meet for Himself—to surround Himself with intelligent and moral beings, on whom He might lift the light of His countenance, who could in some measure understand His thoughts, and sympathise with His ends, who could obey Him, not from the necessity of their being, but from the spontaneous affection of the heart. And, therefore, He made man in His own image, reflecting the spontaneity of the Divine will—not the slave, but the subject, steward, and friend of God. Therefore God blessed him with the visible sovereignty of the earth, taught him language, talked and walked with him in the garden in the cool of the day, at sundry times and in divers manners spake in times past unto the fathers by the prophets, and in these last days to us by His Son. Therefore, the True Vine furnishes Himself with branches which repeat His image, and are partakers of His nature.

It will thus be seen that the symbol of the vine and its branches fails in picturing fully the nature of the union between the believer and Christ. The union of the vine and its branches is one of physical necessity; the union between believers and Christ is one of choice. But defects of this nature must always exist, in tracing the analogy between an object that is lower and one that is higher in the scale of existence. Each thing can be read only by its own light; and the less cannot illuminate the greater. Mountains seen from the plain are foreshortened, and appear smaller than they really are. The intervening ridges and hollows are blended into one uniform imposing outline which dwarfs the summit. To form a correct idea of their size and height they must be seen from their own level; and he who is familiar with the aspect of a mountain from its base only, is astonished to find how it grows in magnitude and grandeur the higher he ascends an opposite mountain.   In like manner, the full significance of a truth can only be estimated from its own level. To express a complete analogy, the objects compared must be equal.   Only a human symbol can convey all that the idea of man implies.   The higher existence involves the lower and something more which makes it higher.   The vegetable is a mineral and something more which makes it a vegetable; the animal is a vegetable and something more which makes it an animal; man is a mineral,* a vegetable, and an animal, and something more which makes him a man.   He sums up in himself all other existences in the world; in his feeding and sleeping he is a mere plant; in his building and movements he is an animal; but, he has in addition his own original and unique humanity, reason, and the power of free will, which make him distinctively man.   Consequently the lower existences, which man never ceases to be, seeing that they are the basis and factors of his perfection, are able to symbolize his being only up to a certain point.   The vine can express all that is peculiar to the vegetable kingdom in man.   Its structure anticipates the human model;

---

* The foundation of man's structure is mineral; most of his skeleton is mineral; there is iron in his blood. It is a significant fact, that in the very core of the human brain— where Des Cartes placed the soul—the microscope discloses a small mineral deposit, consisting of grape-like masses of crystalline matter. Thus, the very functions of thought and of spiritual life are based upon the rocks of the earth. The machinery of the mind and soul, like that of a watch, revolves on jewelled pivots of the mineral kingdom !

the phenomena of its existence prefigure human nature, expressing the same ideas on a lower platform. In every particular connected with organic existence, it is his complete counterpart; but it has nothing corresponding to his intelligence and freedom of will. It is destitute of his nobler organs, and the spiritual powers of which they are the instruments and exponents, because it is destined for a lower sphere of being, and to subserve uses for which a nature higher than the simply vegetative would have rendered it unfit. By the very limitations of its nature, therefore, it is incapable of fully representing all that is involved in the relations of man. Could it do so, it would no longer be a vine, but a man.

No single natural symbol, indeed, can do justice to a subject so peculiar in its nature, and so boundless in its extent as the nature of Christ, and the relations between Him and His people. Hence it is that types and symbols in Scripture are divested of specific imperfections, endowed with attributes not naturally belonging to them, and multiplied in number, so as to accomplish by combination what could not be done by individuality. Under the Old Testament economy, two scape-goats, the one slain and the other set free, were required to symbolize the two great truths, or rather the two-fold aspect of the same truth, united in Christ Jesus—that He who died for our sins rose again for our justification. The prophecies regarding Christ were very multiform and abundant—representing Him from the most varied points of view. Our Saviour, in His parables, compared the kingdom of heaven to a great variety of objects ; and He Himself is said to be a Rock, a Lily, a Lamb, Water of Life, Light of Life ; all these allusions falling short of the glory they are applied to illustrate, yet aiding our meditations. The whole earth is full of His glory; it requires, therefore, the whole earth to express the *pleroma,* or fulness of that Word from which all creation originated—to fill up that grand outline of redemption which had been sketched from eternity. And just as we have four Gospels to portray our Lord's life on earth, and we are thus made to linger amid scenes and incidents, represented from different points of view, until they are thoroughly impressed upon our minds and hearts, instead of hurrying superficially through a single Gospel to the expansion of the epistles; so we have our Saviour represented by multiform types, prophecies, and natural symbols, that seeing Him thus exhibited from the most varied points of view, we may be induced to dwell on the contemplation of His glory, until we are changed into the same image.

In order to make the allegory of the Vine most effectual in its teaching, our Lord therefore endows the plant with the qualities which belong to man. He speaks of the vine as being furnished with the power of choice; the consciousness of its own existence. The branches are represented as remaining in the vine, not by the mechanical necessity of physical law, but by conscious, voluntary election. "As the branch cannot bear fruit of itself, except it abide in the vine : no more can ye, except ye abide in Me." And thus endowing the vine-branches with human power, how strikingly do they teach us the lessons inscribed on all lower nature! How admirably does the patient abiding of the branch in the vine picture what ought to be the constant union and communion of believers in Jesus! The more thoroughly the man imitates, in this respect, the plant, the nearer he reaches perfection. The believer is required to make in him his liberty of choice what in the plant is a matter of necessity. He is to do *consciously* and *willingly*—what the plant does *unconsciously* and *will-lessly*. Scripture frequently appeals to this perfect submission of nature to the Divine will, in contrast to man's waywardness and disobedience. " Hear, O heavens! and give ear, O earth! I have nourished and brought up children, and they have rebelled against me." The stork and the swallow obey their migratory instincts, and know the appointed time of departure for a warmer climate; but God's times and seasons of grace are unknown to and disregarded by man. The sluggard is sent to the ant to learn prudence; those who are exposed to danger are commanded to flee and save their lives, and be as the heath in the wilderness—like the rose of Jericho, which, when its native spot is dried up, is carried by the wind to some moist place where its seed may be sown, and the life of the species perpetuated. Nay, our Saviour even said, on the occasion of His triumphant entrance into Jerusalem, that if the Hosannas of the multitude should be hushed, " the very stones would immediately cry out." All nature obeys God's will; and the capriciousness of man's will is the only uncertain, disturbing element in a world of perfect order and harmony.

Commonest, and apparently least interesting, of all phenomena is the abiding of a branch in a tree; and yet there is a mystery and a wonder in it which familiarity veils from our view. We do not think how it is that an oak or an elm holds out a branch in the air, day and night, summer and winter, year after year, unceasingly. The power which upholds the branch against the combined influences of the weight of the air, and the gravitation of the earth, must in reality be very great, though unappreciated by us. It is a real exercise of vital force, though the tree is unconscious of it, and feels no fatigue from it. Mr. Buckle says, "the power which a plant exercises of holding a leaf erect during an entire day, without pause and without fatigue, is an effort of astonishing vigour, and is one of many proofs that a principle of compensation is at work; so that the same energy which in the animal world is weakened by being directed to many objects, is in the vegetable world strengthened by being concentrated on a few." Marvellous is the mute, steadfast patience of vegetable life. We cannot understand it, or put ourselves *en rapport* with it. David Scott, the great Scottish painter, asked passionately, bending over a flower, why he could not enter into its life. But, though man is sympathetically united to the whole world, vegetable life is, and will ever be, inconceivable to us, because we cannot live it. And yet we seem to see in it something akin to the quality of patience in ourselves. And it is through this patience that all the processes of life are carried on so perfectly in the plant. There is no restlessness, no self-will, no weariness or self-conscious waywardness to frustrate these processes. The most complete harmony is discoverable through all its parts, and woven in the very fabric of its nature. The buds appear in their proper order and place, the leaves have a fixed arrangement, the flowers blossom at determinate points. Not a leaf varies from its position, or a blossom from its order, any more than a star from its orbit. By its patient abiding in the vine, the branch receives without interruption the vital forces and juices that are needful to develop its growth and produce fruitfulness. Through storm and sunshine, through darkness and light, through winter and summer, there is nothing to hinder the intercommunion of vital substances and impulses between the branch and the vine. It is this patience that we are required to imitate; this faithfulness that we are to cherish. What is in the plant a matter of necessity—an unconscious result of unconscious physical powers, should be in the believer the blessed result of a living faith and a devoted love.

Patience is the great lesson taught us by Nature. The orbits of the planets, the order of the seasons, the laws of growth—all teach us the blessed necessity of waiting. Nature never hurries, never takes leaps, never wearies; atom by atom, little by little, perseveringly and steadily, she achieves her work. She is timed not by the hours and minutes of men's watches, but by the stars in their courses. The everlasting mountains are her gnomon, and the shadows cast by their grey, storm-scalped summits mark the hours of her dial. Everything in nature partakes of the majesty of measured progressiveness and slowness—the absence of haste and hurry. The encaustic lichen on the rock endures for centuries, apparently unchanged, while all the time its tiny fangs are crumbling away its matrix into soil for future fields. The yew-tree casts its shadow over the graves of many generations, and seems always the same, while it is insensibly growing in height and girth. And this slowness of growth and steadfastness of purpose, this sure and successive unfolding of creative plan, this advancement in the same uniform line from "the blade to the ear, and from the ear to the full corn in the ear," characteristic of the smallest object, belongs to the development of the great earth itself—extending over immense periods, compared with which the antiquity of recorded time is but as yesterday. How unweariedly does nature produce the same primroses and daisies year after year! She never tires of repeating herself—of wearing the same look generation after generation—of saying the same things over and over again in the sigh of her winds, and the murmur of her waters. What a silent, but powerful rebuke to our love of novelty and change—to the spending of our time in nothing else but either to tell or to hear some new thing! How soothing to our excited feelings is this familiar sameness—this peacefulness of patience— every season! We come, in the restlessness of our losses and wants, to the bosom of our calm mother, and she lays her cool, steady hand upon our hot brow, and stills the fever at our heart, and teaches us to wait, like herself, " till next year for our lily."

Our whole life, in the midst of nature's works and ways, is a discipline of steadfast, immovable waiting. All her tribulations are intended to work patience, and patience a hope that maketh not ashamed. We raise our home by human art in a few months; but we have to wait for years for the noble ancestral trees that are to dignify it. We send our messages to the ends of the earth with the speed of lightning; but we have to wait a whole summer for the growing of our food under the patient heavens. Wonderfully impressive are the lessons of patience which are given to us by nature in these days of steam and electricity, when life is sorely driven and distracted by the multiplicity of its objects. Strangely well-timed, we cannot but think, are the vast discoveries of science in space and time to the moral necessities of our epoch. An age of electricity needed to find out how immensely old the world is, how boundless are the dimensions of the starry heavens. In the slow, deliberate times of our ancestors it was supposed that our earth was only six thousand years old, and the only world in space—sun, moon, and stars being lamps to light its path, fires to warm its hearth. This contraction of the universe, by limiting life's horizon, was fitted to quicken their dull thoughts and hasten their laggard steps. Partaking of the littleness

of nature, they were stimulated to revolve quickly
through their narrow arc. Having such a short tenure
of such a little, transient world, it behoved them to
use all diligence in order to make the most of their
possession. But, on the other hand, in these days of
wonderful activity of body and mind, we have found
out that, for untold ages, nature has been working on,
ushering creation after creation, like the successive
pictures of a panorama, upon the scene; and that, in
the heavens, worlds upon worlds, independent of ours,
grander and more richly endowed, spread on in avenues
of light into infinity. We need the counterpoise of this
discovery to calm the elation of our pride and the fever
of our activity. If our works are now more quickly
done, and our lives lived more intensely, than those of
our ancestors, we feel that they are done and lived
amid larger spaces and in longer eras—we feel that we
have a wider circumference to traverse. Underneath
the field we cultivate so busily are the ages of the
geologist, above it are the spaces of the astronomer.
The grandeur of an immeasurable horizon awes us into
stillness. The earth we inhabit is vaster to us now,
if we can traverse its surface more speedily; and if our
art has taught us to be hasty and impatient, it supplies
its own corrective in the wider and truer views which it
gives us of nature, and which, in their turn, teach us the
slow, patient manners of nature. In every sea we cross,
in every mountain we climb, in every field we sow and
wood we plant, as Emerson says, we see more than
ever now, with our improved methods, that patience is

needed. We cannot get to our end at once; for our feet are still slow and our strength small, while the sea and land are large, and delays of wind and sun, delays of the seasons, delays of the properties of matter, still hinder us. We are "timed to nature," and must tarry the Lord's leisure. We are brought into harmony with the ways of the universe. Our restless human life is adapted to the repose and unity of purpose of the vegetable; and, as the branch abideth in the vine, so are we taught, by our new experiences and grand discoveries, to abide in Christ.

But what is meant by *abiding* in Christ? On this subject we are apt to cherish erroneous ideas. We think that abiding in Christ is mere outward attendance upon the means of grace, engaging in devotional exercises, or doing some religious work in the world. It involves these outward exercises; but it implies much more. These are the forms in which it expresses itself, and is exhibited to the world. But it is not so much action as experience, not so much doing as being. It is an attitude of the soul. It is the habitual direction of the thoughts to Christ, the twining of the affections around Him, resting upon His finished work, and looking to Him as the Author and Finisher of faith. It is faith in Him in lively exercise; love to Him ardently cherished; hope in Him constantly realised. It is forsaking father and mother, houses and lands, and making Him the one moral centre of our being. Such abiding in Christ is not resting in indolence: it tasks all the energies of the soul; brings into intensest action the most vigorous capacities of the spiritual life. It is manifested alike while busy or idle, in solitude or society, when engaged in direct acts of public worship, or when cherishing the spirit of devotion in the absence of its forms.

How seldom does our piety partake of this character! It is usually a fickle thing, subject to fits and starts, frames and feelings. It has little root in itself, and though it springs up rapidly, and looks fair for a while, in the time of temptation it is apt to wither away. We cling to Jesus in certain seasons with ardent devotion, and then let go our hold for some other object, and leave our first love. We get weary at times of the protracted struggle of the Christian life. The freshness and fervour of the early years of our conversion are apt to vanish, the transcendent glory of the Christian faith to become dim, and we are in danger of being drifted away from Christ by the strong tide of worldliness that is running against us. Our religious profession is apt to become like the growth of a foliaceous lichen on a stone; the more the lichen grows and widens its circumference, the more it decays and becomes empty in the centre, leaving a mere rim of living matter. And so the older our profession becomes, the more apt it is to die out at the heart; to become a mere empty hollow rim, whose life is all on the outside; growing more in profession, and less in love, to the Saviour. We run to Jesus in trouble and danger, as a traveller runs to seek shelter from a storm; but we leave Him when the sun shines and all is bright again.

How seldom is it true of us that we make Him our dwelling-place, our continual resort, the home of our soul! He is to us as a wayfaring-man that turneth aside to tarry only for a night, instead of being our familiar friend, the perpetual guest of our heart.

And hence it is that our piety is so stationary and unsatisfactory. Hence it is that we know so little of Him. He becomes a stranger to us, and we make ourselves strangers to Him. Our prayers are formal and mechanical, as addressed to one with whom we have little in common; we are not guided by His eye; and the life which should flow from Him to us is feeble and interrupted. It is only by *patient continuance* in well-doing that we can hope to obtain glory, and honour, and immortality. It is only by perpetuating and increasing the ardent devotion to Christ and His cause which marked the commencement of our Christian life, that we can grow in grace. It is only by abiding in Christ that we can become like Him. A key left upon a sheet of white paper for a few minutes in strong sunshine, leaves a faint spectral impression of itself upon the paper, which becomes visible in the dark. A wafer placed for a little upon a polished plate of steel produces an image of itself, which remains invisible, the polished surface not being in the least degree affected as regards its reflecting powers; but by breathing upon it the dormant image of the wafer develops itself, and fades away again as the moisture evaporates from its surface. And so, a certain likeness to Christ is produced upon our character by a transient contact with

Him during seasons of revival and religious excitement, which likeness speedily fades away again. But in order to become truly and permanently conformed to His image, we must have our hearts prepared and made sensitive, like the photographer's plate, by continuing in faith and love. In order to have our faces shining with His reflected glory, we must, like Moses, be for days alone with Him on the mount of prayer.

"As the branch cannot bear fruit of itself, except it abide in the vine; no more can ye, except ye abide in Me." This truth, so far as the plant is concerned, is so self-evident that it requires only to be stated. We are not impressed by it, because every one believes it. It is one of those first truths on which all reasoning is founded, which are uninteresting to us because of their primary, permanent, and universal force. Every one knows how essential to the fruitfulness, to the very life of the branch, is its continuance in the parent tree— that it dies when separated from the trunk and left to its own resources. Its stock of sap may keep it green for a little while; the echoes of life may reverberate in it for a day or two; but the hostile forces around speedily exhaust this stock, and it has no means of renewing it, and it withers and crumbles away into rottenness. But what is so palpable and simple a truth in regard to the plant, is not so evident in the human world. We do not realize so vividly that our life and fruitfulness are as dependent upon our abiding in Christ, as the life and fruitfulness of the branch are dependent upon its abiding in the vine. We believe in the constancy of natural laws, but our own imperfection makes it difficult for us to believe in the constancy of spiritual laws. We imagine that a certain measure of independence is accorded to us. We shall not surely die though we eat the forbidden fruit. We may not always abide in Christ, and yet somehow we may bring forth fruit; a transient or intermittent union with Him will preserve our spiritual life in all its fulness and freshness. So we think; but our Saviour tells us that the law is as inexorable in the spiritual as in the natural world—nay, more so, for while physical law is dependent solely on the will of God, and therefore may be changed; spiritual law, on the other hand, is dependent upon the very nature of God, and is therefore immutable. Aaron's rod, though separated from its parent almond-tree and dried up, may bud and fruit in a single night; but no man separated from Christ can flourish or bring forth fruit unto holiness. This is a law that admits of no exception. It is impossible to be fruitful or to have life apart from Christ. "Without Me," He says Himself, "ye can do nothing."

It may be said that man can perform good actions of several kinds without Christ, as the heathen did by nature the things contained in the law; but all the good thoughts and feelings and actions of those who know not Christ are, nevertheless, in reality inspired by Him; they are the dawn, or the twilight rays, of the True Light that lighteth every man that cometh into the world. We can do absolutely nothing that is good without Christ. And everything that separates us from Him reduces us to the weakness and impotency of self.*   In the natural world, it is a well-known fact that every dark day, every cloud that intercepts the sunshine, prevents the bringing forth and ripening of the fruit on the tree; and it is equally true that every hour of unbelief, every shadow and cloud of faithlessness that come between Christ and the believer, hinder the development of his fruitfulness.   Every time that the soul is forgetful of Christ's presence, alienated from His love, turning to the world, the process of its ripening is retarded. But on the other hand, when the soul is living in the sunshine of His favour which is life, then it is stimulated to bring forth much fruit.   Without the consciousness of Christ's presence and love it can do nothing; with this consciousness it can do all things.   Without Christ the believer's soul becomes like a besieged city cut off from its supplies, and must surrender to its enemies; with Christ there is no imaginable blessedness that is

---

* The continuous action of faith is very strikingly shown in the 5th chapter of St. John, where our Saviour in the original Greek almost invariably uses the present active participle, when speaking of the relations between Himself and the believer.   It is not as in our version, " He that believeth in Me;" "He that eateth My flesh and drinketh My blood;" "He that cometh unto Me;" but he *believing* in Me; *eating* My flesh and *drinking* My blood; *coming* unto Me;—all indicating that the specific act is continuous, not performed at once and then over for ever, but always going on. Believing in Christ, coming to Him, eating His flesh and drinking His blood is no mere transient act, but a habit.   " Faith is an active, continuous habit of the soul; it is the constant expression of life, and life is eternal."

not within its reach. "If ye abide in Me and My words abide in you, ye shall ask what ye will, and it shall be done unto you." Possessing Him we possess all things; for if we be Christ's all things are ours—the world, and life and death, things present and things to come; all are ours for we are Christ's, and Christ is God's. God hath given us His Son, and how shall He not with Him also freely give us all things.

But it were vain to ask the believer to abide in Christ unless the promise of help were given; as vain as to expect the branch to remain in the vine, unless the vine nourished it with its vital force and sap. Therefore, when Christ says to His disciples, "Abide in Me," He immediately adds, "and I in you." The duty and the means of performing it are placed side by side. And it is the distinguishing feature of the Gospel of St. John that he associates, in the closest manner, everything that the believer does with everything that Jesus does. His Gospel is, indeed, the gospel of communion and fellowship. His writings are full of sayings of reciprocity and mutual endearment between Christ and His disciples. "He that eateth My flesh, and drinketh My blood, dwelleth in Me, and I in him." "At that day ye shall know that I am in My Father, and ye in Me, and I in you." "Behold I stand at the door and knock; if any man hear my voice, and open the door, I will come in to him, and sup with him, and he with Me." All these wondrous sayings reveal the blessed truth that the gospel is not a one-sided scheme, but a system of mutual relations between the believer and Christ. He identifies Himself with us, as we with Him, in the enjoyment of all the blessings of salvation, and in the performance of all the duties of the Christian life. All His commandings are enablings; all His duties are privileges. His very laws are promises; they indicate not the measure of the strength to obey Him which we naturally possess, as the measure of the help which He intends to afford to our obedience. Witness the command given to the disciples, "Give ye them to eat," and the multiplication of the loaves and fishes as they passed from their hands. If He says to us, "Turn ye, turn ye; why will ye die?" we are encouraged to say to Him, "Turn us, and we shall be turned;" if He bids us follow Him, He encourages us to say, "Draw us, and we will run after thee;" if He asks, "Believest thou that I can do this?" we can reciprocate, "Lord, we believe; help thou our unbelief." The Bride prepares a feast for her Beloved, and issues her invitation, "Let my Beloved come into His garden, and eat His pleasant fruits," because He had first prepared a feast for her, "I sat down under His shadow with great delight, and His fruit was sweet to my taste." The mystical meal on the shore of the Lake of Galilee was composed of the fishes which the disciples caught, and the fishes which Jesus had provided. The Lord's Supper is a communion with Jesus,—a mutual feasting, in which the soul sups with Him, and He with the soul—in which the Host becomes the Guest, and the guest the host. And the marriage-supper of the Lamb will be made up of the reward of their own hands, which shall be given to the redeemed, and of the fulness of joy that is at God's right hand—the fulness of receptivity in them, and the fulness of sufficiency in Him. He shall see in them of the travail of His soul, and be satisfied; and they shall find in Him the satisfaction of the mighty longings of eternity.

The fundamental truth upon which the whole science of mechanics rests is equality of pressure. A ship is kept afloat because the pressure of the water from below is equal to the weight of the ship above. The force with which I press my hand against a table at rest, is balanced by an equal pressure of the table against my hand. This law of statics has its counterpart in the spiritual world. In proportion as I abide in Christ, so does He abide in me; in proportion as I believe, so does He help my unbelief. Leaning the weight of my soul upon Him, He sustains me with corresponding power. He gives me grace from Him for grace in me—grace to help, according to my need. It is this abiding of Christ in me that renders my abiding in Him possible. I should speedily relinquish my hold of Him, were His hold of me not so firm and steadfast. Nature is weak, however willing the spirit; and the spirit itself is weak at times, overcome by the evil and distracting influences of the world, and by the reaction of the flesh. But, keeping hold of Him, He keeps hold of me. It is a mutual, reciprocal thing. Abiding in Christ, and Christ abiding in me; my soul, amid-all the passing and perishing things of time and sense, will be in stable equilibrium; the sustaining pressure of the Everlasting Arms underneath will counterbalance the disturbing pressure of the world's cares and sorrows from above. I enter into the rest of God; He lays down His rest as the support of mine; He holds me firm in His own blessed centre of peace, amid the whirl of things; He protects me from being overpowered by outward things, and being disquieted by their terrors. Well, then, may the apostle say, " Let us hold fast the profession of our faith, without wavering (for He is faithful that promised)." The very form of the precept is wonderfully significant; the plain, palpable duty on the one side, and the unseen, but ever-present help of Christ within the parenthesis. Through this abiding in Christ, and Christ abiding in us, our load is divided, our strength is doubled. The strength of Jesus is made perfect in our weakness: we can do greater things than the natural man can do. It was by the union of the Godhead with the manhood in Himself, that He was enabled to perform His mighty works; and so, by the union of the Godhead of Christ with our humanity, we shall be made conquerors and more than conquerors. Through Christ strengthening us we can do all things; we shall be drawn up from our corruption and death to a level that now seems far above us, to the attainment of things which we now behold afar off. Through this abiding in Christ, prayer is not a solitary act, nor a succession of acts, but a continuous going forth of the soul after God—a continual ascending and descending by Christ the living ladder; a continual going in and out by Christ, the living door. It is a habit of the mind, a devotional spirit, a holy communion with God. We dwell in Him and He in us; we are one with Him and He with us. Prayer thus becomes a real power; we shall ask what we will, and it shall be done to us; and as kings under Christ we shall reign on the earth. Work, too, becomes a glorifying of God—a consecration of common things, a linking together of the spiritual and the natural, of heaven and earth; and even suffering becomes a rejoicing in tribulation, a companionship in the kingdom and patience of Jesus Christ.

But a further truth is implied in our abiding in Christ; it also involves our abiding in union and communion with one another as believers in Him. All the branches are no longer isolated units, such as they were in the state of nature, or even a mere aggregate of separate parts; they possess an organic life; they are endowed with a corporate personality. Christ is the Vine, the sum and fulness of the whole; and the believer's life is commingled with that higher social life which flows from the head and the heart of the redeemed Church. It is not enough that the believer should be personally in Christ, and know what as an individual he has in Him, be pardoned, saved and sanctified, serve God, and be accepted in His service. He enters by virtue of his union with Christ into a history and destinies larger than his own; he becomes, as Mr. Bernard says, " a member of a spiritual organization, and shares in a corporate life, in the perfection of which he is to be made perfect, and in the glory of

s

which his Lord is to be glorified." There surely ought to be not only an inward consciousness, but also an outward acknowledgment of this position; not only affections in the heart that associate him with the larger history in which his own is included, but also actions in the life expressive of the association. He should not only abide in Christ, but also in communion with his fellow-Christians—give himself not only to the Lord, but to His people by the will of God— walk with those who profess to continue steadfastly in the apostles' doctrine, and in fellowship, and in breaking of bread and in prayer. His life as a Christian should consist in realising his relation to his Lord, and to his fellow-believers in Him. The Apostle Paul continually urged this thought upon his converts, " Ye are members one of another." Every Christian, therefore, who does not belong to a Christian Church, is not walking according to God's appointment and the order of the gospel; he is living in the loss of privilege and the omission of duty. It fares as ill with the believer who communicates with no Church, who prefers rambling, or at least detachment, to union, as with a branch separated from the vine. In the vine, how greatly does the welfare of each branch depend upon the work of the whole. The sap that pervades each branch is aërated and vitalised by all the branches; the fruit that each branch produces is the product of all the branches. The branch that loses its share of this corporate life speedily loses its own individual life, and withers, and drops off the tree. And so the Christian who separates himself from his fellows is neither safe nor useful. He loses that exercise and development of his spiritual faculties which can only be enjoyed through mutual duties and mutual intercourse—that stimulus of love and contagion of impression which a multitude of congenial spirits communicate. The spirit of the one body does not animate him. Indeed, apart from this sacred incorporation, it is not easy to imagine how we can truly bear one another's burdens, and so fulfil the law of Christ—how we can stimulate one another unto love and to good works, or exhort and edify one another. We frequently hear, from those who forsake the assembling of themselves together, the excuse that they can read their Bibles and say their prayers as well at home; and many of those who attend the public means of grace, imagine that these are observed merely for the sake of church-order and convenience—that the congregation is an aggregate of persons, a mere congeries of independent believers, who join for convenience to do what each is desirous to do personally. But this is an erroneous idea. Our public worship is the outward expression of our corporate unity; it is the action of the *whole* body of Christ; it is the Church realising its own corporate individuality, and, as the bride of Jesus, expressing its love to Him. Chemistry tells us that compound substances exhibit qualities and phenomena which are not found in the individual elements. What was latent in the elements becomes apparent in the compound; what was dormant in the parts is active in the whole. So members of congregations and churches display in their corporate capacity qualities and powers which they do not possess as isolated Christians. And therefore we cannot *individualize* our united worship, or supersede public by private devotion without serious loss and injury.

Abiding thus in the Vine, and in fellowship with one another, the branches are enabled to perform most efficiently the purposes of their existence. Their roots combine, and form the common trunk, which sustains them all.* By their union they are enabled to resist the processes of decay, and the adverse conditions which destroy annual, separate plants. They yield to each other mutual support. The influence that pervades the whole, animates each branch; the sap that circulates through the vessels and cells of the whole economy, reaches the smallest part. One grand, all-pervading wave of growth passes over the whole tree, leaving its little ripple or ring of new wood over every twig. There is no interruption to the formative processes— to the passing up and down of the vital fluids—to the

---

* The woody trunk of a tree is nothing but a mass of aggregate roots, formed by the leaves and buds. We have striking proofs of this in the case of the banyan, the screw-pine, and the mangrove, which, instead of combining the separate roots of their new growths into one dense, uniform trunk—send them down into the ground outside the main stem, and in an independent manner. When a ring of bark is removed from an apple branch, if the wound is muffled in damp moss, roots will invariably push from its upper lip, while the lower will produce none; thus proving that roots are developed from the buds above, and that the trunk of a tree is formed by them.

reciprocal action of the leaves and stem. The stem sends its nourishment to the leaves, and the leaves bring it into contact with the ambient air and light, and then return it endowed with more vital properties to the stem. There is continuous action of endosmose and exosmose; and thus by the mutual help of the vine and its branches all the materials of air and earth are converted into vegetable substances. The light of the sun, the properties of the shower, the impalpable gases and forces of the atmosphere, the crude mineral matter of the soil, are employed by this complicated and delicate machinery, working together towards one common end—to produce rich and nutritious fruit. The rain and dew of heaven are changed into wine; each vineyard becomes a Cana; the sun and the wind, with a laughing mouth, blow from the full sap of the branches "blue bubbles of grapes."

Thus, too, through the branch abiding in the tree, it shares in all its processes of rejuvenescence, by which, however old, the tree becomes young again each season, and displays on the last mere band, or stump of wood— that survives beside a bleached and crumbling skeleton, and that can only stand by the help of a crutch— leaves as large, and fruit as perfect, and life as strong and verdant as in the days of its prime. It is renewed every spring with the renewal of the tree; and when its term of life expires, and it yields to the universal law of death, looking back upon its annual produce, and summing up the accumulated result of its fruitfulness, it may be said, indeed, to have brought forth much fruit.

The branch separated from the tree—supposing it to have an independent existence—is a mere annual plant, and produces only one crop of fruit; but when it is a part of the vine, it becomes perennial, renews its youth season after season, and produces crop after crop of fruit. It is not by the much fruit of a single season that we are to judge it, but by the much fruit of a whole lifetime. There is not a more interesting sight than an old abbey garden, situated in one of the choicest spots as to soil and aspect. Though it is wholly neglected, its walls in ruins, and its area covered with the rankest weeds, there are still the remains of the aged fruit trees—the mellow pears, the delicate little apples, and the luscious black cherries—struggling for existence, and producing fruit, where for centuries destruction only has been at work. How useful each of these venerable fruit trees has been to the generations of man! How great the quantity of fruit, if added up, which it produced altogether! In this respect, it is a beautiful picture of the Christian abiding for years in Christ, and in communion with the brotherhood. He bears much fruit, not merely one season, but many seasons; even in old age he flourishes in the courts of the Lord, and brings forth fruit. Waiting upon the Lord, he renews his youth even as the eagles; he renews his strength, even when the natural force abates; though the outward man perisheth, the inward man is renewed more and more. The star of morning returns in his evening sky; the crocus of spring blooms in his happy autumn fields; the primrose of the sunshine re-appears in his darkness in the Hesperis, or evening primrose; the tree of life, lost in the Eden of youth, he finds again in the paradise of old age. As a subject of the kingdom of heaven, he is always becoming as a little child. His trials are the struggles of rejuvenescence—the soul growing young again—the pains of growth—the casting off the old husk from the new bud—the old skin from the new form. His spiritual work is the exercise by which his strength is renewed; for, just as the body, by every exertion which it puts forth, wears away old material and acquires new, so does the soul, in working for Christ, forget the things that are behind—get rid of old views and feelings, and acquire new and fresh. And how greatly is this continual rejuvenescence helped by his abiding in the community of the Vine—by the Christian sympathy and help of his fellow-believers! Such a combination has power to save him from back-sliding—to keep him steadily looking unto Jesus—to stimulate him to all good works, and to bring out all that is best and noblest in him. The quantity of his being is multiplied and enriched by the life of others; just as the quantity of being in the branch is multi-plied and enriched by the quantity of being in the whole tree. And therefore it is that he brings forth much fruit.

Would that not only individual believers, but also churches and communions, could realise the immense advantages of this Christian solidarity—this abiding together in Christ; associated not merely in spiritual, but in outward form with one another in Him! Our

Saviour speaks, not of several vines, but of one Vine. There is but one Vine, of which all believers, whatever their name or denomination, are branches. We forget this amid our innumerable schisms and divisions. We justify our extreme degree of separation from one another by dreaming of a unity, which we call spiritual —of an inward impalpable union. The same spirit of sinful selfishness which induced Adam, when he had eaten the forbidden fruit to separate himself and his interests from Eve, and to lay the blame of his transgression upon her; which made the younger prodigal son, when about to leave his home, say to his father, "Give *me* the portion of goods which falleth to *me*,"—is doubtless at the root of all the divisions of the Christian Church. The old desire to perfect the individual at the expense of the community, which produced monachism, prevents the amalgamation of sects and denominations. Individual churches become like those *incluses*, or "holy men of the stone," who, during the middle ages, lived for years in a small cell built up around them, beside the wall of a cathedral—connected with the great universal Church, but separated from it by the impervious wall of some speciality of their creed. The slightest reflection will show that more is lost than gained by this policy of selfish isolation. Much of the unfruitfulness of the Vine is owing to this want of unity among the branches. Much force is wasted because there is no concentration of effort, no oneness of aim. Much envy and jealousy are created, because special interests are continually conflicting.

There is reason, indeed, to believe that there is a growing tendency among the most thoughtful and enlightened Christians to draw nearer to each other, and to merge their shibboleths of party in the great watchword of "supreme love to Christ, and fervent love to one another." We see around us growing proofs that the relations between man and man, which sin destroyed, are being re-constituted and enlarged in Christ Jesus. We are advancing farther and farther from the garden, with its selfish, isolated perfection, to the city, the perfect realisation of organized life—of society in its maturity, of the highest well-being of man. But still, we are very far from that blessed consummation, when the various relations of men shall be so combined as to promote the welfare of each individual member, and secure the unity of a common life to the whole. It may not be possible to realise here the outward and visible unity of the One Vine—embracing all who love the Lord Jesus Christ in sincerity and truth. We may never here be able to celebrate the festival of "all saints." It may be with us, so long as we are on earth, as with the plants of the northern zone. These plants are mostly annual and herbaceous. They grow separately in clusters here and there. They are mere *individuals*. They have precisely the same structure, so far as it goes, as trees, as plants that are woody and persistent. They have the same concentrical disposition of the matter of the stem into pith, wood and bark, and the same development of branches in the axils of the leaves. They are trees in miniature—at least the units of trees. But the heat of the sun is not strong or continuous enough, and the period of growth is too short, to allow them to run through all the stages of their development. The whole process is therefore stopped in its first stages, and the stem with its branches and flowers dies down to the ground, and disappears on the approach of winter. That the vegetable machinery would still continue in motion, and simply stops in consequence of the decreasing light and heat of the sun, is evident from the fact, that plants which are annual and herbaceous in temperate climates become ligneous perennials in the tropics. The daisies and dandelions that we trample under foot in our English meadows, become powerful and lofty trees in the torrid zone. The golden rod, the yellow sow-thistle, the blue viper's bugloss, the purple vetch, the knotted bistort, which adorn our woods, or grow as weeds in our cultivated fields—so perishable and herbaceous with us—in the continued warmth and brightness of regions that have no winter in their year, assume the arborescent form, and become the noblest trees of the forest. The annual fern is transformed into the tall enduring tree-fern; and the lowly grass of the field elevates itself majestically into the air in the form of the bamboo.

And is it not thus with churches and individuals? Living in this cold region of earth—we are mere individuals—isolated from one another. Our love is not powerful or persistent enough to unite us and

transform us into one great community. The conditions
amid which we live are unfavourable to our *abiding* in
one another.   The winter of distrust, and jealousy, and
exclusiveness, comes in ever and anon to check all our
approximations to a united state, and to undo all the
work of a summer of co-operation and mutual regard.
We continue, year after year, colonies of separate herbaceous plants, growing in the ground as it were—
instead of branches growing in the same great tree.
Our little love to Christ is the reason of our little
love to the brethren.   But, in the tropical region of
heaven—where the light of the sun shall be sevenfold,
as the light of seven days—the Lord shall bind up
the breach of His people, and heal the stroke of
their wound.   The process of growth arrested on earth,
goes on where there is no interruption of night
or winter.   The continuous shining of the Sun of
Righteousness, that shall no more go down, will gather
the dispersed of Israel into one; transform independent,
isolated plants into branches of one great Vine, a
manifold growth in affiliated parts. The Northman's
fable of the universal tree will be realised in the tree
of life—growing on either side of the river, and in
the midst of the street of the New Jerusalem, and
yet *one* tree—yielding twelve manner of fruits—yielding
its fruit every month—and whose leaves are for the
healing of the nations.   The grain of mustard-seed,
which, when sown in the earth, is less than all the
seeds that be in the earth, there grows up and becomes
greater than all herbs, and shooteth out great branches,

so that the fowls of the air may lodge under the shadow of it. For this transformation, under brighter skies, of the separate, feeble and perishing growths of time into one enduring organization of love, growing from glory to glory, let us now prepare by abiding in Christ, and in one another in Him.

CHAPTER VII.

THE FRUITLESS BRANCHES.

"Every branch in me that beareth not fruit He taketh away."—
JOHN xv. 2.

"If a man abide not in me, he is cast forth as a branch, and is
withered; and men gather them, and cast them into the fire, and
they are burned."—JOHN xv. 6.

NO systematic arrangement exists in nature. Species
cf the same order are not found congregated
together to the exclusion of all others. Sometimes,
indeed, we have vast tracts of country occupied by
social plants; mountain-sides by pine forests; moorlands by heather; arctic wastes by reindeer-moss;
meadows by grass. But even among this uniform
vegetation, other kinds of plants intrude; the winter-
green and the palmy shield-fern creep into the solitude
of the pine wood; the club-moss and the juniper in-
vade the brown wastes of heath; the saxifrage and the
scurvy-grass give a faint tinge of verdure to the snow-
white sterility of the arctic lichens; while the daisy in
spring transfigures the greenness of the meadow with its
dazzling sheen, and the butter-cup in summer spreads

over it its cloth of gold. Upon every square yard of ground, plants that have no relationship to one another, and whose properties are antagonistic, grow in the most intimate nearness; the useful and the poisonous, the highly-organized and the simply cellular, are grouped together. Nay, on every tree there are hosts of other plants growing,—parasites and epiphytes,—making it an island-colony in the air. Woodbine, clematis, and ivy, twine around the trunk; mosses, lichens, and ferns enrich the grandest things in nature with the beauties of the simplest. The law of vegetable distribution is catholic, not exclusive. Every plant carries its own commission to spread itself as widely as it can,—to multiply and replenish the earth. Man, in cultivating the ground, has to contend against this law of universal propagation. He separates a small portion of the earth's surface from the wide common of nature, and within this enclosure he creates an artificial soil and climate, in which certain plants that are useful to him may be reared and develop their prized qualities to the utmost, and from which all other plants may be carefully shut out. But nature will not permit this exclusiveness; she overleaps his boundaries, thrusts upon him her weeds, and strives to bring his guarded domain into harmony with the uncultivated wilds around. In the garden, the chickweed and the groundsel disfigure the beds of lilies and roses; in the field, the blue-bottle, the scarlet poppy and the yellow mustard, relieve the green monotony of the useful corn by their flaunting colours and their unprofitable growth.

In the spiritual world a similar state of things exists. The tendency of human nature is to systematise its knowledge; but the truths of the Bible are arranged like the plants of the field, without any regard to classification.   Doctrines and duties are placed side by side; Divine revelations and historical and domestic incidents are beautifully and harmoniously blended.   In the formation of the Church, Christians try to keep themselves select; they separate into sects and denominations; they make broad their phylacteries, and draw their lines of demarcation clear and distinct. Like the Donatists of old, they seek to make the Church, in its visible form and historic manifestations, identical and co-extensive with the true invisible Church, which the Lord knoweth and not man.   Their fold of salvation is a solemn and sombre pine-wood, in whose frowning shadow no other species of plant is tolerated. No one ever gathers primroses in a pine forest; the ground is never lighted up with starry anemones; nor do blue-bells and forget-me-nots spread the azure reflection of a little heaven below amid its brown needles and empty cones.   And so in their society, none are tolerated save those who pronounce their special shibboleth, and are of kindred views and dispositions. Their idea of the visible Church is a perfectly holy and exclusive body, where all are converted, and no hypocrites or ungodly persons are found—a garden enclosed, where nothing but roses and lilies and useful fruit-trees grow—a field of corn free from every weed. The qualities which belong to the invisible Church are deemed all-essential to the existence of the visible. Absolute purity of communion is the indispensable requisite; and this is sought to be secured by the most rigid exercise of religious surveillance and church discipline.

Now, to this strong tendency to exclusiveness in the visible Church, in all its branches and denominations, the Word of God and the action of Providence alike are opposed. In the world, we see the various changes of society going on by a process of admixture. A similar process of admixture goes on in the Church, and for similar wise and gracious purposes. Our Lord Himself compared the kingdom of heaven on earth to a draw-net that was cast into the sea, and gathered of *every kind*, both good and bad fishes; men of every diversity of moral character having the Gospel preached to them, and finding themselves within the limits of the visible Church. In the parable of the barren fig-tree, He said, " A certain man had a fig-tree *planted in his vineyard*," a tree that was symbolical of evil qualities, growing in the midst of plants symbolical of all that was best and noblest in man. In the parable of the tares He prohibited the servants pulling up the tares, lest they should pull up the wheat with them— lest the removal of the tares might injure, nay, destroy the process by which the wheat was maturing to perfection—and said, " Let both grow together until the harvest;" thereby intimating that the visible Church was to have its admixture of good and evil until the end of time; and this not merely as an historical fact, but as a moral purpose. While, therefore, all Christian churches are to be as precise as possible in defining their boundaries, as select as possible in refusing what they know distinctly to be vile, and accepting only, as far as may be, whatever they distinctly know to be good, yet all self-willed, self-righteous, and impatient attempts to anticipate the perfect communion of saints are expressly forbidden. And every candid mind can see at once the reason of the prohibition. The commingling of the tares and the wheat in the same field is beneficial to both. By association with the righteous, beholding their example, and getting the benefit of their instructions and prayers, the ungodly are brought into the most favourable circumstances for after-repentance and amendment. By association with the ungodly, the righteous are saved from intolerance, bigotry, self-righteous pride, and presumptuous uncharitableness; their feelings of compassion are called forth; their zeal for the conversion of souls is stimulated; their patience and faith are exercised; and by the evils which the association entails upon them, their discipline is carried out, and they are made to long more earnestly for the coming of the kingdom of Christ, when the Canaanite shall be no more in the house of the Lord for ever, and the people shall be all righteous, the branch of His planting, the work of His hands.

The same mixed state of things which the parables of the tares and the draw-net were intended pictorially to represent to us, is seen in the allegory of the Vine. What our Saviour depicted as existing in the wider field and in the outer relations signified by these parables, He exhibits in the more intimate connections of the vine. He shows that the ungodly, as well as the righteous, stand more closely related to Him than the sheep to the shepherd, or fish to the fisherman, or tares and wheat to the farmer. Righteous and unrighteous are not merely tares and wheat growing side by side in the same field ; *they are branches in the same tree.* They are gathered up in Christ. It is this feature of the allegory that is so puzzling to many. They can understand why tares should be found growing in the field of corn ; but they find it more difficult to conceive of fruitless and withered branches in the Vine. How is it possible, they ask, for any to be in Christ, and not produce fruit ? How is it possible for any branch to be once in Christ, and yet afterwards be taken away ? Christ himself said of His disciples, " I give unto them eternal life, and they shall never perish, neither shall any pluck them out of My hands." We read of " the perseverance of the saints," and are told that Jesus is the Author and Finisher of our faith, and that when and where He has begun the good work of faith, He will carry it on and complete it. In the face of these statements, our text says that a man may be in Christ and yet be fruitless ; may be in Christ and yet perish. We must therefore admit that there are different kinds of union with Christ. There is a union that is visible and sacramental, and a union that is real and vital. A man may be in Christ by profession, when he is not in reality ; by a form of godliness when he denies the power thereof. He may be well spoken of, and regarded as a model Christian; may exhibit all the outer manifestations of spiritual life, while yet this show of life only conceals the inward death. He *presses* upon Christ like the thronging multitudes, but he does not *touch* Him, as did that believing woman to whom alone His virtue went forth.

The discipleship of Judas Iscariot is the great impersonation of such a union with Christ. The traitor was, doubtless, present to our Saviour's mind, when He indicated the character and fate of the fruitless branch. He knew well the nature of Judas; He was never deceived or disappointed in him. He was prepared for his treachery; He announced it to His disciples in the prophetic words of the Psalmist, "He that eateth bread with Me hath lifted up his heel against Me." "Have not I chosen you twelve, and one of you is a devil." Why, then, did Jesus admit Judas into intimacy with Him? He gives us the reason in the words, "That the Scripture may be fulfilled." It was necessary that the traitor should live in His company—should go in and out with Him—in order that he might execute his evil purpose, and that God might make his treachery to praise Him in working out, objectively, the scheme of redemption. And if the voice of tradition be true, which identifies Judas with the certain man who said to Jesus, "Lord, I will follow thee whithersoever thou goest;" and who was told, "Foxes have holes, and birds of the air have nests: but the Son of Man hath not where to lay His head," then the objection, which naturally arises in our minds, that Christ should have deliberately and knowingly chosen a deceiver, is removed. We see that, from first to last, Judas was altogether a free agent. He was the only disciple who was not called—the only disciple who volunteered to follow Jesus; and this, too, in spite of the obstacle placed in his way, and the warning given by Him who read his heart, knew his selfish, mercenary motive, and saw the dark future to both that would arise from the connection. And, surely, there is a very solemn lesson to us in the little influence which the intimate association of Judas with Christ produced upon his character. It was proved possible, in his case, to be a companion of Divine, Incarnate Love—to see and feel all the out-flowings of goodness from the very fountain of goodness in the Redeemer's heart—to witness His wonderful miracles, and hear His marvellous words, and yet be little, if at all, sympathetically moved. He lived in the midst of the element of love without imbibing it, like a hollow gourd, floating in the midst of water, and yet empty and dry within.

In many cases, indeed, there is some kind of gain to be got by a professional union with Christ. I speak not of the mere worldly advantages that flow from the respectability of church membership—the good opinion and support of good men. There are higher benefits that flow to the man who is in alliance with Christ by the use of the means of grace than these—benefits not in mere outward things, but even in the very sphere of his soul. If he is something more than a mere formalist; if there is any sincerity and earnestness about him at all, he does get some quickening,—a certain mental and moral elevation, as a natural result of close contact with true religion, — some reflection of the beauty of holiness, some increased tenderness of conscience, some greater perception of the glory of a life lived for Christ. He is like a branch in a vine which has failed to produce fruit, but which, nevertheless, gets from the stock sap to keep it alive—to make it green, and leafy, and symmetrical. It gets enough of the life of the tree to preserve its typical likeness. And thus, though the professor produces no fruit unto holiness from his sacramental union with Christ, He gets some influence which makes him a more sober, more honest, more thoughtful man, than he would otherwise have been. Like the young ruler, Jesus looks on him with love, though he lacks the one thing needful. Like the lawyer who answered the question on the Law aright, he is not far from the kingdom of heaven, though he is not within it. I believe that, even where the work of Christ has failed to produce true conversion, it has not been without some ameliorating effect. Ananias and Sapphira got some good from their association with the infant Christian Church ; the baptism of Pentecost made them somewhat more liberal and self-sacrificing than they would have been naturally. Felix underwent a certain elevation of conscience when he trembled on account of St. Paul's reasonings of righteousness, temperance, and judgment to come. Agrippa was raised above his natural level, when he could permit himself to say to the prisoner who stood before him, " Almost thou persuadest me to be a Christian !" But the sad thing is, that many are contented with this mere moral elevation— this subordinate benefit which a mere professional union with Christ produces. Nay, in not a few cases this benefit is the most serious obstacle in the way of a real union with Christ, and the production of the true fruits of grace. Those who are kept moral and respectable by their profession of religion, imagine that this is all that is demanded of them—that nothing more is required in conversion. They are impressed by a sermon ; they are solemnized at the Lord's table ; they are faithful in the discharge of their religious duties, and liberal in their offerings. They are therefore perfectly satisfied with themselves ; " they are rich and increased with goods, and have need of nothing." And thus their very familiarity with Divine things prevents or destroys their impressiveness ; their very position in Christ secures their consciences from alarm. " There is a way that seemeth right unto a man, but the end thereof are the ways of death."

A fruitless branch resembles a fruitful branch in every respect save in the one quality of producing fruit. Its form, and structure, and foliage are identical. This mutual resemblance is the hinge upon which the parable of the tares and wheat turns. The tares and the wheat both belong to the tribe of grasses, and to the group of *Triticinæ*, or wheat-like grasses. Their structure, mode, and conditions of growth are the same. When in the blade, they present an appearance so precisely similar that the farmer who is careful in weeding his field cannot distinguish between them; and it is only in harvest that the impostor is detected by its smaller and darker ear. The truth presented in this parabolic form is a profound and far-reaching one. Satan, who sows the tares, is not like God, who sows the wheat, an independent Power, existent from all eternity. He is a created being, a fallen spirit, an archangel become an archfiend; and therefore, all that he does is not a separate, specifically distinct, independent working, but an imitation of God. He cannot originate; he can only defile and injure. He cannot work in an independent sphere, and on the same level with God; he works only within the sphere of God, and at a lower level. Sin is not something altogether new and original; it is only a violation of what God has created.

The botanist is struck with the fact, that the most poisonous species of plants do not form groups distinctly separate from those that are happier in function. The potato belongs to the same tribe as the deadly-nightshade; and the purple and yellow blossom of the nightshade is constructed exactly like the flower of the cyclamen—a beautiful and innocent plant of the English meadows—and exhibits a close affinity to the primrose. And so evil belongs to the same genus as goodness—has the same kind of structure and blossom; but its sap and fruit are deadly. Every vice has features of resemblance to some virtue, but terribly degraded. What is covetousness but a misdirected worship? What are extravagance and meanness but an excess and defect of economy ? All moral evil stands in the same relation to all moral good as the tares stand to the wheat. And among the names which have been given to Satan, none contains deeper truth, or conveys a clearer description of his operations, than that of "*Dei simius*," or "ape of God." All that he has ever done has been a caricaturing, defiling, and destroying what God has done—a sowing of tares where God has been sowing wheat. Under the same law to which Satan himself is subject, the barren branches in the vine are placed. They are imitations of the fruitful branches. It is because there are true Christians that hypocrites exist.

But the fruit is a sure discriminating test: " By their fruits ye shall know them." In nature there are some plants, belonging to entirely different orders, so remarkably like each other that they can only be distinguished when they flower and fruit. The foliage of the holly, for instance, is exactly repeated in the *Desfontainea* of Chili, a shrub of the gentian family ; and the leaves of the bat-wing passion-flower are absolutely identical with those of the *Lourea*, a member of the pea family, and totally unconnected.* And so, how-

* The vine-worts, distinguished for their wholesome and nutritious qualities, seem closely allied to the *Umbelliferæ*—a tribe distinguished for its poisonous properties. The foliage of many of the vines is like that of many of the *Umbelliferæ*. The blossoms of the vines are usually small, greenish coloured, and arranged in corymbs, umbels, or panicles ; and in this respect bear a close resemblance to those of the *Umbelliferæ*, which are mean and poor, and lose what beauty they have by too close crowding ; while the petals of one species of vine, the *Ampelopsis*, are turned inwards at the points—a peculiarity specially belonging to the petals of the

ever like in outward appearance and manner of life
the true Christian and the mere formalist may be, by
the fruits which they produce they are easily distinguish-
able.   The barren branches are at once discerned
when the fertile are loaded with fruit; all alike during
the growing stage—indistinguishable in the blade—the
harvest displays their real character.   It is the contrast of good which first makes evil to appear.

It will be observed that the fruitfulness of which our
Saviour speaks is not an *immature* or *latent* condition.
The young vine is three or four years old before it
begins to bear; and if the husbandman came to seek
fruit on it before this stage of growth, he would be disappointed.   And so the Christian has a certain
brooding period, during which the powers necessary
to produce fruitfulness are being matured.   There is
no fruit on the branch as yet; but it is latent; the
conditions necessary for it are present—and only
require time for their development.   It is not of
this immature stage that our Saviour speaks.   It is
not such a branch that He threatens to take away.   He
is long-suffering wherever there is the slightest prospect
of fruit.   He who sought fruit for a thousand years from
Israel, and in His wonderful patience called the long
interval between Moses and Christ only one day,—

Umbelliferæ.   Further, the sensible properties of the two families
approximate to one another in the acrid berries of the *Cissus*, a
species of vine.   Thus the parsley-crown and the vine-wreath, the
wine-cup and the hemlock-drink, are as closely connected in physical qualities as they have been in their effects upon human history.

"All day have I stretched forth my hands to a disobedient and gainsaying people"—will willingly wait for the growth and development of the tender branch. His patience with the tree that has any hope of God in it is beautifully seen in the parable of the barren fig-tree,—"Lord, let it alone this year also, till I dig about it and dress it." No pains will be spared to bring out any tendency to fruitfulness that is in it; it will have the best cultivation, and be placed in the most likely circumstances to cure its barrenness. Neither is it of fruitfulness as a *transition* state that our Saviour speaks. Every tree has its stage of rest, its winter condition, during which it produces no fruit. Through this period of inactivity and barrenness, it must pass to greater productiveness in summer and autumn. And, corresponding with this natural torpor of the tree, the Christian has many barren and unprofitable seasons—winter-states of soul, when his feelings toward God seem to lose their warmth, and in the midst, it may be of much outward activity, his religious life is listless and dull. Such seasons are needed for calmer meditation, for firmer trust, for truer and deeper insight. Through them he returns to the ardour of first love, and performs the works which that love taught; and thus, through overcoming, finds the tree of life which is in the midst of the paradise of God.

It is not fruitlessness, therefore, as an *immature* or *transitional* state that is condemned; it is *fruitlessness as a fixed and final state*, as a permanent condition of life. The branch that is unfruitful, in the sense that our Saviour means, is one upon which the experiment of grace has been tried and failed—one that has remained during the three probationary years in the vineyard without benefit—and has had all the advantages of special cultivation during the additional year of respite in vain. There is no dormant capability to develop, no possibility of fruitfulness to change into an actuality. It is in the condition of the Church of Laodicea, of which Christ said, "I would thou wert cold or hot," whose lukewarmness was not a stage through which it was passing into greater heat, but a final and enduring state. It is a solemn thought, that it is more from the ranks of the godless and the profligate that converts to the gospel are drawn, than from the ranks of decent church-going professors, who are gospel-hardened. It was among the publicans and sinners of Galilee that Christ wrought His greatest miracles of grace; while the scrupulous, self-righteous Scribes and Pharisees of Judæa were utterly untouched by His quickening power. Zaccheus, Mary Magdalene, Matthew—those who were cold in the estimation of a hypocritical sect, were subjects of Divine grace; while Simon the Pharisee, and others like him, who were lukewarm professors, continued in the same state of spiritual coldness and torpor. The former readily passed from their coldness to the fervency of a Divine heat, while no amount of heat ever set on fire the torpid hearts of those who were satisfied with their own condition. "Verily, I say unto you, that publicans and harlots shall enter into the kingdom of heaven, while ye shall be shut out." These social outcasts are neglected plants, growing wild beyond the pale of the kingdom of heaven at present; but they may be brought in and engrafted in the Vine, and bear fruit meet unto repentance. Their condition, therefore, is hopeful. But the condition of branches long fruitless in Christ, which have shared for years in all the discipline of the Vine in vain, is indeed hopeless. How *can* such be made fruitful? What is there to change them? If all has been tried already that can be tried; if God Himself is driven to say, "What more could I have done to My vineyard that I have not done to it;" what can be hoped for from the years to come? What can we expect but that this fruitless condition should continue in the face of heaven unchanged and unabashed, and God be compelled at length in strictest justice—in tenderest mercy for the good of the whole Vine—to take away these barren, encumbering branches.

It will also be observed, that it is not of the branches which forsake Christ openly—which fall away from ordinances, and disconnect themselves with His Church —that He speaks in the second verse. He speaks of these apostates farther on; and such branches as abide not in Christ get dry and withered; every one sees their condition; and not God, but men, their fellow-men, gather them and cast them into the fire, and they are burnt. Here, on the other hand, He speaks of those who are members of churches, who attend regularly the means of grace, who *continue* in Christ by profession and by keeping up their interest in the Church. As the unfruitful branch continues year after year green and leafy and flourishing; so year after year they maintain their religious character; they seem fair and good in the eyes of their fellow-worshippers; their true condition is seen only by God; and they are therefore taken away from the Vine not by men, but by God. It is not dry and withered branches that are taken away; but sappy, leafy, unfruitful branches. If the place of woe should open and disclose the former condition of its occupants, it would reveal the awful fact, that many of those who enter it from this Christian land are not the profligate and profane dregs of the population, but those who had known the gospel and gone all the round of ordinances, but who continued fruitless to the end. "And so I saw the wicked buried who had come and gone"— not, as we should say, from the haunts of vice and profligacy, but—"from *the place of the holy*, and they were forgotten in the city where they had so done." The greatness of their privileges only aggravated the awfulness of their condemnation. They not only perished "from the way," but from the holy hill of Zion, from the table of the Lord. They were taken away *from the Vine*. Like the lukewarm Laodiceans of old, they were spued *out of the very mouth of Christ*—rejected with moral loathing and nausea—exchanging the greatest possible nearness for the remotest distance. Like Judas, they rose from

the Supper of love to consummate an act of betrayal—
to lift up against Him the heel of the very feet which
Jesus washed with His own hands. And like Judas,
they went out from the upper chamber, which was a
very gate of heaven,—from the sacrifice of the cross,
which might have saved them,—to the suicide of their
own cross, the Aceldama of their own blood. "What
is the hope of the hypocrite though he hath gained,
when God taketh away his soul?"

Most sorrowful indeed is this continuing in Christ,
and yet bearing no fruit, because it shows that for such
Christ died in vain. If it be true that Christ died that
they which live should henceforth live no more unto
themselves, but unto Him that died for them and rose
again, then that object has been frustrated so far as
these fruitless branches are concerned. I have already
shown that the fruit of a tree just means this—that the
branch no longer grows for itself, that it sacrifices its
own selfish life for the sake of the seed that is to spring
from it. A branch which puts forth leaves only lives
for itself; all the sap it gets is converted into nourishment for its own tissues, to multiply and enlarge its own
leaves, and to extend its own stem. A branch, on the
other hand, which produces fruit, has its own selfish life
changed into an unselfish growth for the use of others;
the sap that would have fed its own parts is converted
into nourishment for an independent life that is to
spring from it. The branch which thus produces fruit
sacrifices itself for the sake of others, and repeats in its
own life the process of self-sacrifice by which it was

itself formed. "Greater love hath no man than this, that a man lay down his life for his friends. Ye are My friends if ye do whatsoever I command you." It will thus be seen that the professor in Christ who produces no fruit is living for himself—converting all the blessings of heaven to base, selfish uses. He is not actuated by the spirit of self-sacrifice which Christ displayed; the mind of devotion that was in Christ is not in him. The example, as well as the efficacy, of the death of Christ, are thrown away upon him. He cannot imitate—he cannot even appreciate or understand them. The first step into life in Christ is self-sacrifice, and this step he has never taken. It is most mournful to think that an external union with the Church, and a moral propriety of life, are all that Christ has done for such—all that God's goodness in providence, and the unspeakable gift of His Son, have succeeded in effecting in them. Surely such a result might have been obtained at less cost! Surely it needed not a sacrifice so awful as the death of God's Son to produce a mere profession of religion—the mere natural products of the unsanctified heart—virtues which paganism itself might have taught, although the Son of God had never become incarnate, or suffered on the cross. Is this all the fruit of the Redeemer's travail? Is this pitiable profession the repayment of all that mighty expenditure of blood and tears? Was it to produce a mere leafy, fruitless branch like this that the True Vine was cultivated by the Husbandman, and made perfect through sufferings

—that it pleased the Lord to bruise His own Son, and to put Him to grief?

Is it to be wondered at that God should take such a fruitless branch away? "Every branch in Me that beareth not fruit He taketh away." The Husbandman of souls is very patient and long-suffering; but His Spirit will not always strive with callous-hearted men. He has no pleasure in the death of him that dieth, but such a death may be forced upon Him, as a matter of stern and solemn necessity. For many years He has digged about and dressed the barren fig-tree; for many years Christ has come seeking fruit, and finding none— hungry for some answering token of love, some return of life for His sore travail of soul, and always disappointed. But the parable of the barren fig-tree, uttered in warning, will become at last the miracle of the blasting of the barren fig-tree, executed in judgment. The axe that was laid at the root of the tree for immediate use, "that this sign of what was threatened might avert the actual fulfilment of the threat," is at last lifted up to cut it down as a cumberer of the ground. The season of grace is over; and Christ comes no more seeking fruit—hungry for love; but to execute vengeance— filled with wrath. On the one side, all the resources, even of heavenly love, are exhausted; on the other, the measure of guilt is filled up. The harvest has come, when the tares and the wheat, growing together, display their characteristic qualities in unmistakable plainness and fulness; and this is the time for gathering the one from the other without risk of confusion and loss. The draw-net is full, and brought to shore, and now the work of separating the good fishes from the bad can be deliberately * accomplished. Do we say that the "taking away" of the branch is a mere idle threatening—that God is too merciful to proceed to such an extremity? Does the devil whisper in our ear, "Ye shall not surely die?" This is the doctrine of the world, which administers comfort to souls rushing blindly to destruction with a lie in their right hand. Do we say that it is God who threatens to take the branch away, while Christ will perhaps spare it? But do not the very words, "Every branch in Me that beareth not fruit *He* taketh away," show that Christ acquiesces in the doom? In the parable of the barren fig-tree, the great Intercessor who pleaded for the life of the tree said, after three years' probation, "if it bear fruit then, well, and if not, *then after that thou shalt cut it down.*" He will allow its doom as just and good, should it abide unfruitful. And what a thought is this! The wrath of the Lamb as well as the wrath of God! When He who has given His very life to save comes for judgment, it is the awful sign that all responses to mercy are for ever silent—that every germ of spiritual faculty is not torpid only, but dead—that even the love of Christ has done its utmost, and now rises to put the barren, useless branch decisively and for ever away.

The word in the original translated in our version "taketh away" is *airei;* while the word in the original

---

* "And *sat down*, and gathered the good into vessels, but cast the bad away."—Matt. xiii. 48.

for "purgeth" in the same verse, as already mentioned, is *kathairei*. We have here an interesting example of paronomasia or assonance, which cannot be retained in our translation, but is well rendered by the German words *abschneiden, beschneiden*. The Hebrew language abounds in such assonances, or plays upon words. The words "without form and void," in the second verse of the first chapter of Genesis, are in the original *thohoo, vabhohoo;* the words *fruit* and *end* in the second verse of the eighth chapter of Amos are, in the original, *kaytz* and *ketz*. This is also a peculiarity of the Arabic language ; many of the ornaments and images of the Koran are these assonances, or words with a similar sound. A sermon on death preached by an Arab, might be thus parodied in English. "When the sad hour shall *arrive*, what pious work will *survive*. When in the tomb you shall *repose*, what will you *oppose* to the questions that He then will *propose ?*" The Puritan writers were also addicted to such assonances as "*give* us and *forgive* us much." Our Saviour's *airo* and *kathairo* indicate the subtle connection between the two processes of taking away and purging. In form they appear the same. God, as already said, often employs the same providential means to confirm the faith of His own people and to reveal the true state of the hypocrite. The pruning of the vine is just the taking away of the fruitless branches, in order that the fruitful branches may be made more fruitful; the *airei* is a *kathairei*. The hard sayings which caused some of the disciples to go back and walk no more with Jesus, elicited the triumphant confession

of St. Peter's faith: "Lord, to whom shall we go?   Thou
hast the words of eternal life."   The tribulation that
blows away the chaff purifies the wheat.   The same
temptations which are a trial of the faith of God's
people cause mere professors of religion to fall away.
The heat which ripens the corn rooted in deep soil,
scorches and withers the corn on stony ground, that
springs up rapidly because it has no depth of soil.
The judgment that is a *fire* to burn the tares is a light
to cause the righteous to shine forth as the sun in the
kingdom of their Father.

The words, "He taketh away," are very calm and
quiet; but it is because of their great depth of solemn
significance.   Methinks they indicate the silent and
outwardly unsensational way in which God's judgment
is usually executed.   For once, in order to give the
world an awful and emphatic proof of the fierceness of
His indignation against evil, He will drown the world
with a flood, or burn up the wicked cities of the plain
with fire, or send His destroying angel to smite the first-
born of Egypt.   But usually it is not by catastrophes,
or crises, or violent measures, that He punishes the
ungodly.   He "taketh them away" quietly—gradually,
it may be, and those around them may not know of it.
They go out as at other times, and they wist not that
the Lord hath departed from them.   The taking away
may be in strange contrast to the purging.   The one
may be painless; while the other is not joyous, but
grievous.   The fruitless branch may be taken away
from Christ by its prosperity, its pleasure, its success.

Ephraim joined to his idols may be let alone, with no accusing conscience, no unsatisfied desire—all on earth going well with him, and no voice from heaven reaching him. On the other hand, the fruitful branch, that it may not be condemned with the world, is pruned by sore trial—poor, oppressed, and afflicted; plagued every morning and chastened every moment. It is not death alone that takes away the fruitless branch; it may be taken away in life. Though not severed in form from the vine, the ungodly are separated in spirit; though outwardly enjoying the use of all the ordinances and means of grace, they may be spiritually excommunicated by Him who sees not as man seeth, and who shuts, and no man opens. The body of man is not dead when the breath leaves it. It ceases to be the instrument of the soul; it is dead as the body of a man, but it is not dead in itself. The life is in each portion more or less completely. It has lost its human life— its animal life; but it still retains its vegetable life, as is proved by the fact, that for a time the beard or nails will grow, the limbs move, the glands secrete their peculiar fluids. And so the fruitless branch may maintain for a long time the appearance of vitality— retain a species of low vegetable life. The forms of religion may be kept up; but only as forms, without joy, and without unction. The profession of a Christian may continue to bind him to their performance, even when the heart is gone out of them. It may keep him appearing as a Christian for a long time, just as a thick rind will keep a decaying tree standing apparently green and flourishing among other trees of the forest. And this thick bark of the forms of piety may prevent the man himself from discovering his inward decay.   His religious delusion may even continue till that solemn moment when Christ shall say to those who stand without, knocking at the door of heaven, entreating to be let in, on the plea that they had eaten and drunk in His presence, and He had taught in their streets, "I tell you, I know not whence ye are ; depart from me all ye workers of iniquity."

But all fruitless branches do not keep continually green and flourishing.   Some cease to abide in Christ —forsake the outward fellowship of the Church—and, even to the eyes of man, appear dead as they are in reality.   "If a man abide not in Me, he is cast forth as a branch and is withered ; and men gather them and cast them into the fire, and they are burned."*   On almost every tree may be seen branches that are dead

---

* Three summers ago, a young man, who lay under the shadow of one of the elm trees in the forest of Windsor, was killed by the falling down upon him of one of the largest branches.   There was no storm of wind at the time ; on the contrary, the air was calm and motionless, and not a leaf in the forest stirred ; the branch was not old and rotten ; on the contrary, it was fresh, full of sap, and covered with rich green foliage.   This strange thing not unfrequently happens to the elm during the long continuance of dry and sultry weather, which has the effect of making its wood brittle, so that the branches part easily from the tree, and fall down by their own weight.   How many professing Christians are made fickle and unsteadfast during a period of trial, so that they lose their hold of the Church, and fall away from it at once, while apparently green and flourishing !

and dry. They are no longer stimulated by the sap of the tree; no longer partake of its general life and growth. They have ceased to grow, and therefore have ceased to live. They are only mechanically united to the tree, and are mere excrescences, disfigurements upon its beauty. The influences of the weather, which call forth the latent life that is in the other branches, and stimulate them to greater luxuriance of foliage and richness of blossom and fruit, only wither and blanch the dead branches. What is favourable to the others is unfavourable to them; what hastens the growth of the others only hastens their decay. The ripeness of the one is the rottenness of the other. And a time comes, sooner or later, when even their mechanical attachment to the tree gives way—and they fall to the ground, strewing it with melancholy ruins. These fallen branches form the fuel which the woodman gathers for his fire. They are at once fit for the burning, for there is no sap, no resisting element of life in them; the burning fitly consummates the process of oxidation long ago begun and carried on in them. In a similar way, there are in the True Vine dry and withered branches that are called by His name, but have no share in His vitality—whose connection with Him is a purely mechanical one. They are deformities upon Him. The dispensations of God's providence that help to develop the growth and fruitfulness of Christ's true disciples, only wither them into greater deadness and blanch them into greater deformity, and cause to grow upon them the noxious parasitic growths of worldly lusts. The same processes of grace which prove a savour of life unto life in true believers, is a savour of death unto death in them. And the time comes when even their mechanical attachment to Christ gives way. They renounce in the end even their nominal profession, and fall to the lowest point of worldliness and unbelief. And in this state they are fit fuel for the burning. The flame of Tophet is the fit consummation of the spiritual oxidation and decay that have been going on for years.

The withered branches on a tree were once full of life and beauty. There was a time when they had a vital connection with the tree, and partook of its sap and general force. The spring clothed them with foliage, and the summer with blossoms, and the autumn with fruit like the rest of the branches. They, too, helped to develop the general structure of the tree, and contributed to the perfection of its symmetry. But a time came when, owing to some unfavourable circumstance, their terminal buds lost the power of unfolding themselves, and finally died. With the death of the terminal buds and the cessation of the formation of new leaves, the further growth of the branches was necessarily arrested. The wave of general life went past them to other branches higher up the tree, and they were left behind. And now, although they remain in the tree, they have no part in the movements that go on in its living economy. No future spring can revive or quicken them. They are irretrievably withered and dead. We see this retrogression very strikingly displayed in pine trees growing in a dense wood. Tier after tier of branches, once green and flourishing, and forming the leading shoots, are left behind in the upward and onward growth of the tree, and become ragged and leafless sticks, gradually falling off and strewing the ground, while only the top branches are living and verdant. Thus is it with the True Vine. In its upward and onward growth, some professors of Christ's name are left behind. They do not grow with the growth of the tree, and therefore they perish. Demas was a striking example of such retrogression. The Apostle Paul mentions him as at one time the most conspicuous and faithful of his friends and fellow-labourers in the Gospel. Four sorrowful years of persecution passed away, and the apostle, still a prisoner at Rome, says, in his Epistle to Timothy, "Demas hath forsaken me, having loved this present world." We have no reason to suppose that the apostate ever returned to his forsaken Lord. He was too intent upon his husks to think of his Father's house, and therefore never came back from the far country. And how many professors as prominent and useful in the Church as Demas, since then have backslided hopelessly like him! The process of declension is a gradual one. Before me, while writing these words, I see an elder tree growing in the narrow plot of a town garden, where it is pinched for want of room. It is covered with dark green foliage, but projecting from the midst of the verdant mass are numerous ragged summits of branches destitute of leaves, and presenting an unsightly appearance. These leafless twigs indicate how far the growth of the tree had reached. They were once covered to their extremities with foliage, but the wave of life has receded from them, and left them dry and leafless. They produce foliage now at a lower point, and this retrogression will continue until the life of the tree ebbs away from the extremities to the centre, and the whole tree at length becomes leafless and dead. An analogous process takes place in many professing Christians. They recede from the positions they once occupied; they are incapable of keeping the heights of grace they were once competent to.win. They fall to lower levels, and produce feebler growths. They leave their first love, and no longer do the first works. And when the light of love goes out, the candlestick itself is soon removed out of its place. When the reality of the Christian religion dies out in their hearts, the form cannot long be maintained amid the corrupting influences of the world. There may be a few spasmodic efforts at repentance, but they are like the flashes of a candle expiring in its socket. And from stage to stage, on the melancholy incline, they fall lower and lower, until ultimately they lose even the outward semblance of religion.

The extremest cold known is that which is caused by the condensation of carbonic acid gas—that gas whose ingredients, in the solid form, we burn on our hearths, and in our bodies. And so the greatest spiritual coldness is caused by the subsidence of once glowing and devoted piety. The greatest love to Christ passes into the allotropic condition of the greatest hatred. Scientific men tell us that substances which once were sources of power, are sources of power no longer. Ages ago, their atoms closed in chemical union—their mutual attractions were satisfied. The atoms of granite, of limestone, of most of the substances that compose the crust of the earth, met long ago in chemical combination, and as dynamical agents they are dead. We cannot use them as food to enable us to perform the functions of life; we cannot burn them as fuel in our engines as sources of mechanical power. A granite mountain, or a limestone cliff, speaks to us of forces once potential that might have been utilised, but which have now become utterly inert. They are the cold ashes of a fire that can no more be kindled. It is impossible to bring them back to the condition in which they were before the mutual attractions of their molecules were unsatisfied. And thus it is with those who, from their union with Christ, have sunk into a state of spiritual torpor and deadness—who have passed through, and rejected for themselves God's appointed means of renewal. The spiritual powers that might have enabled them to endure unto the end have passed away; their desires and longings after Christ have subsided, after a profitless fruition of them; they have come as near as possible to the Saviour, and the experience of the union has left them cold and dead. And therefore it is as impossible to renew them again to repentance—to make them spiritually living and potential—to bring them back even to the condition of those who are unconverted, because the experiment of grace has not yet been tried upon them—as it is to make the particles of a cold, hard granite stone unite with the oxygen of the atmosphere, and so become a source of motive power.*

"That which beareth thorns and briers is rejected, and is nigh unto cursing, whose end is to be burned." The barren branch, ceasing to abide in Christ, falls under the full effects of the curse pronounced upon the ground for the sin of man. Instead of bearing acceptable fruit, it brings forth thorns and briers. Apostates

* Of course, in these remarks, I must not be understood as limiting the mercy of God. All things are possible with Him. His thoughts are not as our thoughts, nor His ways as our ways. Natural analogies from objects that are subject to fixed law cannot picture forth fully the processes and expressions of God's free grace. We cannot pronounce infallibly of any soul, even the most depraved--even at the eleventh hour of life—that it is hopelessly lost. Even the threatenings and punishments of Scripture, that are expressly said to be *for ever*, are conditional and contingent, and can be averted or removed, as they have been repeatedly by repentance of the sin which caused them. Still, notwithstanding this, we cannot obliterate the awful hypothesis to which the Apostle alludes in the Epistle to the Hebrews : "For it is impossible for those who were once enlightened, and have tasted of the heavenly gift, and were made partakers of the Holy Ghost, and have tasted the good Word of God, and the powers of the world to come, if they shall fall away, to renew them again unto repentance ; seeing they crucify to themselves the Son of God afresh, and put Him to an open shame." So long as the apostacy lasts the impossibility continues. While they are crucifying the Son of God they cannot, according to the laws of the human spirit, which God established and which God respects, be renewed unto repentance ; but if they cease to do this—if they long for pardon and cry for mercy to Him who is able to save to the very uttermost—then He will make known to them "the exceeding riches of His grace."

are not merely unprofitable servants, they are represented as inveterate and malicious enemies of the Son
of God. The most cruel persecutors of the faith as it is
in Christ Jesus are renegades from it. In the natural
world thorns are undeveloped branches. Just as fruit
is the arrestment and metamorphosis of the branch, so
are thorns an arrestment and blight in the formation of
branches. This is clearly proved by the fact that thorns,
like other branches, are connected with the centre of the
woody stem—that they sometimes bear leaves, and are
often converted, under cultivation, into true branches.
Many plants, such as the plum and the pear tree,
which are thorny in their wild state, lose their thorns
when cultivated in the garden, by having them transformed into fruitful branches. The converse is also
true, that many cultivated plants which had lost their
thorns, revert to the thorny state when abandoned to
the care of nature—their fruitful branches being transformed into formidable spines. Thus, we have in nature
analogies for the consequences of the two opposite spiritual states of fruitfulness and barrenness. The selfish life
of the true Christian is arrested to bring forth the fruit of
self-sacrifice, pleasing to God and man ; the selfish life of
the apostate changes into thorns, that pierce his own heart
and wound others. Very eloquently does the present
state of Palestine speak of the spiritual barrenness of
God's ancient people. Every traveller marks the
strange abundance of prickly and thorny plants in the
land. It failed to become a fruitful vineyard to the
Lord, and it was transformed into a wilderness of thorns

and thistles, rendering many of the hills impassable, and entangling the foot of the traveller on spots formerly rich in culture. "They shall lament for the teats, for the pleasant fields, for the fruitful vine. Upon the land of My people shall come up thorns and briers." And what is thus true of the natural field, is true of the spiritual field in the heart of man. That which is barren bears thorns and thistles, and is nigh unto cursing; the branch that does not abide in Christ, but passes out of His cultivation into the wild or natural state, produces thorns.

I know nothing more strikingly significant than the degenerations of the vegetable kingdom. The parallelism between them and spiritual things is complete and patent to all. God has connected the consequences of sin with them in a way that he who runs may read. Degeneration in plants applies to all those cases in which, not only is the absolute bulk diminished, but the whole form is altered and depauperated. It is the result not so much of a deficiency in growth as of a perversion of development. And thus understood, it is a most interesting circumstance that all the peculiar noxious growths of the wilderness into which man was driven by his sin, and in whose ragged and thorny aspect he saw the new image of his new self, are degenerated forms. The thorns, thistles and briers with which the ground is cursed, and which make the conditions of cultivation so hard and toilsome to man, are not normal structures—perfect in type—but abnormal degradations and arrestments of structure. As man himself changed from the law of his being, and fell into a state of sinful degeneration, so the outward witnesses against him in the soil, from which he wins his daily bread, have deviated from the modes of growth in other plants of brighter nature and happier fortune. The order of creation is departed from, that man's breach of the order of creation may be punished—that the abnormal departure may be in terrible array against the sinner.

We have seen that thorns are arrested branches; instead of going on to produce foliage, blossoms, and fruit, they stop short and sharpen themselves into cruel and wounding spines. And thorns, as a rule, are chiefly found in rosaceous and leguminous plants, in roses, pears, plums, and beans,—those plants which man specially cultivates for food, for beauty, or for luxury. The prickles of briers are also an alteration in the development of the hairs, with which the stems of plants are often covered; a change on them which is connected with injury to man. Prickles are mere woody hairs, superficially connected with the stem; and the adventitious production of hairs is due to an arrested growth, generally arising from pressure impeding the proper development of the organ. The stems of the gooseberry bush, escaping from the garden into the woods, and becoming wild, are thickly covered with prickles, and seldom produce flowers or fruit; while the strange *wig-tree* is so called, because its flowering stalks bear hairs instead of flowers—clearly showing that the production of hairs indicates a degeneration of parts, or an abortive state of them. So also in thistles, what is called the seed is in reality the fruit, containing the seed in its interior; while the hairy pappus or downy parachute attached to it, by which it floats in the air and is carried from place to place, is, in reality a degenerated calyx. Instead of the green rosettes of leaves which we see immediately under the petals of the rose, or which clasp round the ripe strawberry fruit like the setting of a jewel, we have this tuft of silken hairs growing from *the top* of the thistle seed. Thus, what is distinctly an abortion or a degeneration of the calyx—a departure from the type upon which plants are constructed—a transgression of floral law—is made under natural, that is, habitual circumstances, subservient to the scattering of the seed, the means of diffusing extensively this noxious weed, and punishing man for his violation of the Divine law. And it is a remarkable fact that this curious arrangement is peculiar to most of the composite plants—an order to which the thistle belongs, and which is by far the largest and most generally diffused of all known tribes of plants. In very many cases they are found as weeds, growing on cultivated soil, or in close connection with man. It seems as if God had arranged the smaller class of plants to furnish man with food and beauty, and the larger to be weeds, —disputing the soil with them, making cultivation difficult, and the need of labour constant, and thus punishing and disciplining man. And how wonderfully have these composite plants, these thistles and dandelions, been furnished for their special task! Besides

the degeneration of their calyx, in order more effectually and widely to sow them, and their large number
and wide diffusion of species, they produce compound
flowers—hundreds of single flowers clustered on a
common receptacle, so as to economise space, and
crowd them as close as possible; each separate flower
producing its fruit and its marvellous self-sowing ap-
pendage.   In the common spear-thistle, each plant
produces upwards of a hundred seed-vessels, or heads
of flowers, yielding twenty-five thousand seeds! Thus,
even in the very deteriorations and degenerations of
creation, we see strange beauty and meaning: we see
the wonderful fitness between the curse on the ground
and the means by which it is accomplished. And
through the very marvel of the curse, we are led to
look for the wonder of the blessing: by the beauty
that we see, even in degeneration, we are enabled to
picture the surpassing glory of the palingenesis, when
"instead of the thorn shall come up the fir-tree,
and instead of the brier shall come up the myrtle-
tree;" "when the Branch of the Lord shall be
beautiful and glorious, and the fruit of the earth shall
be excellent and comely, for them that are escaped of
Israel." *

* It is worthy of notice, that the tabernacle, with its sacred furniture, was constructed of Shittim wood, or the wild acacia—the
most frequent and characteristic tree of the wilderness. This tree
is a stunted and shaggy *thorn bush.* Out of the natural symbol of
the curse God constructed the divine symbol of grace. In the
midst of this thorny growth of the desert He appeared in a flame of
fire to Moses, and gave him the blessing of Him that dwelt in the

The arrestment of the branch, in the case of the righteous, we found, led to the production of blossoms and fruit; the arrestment of the branch, in the case of the ungodly, we have just seen, leads to the production of thorns. The wild, thorny plant, changed by grace, abiding in Christ, and cultivated by the Husbandman, loses its thorns, and produces fruit instead; the cultivated plant, ceasing to abide in Christ, and going out of cultivation, back to its original wild state, produces even worse thorns than it had before. He that overcometh—that endureth to the end—shall eat of the tree of life,* which is in the midst of the paradise of God; he that falleth away, and apostatises from Christ, shall be wounded with the thorns which he himself brings forth. "He that abideth not in Christ is cast forth as a branch, and is withered; and men gather them, and cast them into the fire, and they are burned." "Every plant which My heavenly Father hath not planted shall be rooted out." The doom is thorough and irrevocable. It will not be merely a leaf or a twig taken away, and

bush. In the midst of the tabernacle, constructed of this thorny growth of the desert, He manifested His glory, and appointed His trysting-place with man. Out of the thorns of the wilderness grow the purple blossoms of the world's restoration.

* The Greek word for tree in Rev. ii. 7, is not *dendron*,—the living tree; but *Ksulon*—dead timber. It is coupled with the words "of life," to indicate that the tree, dead in itself, is, nevertheless, a tree of life. There is surely here a distinct reference to the cross,—the tree of death to Christ, but of life to all who believe in His name. The fruit of the cross—the blessings of redemption —are what the faithful shall enjoy in heaven.

X

the rest of the branch allowed to grow and repair the injury; it will be complete extirpation. The Husbandman subjected him to occasional chastisement, if perchance His severity might accomplish what His goodness failed to do—viz., lead him to repentance. This leaf and that twig were taken away, and the whole branch pruned. The blow first affected his property, then his relations, then the inner circle of home, and finally descended upon his own person, bringing him near to the perillous edge of death. But he recovered, and returned again to worldliness. All the heaven-sent discipline proved vain and futile—it only hardened his heart the more. But the final blow will be as complete as it will be terrible. He will be cast forth from the Vine; he will be rooted up from the vineyard. "For he that, being often reproved, hardeneth his neck, shall be cut off suddenly, and that without remedy."

In the case of the branch in Christ that beareth not fruit, mentioned in the second verse, it is said that the Husbandman Himself will take it away. Continuing green and flourishing in the Vine, though fruitless—abiding in Christ by outward profession and zealous attendance upon the means of grace—it is only God who can excommunicate him, for man sees not his hollowness and hypocrisy. To the last he retains the esteem of good men; and he is only separated from the fellowship of the Church when Christ says, "Depart from Me, I never knew you." But in the case of the branch that abideth not in Christ, mentioned in the sixth verse, it is said that *men* gather it and cast it into the fire. It falls withered from the tree; its dry, dead, useless condition is manifest to all; and, therefore, the Church in the exercise of a godly discipline, separates it from its communion. Like suckers of the vine, cut off by the pruner, and left on the ground until, dry and dead, the peasants come to gather them out of the vineyard, and burn them as fuel in their cottage fires—so the branches that abide not in Christ are gathered dry, and withered, for the burning, by those who have authority in the Church. Thus Nadab and Abihu were gathered out of the vineyard by Moses, Achan by Joshua, Ananias and Sapphira by St. Peter, and Alexander the coppersmith by St. Paul.

The Scripture phrase which describes this work of judgment is remarkable. When the branch is spoken of as not abiding in Christ, as cast out and withered, the singular number is used; but when gathering is spoken of, the words are plural, "men gather *them*, and cast *them* into the fire, and *they* are burned." The branch is cast out and withered as an individual, solitary, isolated—but it is gathered as one of many. Very expressive is the Greek word for this gathering; it is *sunagousin*, from which the word "synagogue"* is

---

* It is interesting to notice, as Archbishop Trench remarks, that throughout all the New Testament, the word *synagogue* is never used for the body of the faithful in Christ Jesus. It is abandoned to the Jews. The chosen people might have been the Church of Christ had they remained in Him and borne fruit; but ceasing to abide in Christ and to bring forth fruit, they became dry and withered, and formed the synagogue of Satan. They could not be like the heathen, merely non-Christian, they must be anti-Christian.

derived. It is cast out from the Church of Christ, but it is received into the "synagogue of Satan." The blind man whose eyes Jesus opened was cast out of the synagogue by the Jews, but he was received into the fold of salvation by Him who said, "I am the door of the sheep;" whereas those who fancied they saw, and therefore were made blind in judgment, belonged to the synagogue of the Jews, but they were cast out of the fold of salvation by Him whose fan is in His hand, and who will thoroughly purge His floor and winnow the chaff from the wheat. And just as those who turn away from the world, and forsake father and mother and friends for the kingdom of Christ's sake, do not find themselves in a state of destitution and abandonment, but are taken up by Him who said, "Come out from among them and be ye separate, and I will be your Father, and ye shall be My sons and daughters ;" so, on the other hand, those who forsake Christ for the sake of the world and of earthly relationships, are not lonely outcasts, but find those who are like-minded with themselves; they go, like Judas, to their own, and make with them a synagogue of Satan. The withered branches are gathered together; the tares are bound up in bundles. They are finally separated from the vine and the wheat. The kingdom of darkness and of light no more shade unto each other, but are distinct in their meridian brightness and midnight gloom. The

Probably there is an occult reference to them in the word which Jesus chose to indicate the gathering of the withered branches that abide not in Him.

different orders of plants no more grow together on the same soil; they are separated, each kind to its own. The Church of Christ and the synagogue of Satan no more occupy common ground; that which divides them is not a solid, but "a great gulf fixed."

And what a vista of dread does this image of a synagogue in connection with the apostate branches open up to us! How will the gathering of the withered branches together, and the binding of the tares into bundles, aggravate the misery of their doom! The gathering together of the redeemed, of the multitude which no man can number before the throne, will enhance their happiness; the renewal, with those whom they loved and lost, of the fellowship of earth perfected for ever—the communion with the wise, and great, and good of all ages, whom they knew not here, but admired and reverenced—will add bliss to bliss. They shall sit down with Abraham, Isaac, Jacob, and Moses, and with prophets, apostles, martyrs and reformers, in the kingdom of God. But the gathering together of the ungodly will increase their mutual sufferings. Ponder the awful description of that society to which the finally impenitent shall belong: "The fearful, and unbelieving, and abominable, and murderers, and whoremongers, and sorcerers, and idolators, and all liers, shall have their part in the lake that burneth with fire and brimstone, which is the second death." The gathering of the fruitful branches will be into an organic, a living union with each other which nothing can break—the formation of a tree of life which will blossom and fruit throughout eternity. The gathering of the withered branches will be a mere heaping together of fuel that cannot unite,—for the disruptive effects of sin will continue in spite of the outward aggregation,—and whose burning together will only increase the fierceness of the flame that consumes them all.

But these hard and painful sayings our Saviour utters, not for the purpose of inspiring a slavish fear, but to produce a salutary caution. Not in wrath, but in love He speaks. "These things"—the words of doom, as well as the words of comfort—"have I spoken unto you, that My joy might remain in you, and that your joy might be full." This is the gracious purpose of even the most grievous parts of His discourse. He draws the shadows dark that the lights of the picture may be more clearly and brightly defined. He mingles one drop of wholesome fear in the full cup of blessing which He proffers to them, that it may prove sweeter and healthier in the drinking. He desires that every element which would hinder their perfect conformity to His image and experience, may be removed—that, pure as He is pure, and perfect as their Father in heaven is perfect, His joy may remain in them, and their joy may be full. Our Lord addresses us, too, in the same strain —speaks to us of the danger of mistaking a mere profession of religion for a change of heart and life —of substituting the mere confession of love with the lips, for the doing of His commandments. He warns us against the sin of backsliding—of the awful doom of apostacy. But it is His very anxiety that we should use all diligence in making our calling and election sure which brings this sternness over His loving face; it is His tender voice rising in the distance into loudness and harshness, to recall us from our backsliding into "the far country," which thus speaks to us of the lightning hid in the soft bosom of the fertilizing cloud—of the fire, kindled by the Sun of Righteousness Himself, in which the faithless, fruitless branches shall be burnt. He wishes us to be purified from all the remains of selfishness and pride, and from the distrustfulness and false humility, or will-worship, which were the dark, disturbing elements in the repentance of the prodigal, when he came to himself, and said, "I will arise, and go to my Father, and will say unto him, Father, I have sinned against Heaven, and before thee, and am no more worthy to be called thy son; *make me as one of thy hired servants.*" He wishes us to make our repentance perfect, by the omission of these words—to draw near, and be willing to be blessed up to God's willingness to bless—to accept the position, and bear the character, and do the work, not of servants, but of sons. "Henceforth I call you not servants, for the servant knoweth not what his lord doeth; but I have called you friends; for all things that I have heard of my Father I have made known unto you." "As the Father hath loved Me, even so have I loved you : continue ye in My love." His own nature—which is pure, self-sacrificing love itself—He wishes to be in us, that His own joy may remain in us, not as a mere transient emotion, but as the very element of our being—the very life of our life. In proportion as we keep His commandments does our friendship with the Redeemer become closer and more tender. In proportion as we continue in His love—in the element of His Spirit—shall our joy be full ; for even as the " Man of Sorrows " could speak of His joy ; so, in the midst of our sorrows—not in spite of them, but because of them—we, too, can speak of the fulness of joy that we have in Christ. And thus, as branches in the True Vine, we shall be assimilated to Him in heart and life—in inward faithfulness and outward fruitfulness. Our personality, through our union with Him, and the partaking of His fulness and holiness, shall be, here and hereafter—not lost and absorbed, like a drop in the ocean, as the eastern mystics dream that the individual shall be lost in the Absolute—but truly perfected, each in its own peculiarity, and all combined, perfect branches in a Perfect Vine.

THE END.